CHARLES AND JOSIAH:

OR

FRIENDLY CONVERSATIONS BETWEEN A CHURCHMAN AND A QUAKER.

Prove all things ; hold fast that which is good.—1 *Thess.* v. 21.

LONDON :
BELL AND DALDY, FLEET-STREET.
DUBLIN :—HODGES, SMITH, & CO.
1862.

Tolerate no Belief, that you judge false and of injurious tendency : and arraign no Believer. The man is more and other than his Belief : and God only knows, how small or how large a part of him the Belief in question may be, for good or for evil. Resist every false doctrine : and call no man heretic. The false doctrine does not necessarily make a man a heretic ; but an evil heart can make any doctrine heretical.—*Coleridge.*

R. D. WEBB AND SON, PRINTERS, DUBLIN.

INTRODUCTION.

THESE imaginary "Conversations" were chiefly written
in the latter half of 1854, and finished in January 1855,
during a tour in Australia connected with investigations
in Natural History. An accidental and very trifling circumstance turned my thoughts in the direction they have
taken. I was staying for some weeks, for the purpose of
botanical explorations, on the little island called Rottnest,
off the coast of Western Australia. I occupied a house
belonging to the government, but boarded with the pilot,
whose small cottage hard by was one of the very few in-
habited houses on the island. One Sunday evening, whilst
waiting for dinner, I chanced to pick up an old number
of the *Family Herald*, and my eye rested upon a leading
article on Quakerism, which struck me as being sensibly
and fairly written. Yielding to a train of thought, not
unnatural in one who had been born of Quaker parents,
but who had left the Society, I began to think over the
plan of an Essay on Quakerism ; but soon abandoned
the essay for the dialogue. The dialogue seemed to possess many advantages, particularly as it offered scope for

free discussion of *both* sides of the question. Having
determined on the conversational form, my mind flew
back to byegone times, and to a dear friend of my youth,
long since entered into his rest, with whom, when growing out of boyhood, I had been accustomed to hold religious discussions. He was my senior by six years, and
a consistent member of the Society of Friends ; a man
of blameless life and conversation ; constant to what he
believed to be his moral and religious duty; well informed
on the doctrines of his sect ; one whose Christianity
showed itself in action rather than word ; liberal in mind,
and charitable to the opinions of others ; humble ; not
over-confident, but ever firmly upholding what he believed
to be the truth. Here, then, I found in this my early
friend (whose name was JOSIAH) what I wished for in the
ideal Quaker of my projected dialogue, in whose mouth
I designed to put nothing but such arguments and statements as a consistent but well-informed Quaker might
advance in defence of his belief. Into the mouth of
CHARLES I proposed to put whatever reasons I could
myself advance in defence of the doctrine of the English
branch of the Church Catholic ;—my simple desire being
to uphold all that ought to be upheld, and to defend no
doctrine which I did not believe. I trust that I have
not lowered the standard of Catholicism by anything here
written.

Having shown the manuscript to some of my Quaker
friends, the remarks they made led me to believe that its
publication would be of use.

Thus encouraged, in the spring of last year, I placed
the manuscript in the hands of my relative J. P., of this
city, who expressed his warm approval of the general

spirit in which it was written, but said that, in several parts, sentiments and opinions had been put into the mouth of JOSIAH with which he could not, as a Quaker, coincide. Finally, he offered to go through the work, and suggest such changes as he thought were necessary, in stating the Quaker side of the argument.

To this offer I willingly assented, and the result has been a *real* discussion, in which we both have sought to maintain, by the best arguments in our power, the views of Christian doctrine to which we are severally attached. I trust we have done so in a fair and candid spirit.

In the prosecution of this work, which has proved to both of us a heavier task than we had anticipated, we have been encouraged by the hope that our honest endeavours to state the arguments on each side fairly, if not fully, would tend to the elucidation of truth ; we think also that, by placing them in juxtaposition, their respective value and force can be better estimated than when they are found separated in different treatises. How far we have succeeded it is not for us to decide.

The dialogues, as they passed through the press, have been revised by a clerical friend, to whom I am indebted for valuable criticism and assistance, which have materially improved what had been written in the character of CHARLES. The proofs were also shown by J. P. to some of his friends, from whom he derived considerable assistance in the defence of Quakerism put into the mouth of JOSIAH. But, as neither of us has adopted any thing that we do not ourselves approve of, we alone are responsible for the opinions or arguments advanced in these conversations.

A few words must be said regarding what I had originally written for "Quakerism," but which has been repudiated and cut out by J. P.. Every one who knows anything of the ebbing and flowing of religious thought, must be aware that different "phases of faith" prevail, at different times, in what appears to be outwardly the same body. Even within our Church, notwithstanding its fixed creeds and formularies, how many *fashions* of popular theology have prevailed since the Prayer Book was settled. The members of the Society of Friends, as will be seen in the following pages, refuse to be bound by the opinions, either of their founder George Fox, or of those who have written in defence or explanation of their doctrines; and therefore the only writings for which they can be held responsible are the "epistles," or pastorals, annually put forth by the Yearly Meeting; and the " Book of Minutes and Advices" sanctioned by the same authority. But the popular preachers of the day,—for Friends like other folk have their " popular preachers,"—have immense power over the faith of their hearers. Though their preaching is liable to be checked by the " elders," appointed to watch over the doctrine preached, yet this check on false teaching is obviously insufficient, considering the high authority with which the Quakers believe their ministers to be invested; and on more than one occasion the elders have been carried away by the eloquence of the preacher, and instead of checking his errors, have encouraged him in them. Thus, in Ireland, at the time of the "new-light" or unitarian secession, many of the elders followed the false teachings of fluent ministers: and in America, Elias Hicks, an eloquent man claiming divine illumination and guidance, and professing to uphold the doctrines of Fox and Barclay in renovated purity, per-

suaded one-half of the American Quaker community to
adopt his unitarian, or rather his deistic views, and to
sever their connection with the original body.

But it was not against unitarian Quakerism that I had
contended in the passages which have been cut out as
being inapplicable to the principles now held by the
Friends. I had put into the mouth of "Josiah" too
much, it seems, of what is called "quietism;" a phase
of belief which results from peculiar interpretations
of such texts as "Keep silence before me, O islands;"
"Be still and know that I am God;" "We are the
clay, and thou our potter;" or, "In quietness and confidence shall be your strength;" &c. These, and similar
texts, when I was in the habit of attending Friend's meetings some thirty years ago, were favourite or at least
frequent subjects of the sermons delivered: not that a
Quaker sermon is necessarily, or indeed often, a discourse
on a single text, for frequently it consists of loose observations strung together by texts, as the mind of the
speaker rambles on from text to text and subject to subject. The abnegation of the creature, the necessity of
introversion of spirit, the continual waiting in expectation
of "a dayspring from on high," were habitually enforced
from the preachers' gallery. In consequence of such a
style of preaching, the Friends, at least in Ireland, had
largely embraced quietism; and accordingly the writings
of Madame Guion, Fenelon, and other quietists were frequently to be found in Friends' families, and recommended by Friends for the perusal of young persons.
Hence the Quakerism that I myself had imbibed was
quietistic; and hence, when, after many years of estrangement, I began to write of Quakerism, I naturally reverted

(like a newly awakened Rip van Winkle) to what had been in vogue when I was a boy. But, meantime, the Quakers had changed with the times ; not only in the less rigid enforcement of the time-hallowed forms of dress and address, but in many other respects. A style of evangelical (I do not mean *calvinistic*) preaching, of which the late J. J. Gurney's preaching was the type, had gradually arisen. The old style, after many struggles with "Gurneyism," had gradually declined ; and, as I am informed, has now lost much of its prestige, though it is by no means extinct, and often makes a vigorous protest against modern innovations.

Several Essays have recently been written on the gradual decline of Quakerism, and various causes have been assigned for what is a generally admitted fact. Many elements of decay may be at work, but the chief cause of weakness seems to me to be a gradually failing faith in the truth of the doctrines held by Fox and Barclay. The proportion of Friends who *distinctly* hold the distinctive dogmas of Quakerism to those who hold them *loosely* or in a new sense, is yearly diminishing. In another generation or two, unless renovated, the dogmatic teaching of Fox and Barclay will die out.

Of this decay in doctrine the leading Quaker dogma of "Immediate Inspiration," or as they term it, "the immediate influence of the Holy Spirit," is a striking example. It is no longer held in the strong and full manner in which it was regarded even within my own memory, much less in the *paramount* form in which George Fox and his associates taught it. As now held, it is so little different from the parallel doctrine of the Church—the sensible influence of the Holy Spirit on the faithful heart

—that it is hardly worth upholding as a ground of separation from the Church's communion.

Of late it has become a frequent custom with many of the younger members of the Society of Friends to go on Sunday mornings to the Quaker meeting, and in the evening either to church or to some dissenting chapel, where they may hear a sermon. Such conduct, twenty years ago, would have subjected the offenders to admonition, as it would have been looked on as acknowledging "a hireling ministry," and therefore as infringing a vital principle of Quakerism. But a still wider departure from former practice is now beginning to be tolerated ; for marriage to a member of another communion, even though solemnized by the blessing of "a priest," no longer necessarily involves the loss of membership. And, having so far *sanctioned* the authority of "a man-made priesthood," it only further remains that Friends should abandon what they have called their "ancient testimony against the payment of tithes," and this in fact is taking place, at least in Ireland, where the conversion of the tithe into a rent-charge has demonstrated to many the unsound basis on which their scruple rested.

Such, I apprehend, will be the fate of all the other "ancient testimonies" of Quakerism. A more enlightened and better educated generation is beginning to discover that, though the doctrines of Fox and Barclay have in them "much that is true, and much that is new," yet that "what is true is not new," and what is new is only true in a very restricted sense. The natural result of such a discovery ought to be just what is actually in progress, namely, a gradual loosening of the bonds which hitherto have bound together the members of the sect ; and I trust it will result in a gradual gathering into the Church's communion.

It is my earnest wish that this work may prove useful. I can truly say that it has been written neither for fame, nor for profit, nor yet for amusement, but to advance what I believe to be the cause of truth. Hence, I have freely sacrificed to J. P.'s criticism every passage which in his judgment was deemed offensive or unjust; although I still think that some of the passages cut out were directed not at chimeras of my own brain, but at opinions which once largely obtained, and which do yet, in several localities, prevail among "Friends." But I am quite willing that these misty opinions should be allowed to dissolve naturally, as morning fogs disappear before the rising sun.

W. H. H.

Trin. Coll. Dublin.
Feb. 5th, 1862.

CONTENTS.

CONVERSATION III.

CONVERSATION VI.

CONVERSATION VII.

b

CONVERSATION I.

"Your garments are moth-eaten."—*James* v. 2.

JOSIAH. I have often wondered, Charles, at thy leaving us. Thou never seemed to have much taste for those gaieties and amusements which tempt so many young men to quit our religious Society.

CHARLES. It certainly was no predilection for what Friends call "vain sports and places of diversion" that induced me to throw up my "birthright" of membership. I left the Society as I should leave a crazy ship whose timbers were unsound; in other words, because I had satisfied myself that its *peculiar* or *distinctive* doctrines were not founded on a right interpretation of Scripture, and that the Church of my forefathers had higher claims on my obedience than the sect among whose members I happened to have been born and educated.

JOSIAH. Thou once thought very differently of our principles.

CHARLES. True. There was a time when I did think very differently of the principles of the Society, that is, of the *theory* of Quakerism; but this was before I had fairly examined the question, and while I remained bound up in the *prejudices of education.*

JOSIAH. I fear thou hast never thoroughly examined the question : few of those who leave us really understand the principles they reject. I am truly sorry to hear thee calling the instruction of thy excellent parents, the prejudices of education.

CHARLES. The word may sound harsh, and yet I have used it in sober earnestness, after calm deliberation. Nevertheless I honour my parents' memory. But love and reverence for individual worth ought not, in matters of faith, to sway the judgment, which should be formed after examining the evidence. The question is, " What is truth ?" My quarrel is not with the Christian lives of Christian Quakers, such as my dear parents were, but with the ISM—the *principles* on which the Quaker Society, as a society, is founded ;—the rock, or rather the sand on which it stands. If anything could have retained me in membership, it would have been the witnessing among Friends such lives as those of my father and mother.

JOSIAH. Now, Charles, is this consistent ? Thou speaks* with reverence of thy parents, and admits that such are still to be found amongst Friends, yet thou leaves the Society because thou hast persuaded thyself that its doctrines rest on a sandy foundation. Hast thou forgotten Who says, " Men do not gather grapes of thorns, or figs of thistles"—" By their fruits ye shall know them" ?

---

* Even since the translation of the Bible, the third person singular of the verb has been simplified, thus " hath," "seeketh." " hindereth," have been changed into "has," " seeks," "hinders," and no doubt the inflection of the second person would also have been cut off, if it had continued in common use. Josiah, therefore, considers himself entitled to make this change, which is in *unison with the* tendency of the English language.

Judge the Society by its fruits,—by such fruits as all the world admits that it has borne. Judge it by the philanthropy of William Penn; by the benevolence of Richard Reynolds; and by the Christian graces of Elizabeth Fry, who realized to my mind the "pure and undefiled" religion which "visits the fatherless and widows "in their affliction, and keeps itself unspotted from the "world;" and yet she moved in that world among the rich and great. I might instance many others; but these, thou wilt say, are individual examples. Then, look at the Society as a body. See its action on the public mind on the subject of slavery, of war, of capital punishments, of judicial swearing; foremost in every work of amelioration. Where, among other professors, canst thou find a higher standard of morality, or more abundant fruit, more freely offered in the Master's service?

CHARLES. My dear Josiah, I admit all this. I admit the beauty of the individual characters you have referred to, and admire the philanthropy of which you have spoken. I know too that men do not gather such grapes of thorns, or such figs of thistles. Yet all this does not bring me a step nearer to Quakerism; to those peculiar dogmas which separate the Society from the Church. You have challenged me to name any Christian professors who exhibit richer fruits of piety and charity. God forbid that I should exclude any, "who profess and call themselves Christians," from a participation in the fruits of the Gospel, such as you have named. It is not the Quakerism of these persons, but their Christianity, that bore these fruits. Their holy lives and conversation do not make the distinctive dogmas they held a whit more true, though they do prove that their hearts were centred upon that which *is* true,—our common Faith.

JOSIAH. By Quakerism thou seems to understand merely those peculiarities which distinguish our Society from other Christian sects. I, on the contrary, regard this term to mean the Christian doctrine divested of superstitious inventions.

CHARLES. In estimating the value of any "*ism*," I must needs confine myself to its specific characters, or those which distinguish it from every other "*ism*." Christian doctrine is generic, not specific ; the common property of all alike, even of those who most differ from both of us. Neither of us, for instance, values the *peculiarities* of Romanism. We both believe that the worship of the blessed Virgin is a "fond thing," an aftergrowth without warrant from Scripture or from apostolic times; that prayers and offerings at the shrines of beatified mortals are worse than useless; and that the dogmatic teaching of the Roman Church is in many cases false, and some of her devotional books (as those of Liguori) bordering on blasphemous. And yet, notwithstanding this, I doubt not you will agree with me, in believing that the Christian lives of good Roman Catholics are as beautiful as any you can quote among any sect of Christians;—and more, that the Roman Church can point back, through past ages, to a succession of such within her pale. But does this prove the truth of those dogmas which she has dared to add to the Catholic creed ? Certainly not. It proves that Christianity still exists within her borders, and nothing more. The pure within her pale have built upon the everlasting Rock;— and though they may be "cumbered with much serving," "*careful* and *troubled* about many things" beside the "one thing needful," and though many of their dearest fancies may be " wood, hay, stubble," to perish in the day of trial, yet if they look through all and above all to the one great atonement, all the rest will pass away, and they shall be received into His everlasting arms. " God is love," " and he that loveth is born of God." They who love Him " with a pure heart fervently," though they may not see all things clearly, and though much that they think they see may be a hallucination, yet with the love of God in their hearts, " No man shall pluck them out of His hand!" Do you not think so ?

JOSIAH. Certainly. I should be sorry to suppose that there may not be—nay, that there are not—many bright examples of holy living among every body of professing Christians.

CHARLES. Precisely my opinion. And as we so well agree in this, you must allow me to refer the holiness of life, which we all admire, to that Body to which we all, of every denomination, profess to belong, and not to regard it as the particular fruit of any particular branch. There is but *one* Vine from which ability to yield such fruit can be derived ; and while any branch, however cankered, has still a living connection with the trunk, fruit will be produced, though it may be but like " the two or three on the topmost bough." When a branch ceases to bear fruit, it is cut off and withers. Were such holiness as we have been speaking of *peculiar* to the Society of Friends, then indeed you might ask me to regard it as the fruit of their " peculiarities ;" but as it is not, you must even permit me to look on it as fruit yielded, either without reference to the peculiarities, or in spite of them.

JOSIAH. I certainly do not regard it as the fruit of our

peculiarities, yet even the smallest matter is important if it be an item of Christian duty. "He that is faithful in that which is least is faithful also in much." The faithful Christian must ever be peculiar in a world of self-indulgers.

CHARLES. Your peculiarities of dress and address have been held to be a hedge and defence from the snares of the world, on the principle that a good fence is necessary for a garden.

JOSIAH. They have been often advocated on this ground, but only as a collateral advantage, not as the reason for adopting them.

CHARLES. A peculiarity of dress and address, certainly, when strictly adhered to, may act as a hedge and defence to young persons who would be ashamed that a Quaker's coat should be seen at a gaming-table, or on a race-course, or at the theatre. But unless your young folk have some better fence against the temptations of the world than the cut of a coat, I fear your garden screen will scarcely shield the " tender grapes" from the " little foxes." You may rear a race of formalists, whose coats, waist-coats, and breeches may all be of the most faultless cut, with the proper number of buttons, and the orthodox depth of pockets, but who, for all that, may have put off " the whole armour of faith," and may be as " miserable, and poor, and blind, and naked" as the most degraded victim of superstitious folly. I think you must admit that "very plain" Friends are not always the brightest examples of a Christian life,—nay, that what is called " plainness" may co-exist with deadness to the spirituality of true religion.

JOSIAH. Plainness of dress may well exist, and doubtless has often existed, without spiritual life; but it is hard to believe in the existence of spiritual life where dress and other vanities evidently occupy the thoughts. A heart-felt Christianity must show itself in the outward bearing.

CHARLES. Certainly. Nevertheless the hedge may be well trimmed, yet the garden empty or full of weeds.

JOSIAH. We have not upheld this plainness of dress and address because it is a hedge, although many Friends may have advocated it as such. We have upheld it, as thou must know, on much higher grounds. At the time that our Society arose, the most absurd and lavish compliments of speech were commonly addressed not only from inferiors to the great, but, by a mock affectation of humility, they passed current among equals. Uncovering the head and bending the body, almost as in the act of solemn worship, one to another, and fifty senseless forms of " bated breath and whispering humbleness" were universal. Our founders felt called upon to protest against this torrent of absurdity, and to restore the language of conversation to the simplicity of truth. The same period witnessed the greatest extravagance of apparel, and a sad laxity of morals amongst those who ought to have been the guides of the people, namely, the higher classes of society, and even too many of the ministers of religion. Our early Friends did not institute any particular mode of dress, they but called upon all to renounce everything that might minister to pride and vanity, and to reject all superfluous ornaments. Their dress was like that worn by other sober-minded men and women of their day, and the *peculiarity* arose afterwards, because they refused to follow the ever-changing fashions of the world.

CHARLES. Well, it soon became peculiar, and apparently was valued as such.

JOSIAH. That may be. I only wish to show how the peculiarity arose. Our Society was not the only offspring of those times. The different sects of fighting professors into which the Puritans divided, and which at length overturned the government, in what is called "the Great Rebellion," were brought into existence by the same causes as those from which our Religious Society first arose. But there was this difference between them and our early Friends, that these sects fought one with another, and those that rose to the mastery imposed their yoke, with unpitying severity, on the rest : but our Friends, following the Great Exemplar, gave "their backs to the smiters; their cheeks to them that plucked off the hair :"—they alone bore persecution, even unto death, without flinching, and quietly continued in their own course through all.

CHARLES. I am well aware of all this, and no man honours the noble conduct of those true martyrs more than I do. It was not without a cause, and a strong one, that they set themselves against the follies and impieties of that troublous time, and none ever more steadfastly upheld what they believed to be the Christian banner than did those sturdy testifiers. Passive resistance is the true weapon in religious warfare. Friends made it a fundamental principle of their Society, and to its aid much of the rise and progress of the Society may be attributed.

JOSIAH. Thou dost not, then, attribute the success of our early Friends to the truth of the principles they preached, and for which they suffered.

CHARLES. Not to their truth in the extreme sense in

which the early Friends held them, though no doubt to a large extent their principles were true. Friends were right in upholding the spirituality of Christian worship against the formalism of "professors" of those days—right in opposing the fulsomeness and extravagance and debauchery around them—right in claiming liberty to obey God after their conscience. Every one of their "testimonies" had in it a nucleus of truth which appealed to the hearts of the hearers, when urged with the zeal of your early preachers, and illustrated by their patient endurance of obloquy, fine, imprisonment, death itself. There could be no doubt of the sincerity of men who forsook their all, and endured persecutions for the sake of what they believed to be "the Truth." This was a powerful introduction to the many among the poorer and middle classes of society, who, without much education or refinement, were disgusted with the professions of the times, and earnestly seeking a way of true religion. When they found that Friends held all the leading doctrines of Christianity, though denying the outward rites and ceremonies in use among others of the Christian name, and when they saw them suffer persecution without a murmur, for the sake of their belief,—not, like others, meeting in holes and corners to practise religious rites, but going boldly to their customary place of worship, at the customary hour, and, when the doors were locked against them, standing patiently in the open street, absorbed in solemn spiritual exercise, until taken to prison or driven away by constables and dragoons—when they saw *passive resistance* like this, in so sacred a cause as that of religion, it was impossible not to be moved by it. It was almost enough to cause " the very stones to cry out;" and

doubtless attracted to the body many who were already
wavering in their faith. I own that, in reading the
lives of the early Friends, their patience under unmerited suffering is that feature of the history which most
affects me in their favour. And if to read of those sufferings has still such an effect on the imagination and
sympathy, how much more must the daily witnessing
them have had. Hence I refer to the influence of this
cause alone a great proportion of the early "convince-
ments;" and I am the more warranted in doing so from
the notorious fact that, as persecution of the Society
slackened, accessions to its numbers from without decreased; and when it ceased altogether, the Society made
no progress worth speaking of.

JOSIAH. Thy attempt to account for the rapid increase
of the Society of Friends in early times, as being due, not
to the purity of their doctrines, but to the persecution
they suffered, reminds me of the celebrated argument of
Gibbon, that secondary causes will account for the rapid
increase of Christianity. It is true, in the case of our religious Society as in that of the Christian Church, that
when persecution slackened, zeal diminished. The relief
afforded to us by more equitable legislation has not, I fear,
been accompanied by an increase of religious life in the
body: through the cares of this world and the deceitful-
ness of riches the love of many has waxed cold.

CHARLES. You allow then that there are few signs of
growth exhibited by the Society in these days?

JOSIAH. As respects numbers, the census shows that
Friends have decreased in this country; but this is not
the case in America. The spiritual condition of the
body is a more difficult question. I do not wish to specu-

late on the attainment of living persons, but I appeal to thee, if we both have not known many, now departed to their rest, whose lives showed the genuine "fruits of the Spirit:" nor do I see any reason to think that there is less of vital religion amongst us now. But though our numbers have not increased, or have even declined, this is no proof against the truths of Quakerism. It is but another example of those alternations of vitality and deadness, of revival and decay, which have marked the history of the Christian Church from the days of the apostles to the present time. And is not the note of revival even now to be heard amongst us? Our Society may never become popular; it may never count its numbers by hundreds of thousands, or enrol the great and wealthy under its name; but I believe that it will still exist as a Church, as an integral portion of the Christian Church, of which the Lord Jesus is the High Priest and living Head.

CHARLES. We shall speak of this hereafter. Let us now return to the "peculiarities." You are prepared, I suppose, to defend them, not on the ground of their usefulness as a hedge, but on the higher ground as professed by your founder, George Fox.

JOSIAH. I have already shown that there was no peculiarity of dress in George Fox's days. He and our early Friends based their testimony to "plainness of speech, behaviour, and apparel" on the grounds of truth and seemliness. They acted in the spirit of our Lord's declaration, "One is your master, even Christ, and all ye are brethren." They were not "to receive honour one of another," but to seek "the honour which cometh from God only." They refused to call any man their master who was not so, or to subscribe themselves his "humble

and obedient servants." Nor could they conscientiously
style men " honorable" or "reverend" who might neither
be the one nor the other, lest they should derogate from
the dignity of truth, and by flattering titles minister food
to the pride or vanity of their fellow men. The same
principle led them to use the singular number in addressing any one, whether he were their inferior, or a person
of the very highest rank. They refused to kneel or to
uncover their heads as a mark of respect to man, because
they considered these signs of respect to be consecrated
to the worship of God. Many were the imprisonments
and persecutions to which these and similar scruples subjected them. Then, as to dress, thou must grant that
the Holy Scriptures contain many precepts against su-
perfluities; thus Peter, speaking of the adorning of women, says that it should not be "the outward adorning
" of plaiting the hair, and of wearing of gold, or of put-
" ting on of apparel ;" but " the ornament of a meek
" and quiet spirit." Thou hast admitted that Friends
were right in upholding the purity and simplicity of
truth against the spirit of a corrupt age : now truth is
unchanging, and what was right in our early testimony
is equally so at the present day.

CHARLES. Yes, Josiah, the *spirit* of that early testimony was and is right and good, and is unchangeably so.
But outward circumstances have so greatly altered, that
the *letter* of your testimony has degenerated into mere
formalism, and is not worth contending for. The use
of the pronoun " *you*" to individuals is no longer a mark
of fulsome respect : it is given indifferently to all classes,
from the highest to the lowest. The names of the week-
days and of the months, though heathen in their deri-

vation, have no more reference now to heathen worship than have the names of the planets to heathen gods, and it is just as sinful to call the planets *Mercury, Venus, Mars, Jupiter,* &c., which Friends do not object to do, as it is to say *Sunday, Monday, January, February,* which names have a smack of idolatry to their ears. As to complimentary modes of address, your objection is certainly more rational than that raised against the names of the days and months, yet I cannot allow that there is impropriety in using titles of respect which are well understood. St. Paul directs us to " render to all their dues"— not only " tribute to whom tribute is due," but also " fear to whom fear, honour to whom honour ;" and he acts on the latter maxim by addressing Festus as " most noble," which is evidently a complimentary title, and the same which was given to that Roman governor by Tertullus, as it was also by Claudius Lysias to Felix, and by St. Luke to the Christian Theophilus, who was probably a man of rank.

JOSIAH. The original denotes a high degree of power, rather than of moral excellence, and it was in that sense properly applicable to Festus, and probably also to Theophilus, of whom we know almost nothing, but who, from being thus addressed, may be inferred to have been the governor of some province.

CHARLES. A similar reasoning will apply to the ordinary titles of courtesy now in use, which are descriptive of the office, or denote the rank or social position of the person addressed. They cannot well be relinquished, as society is constituted, being useful to mark different degrees of intimacy, and the respect due to age and station. The disuse of these forms gives to your intercourse with strangers an appearance of bluntness, which

c

is not always redeemed by that courtesy which ought invariably to accompany true religion.

JOSIAH. Many feel the want of some such form, when addressing those with whom they are not intimately acquainted : and, for my part, I see no objection to the use of the conventional modes of address to which thou hast alluded. Courtesy is certainly one of the fruits of genuine Christianity.

CHARLES. If all men were under the influence of Christian principle, many forms might perhaps be dispensed with which are now required; but with men as we find them, both within and without your "hedge," some "buffers" are required to prevent the unpleasant jostling of man and man. The forms of the House of Commons, though at first sight unnecessary, do in fact tend much to prevent the personal animosities which would otherwise spring up in the heat of debate. To address an unknown person by letter as "Respected friend;" or a person to whom you are indifferent as "Esteemed friend," is quite as inconsistent with "the dignity of truth" as to write "Sir" or "Dear Sir" under similar circumstances.

JOSIAH. I quite agree with thee. I never liked these forms of address, which have been unmeaningly used by too many Friends in their ordinary business letters, and even printed in circulars intended to be sent to men of whom they know nothing personally.

CHARLES. But, to revert to simplicity of dress, you surely must admit that the modern costume worn by most gentlemen is simple, and much more convenient than a "Friend's coat." In this respect the world has not only come up to your Society, but has outstripped it. Your "plain" dress is therefore no longer defensible on the ground of its greater simplicity. It can only be upheld as a *badge*, a uniform to proclaim to the passer-by, "Here comes a Quaker." And so also, I apprehend, of the female dress, though that is a delicate subject to handle. Still I cannot help saying that had I commenced making a collection of "Friends' bonnets," when I first went to meeting, and continued it year by year, I should by this time have a museum worth exhibiting. So greatly does fashion influence your female Friends, that the only un-changing matter in their head-dress is the material. The bonnets are still made of pasteboard, and covered with silk. I have seen a few, very few, covered with cotton. I do not remember ever to have seen a velvet "Friend's bonnet," which I wonder at, as every other silken ma-terial, from the plainest lutestring to the richest satin, has had its day, within my memory. Then the nice variations in colour and in shape ;—the high crowns and the low crowns ; the long fronts and the short fronts ; the broad plaits and the narrow plaits, and the puckers ; the frill behind and the plain back ;—why, "Vanity Fair" itself, with all its butterflies, cannot surpass the variety of these sober moths.

JOSIAH. I grant the changes of fashion among the bonnets, and thou might have said as much about hats, which have *revolved* within our memory too. Thou may remember the round-topped, unbound, broad-brims of our schoolboy days, and the few three-cornered looped hats remaining from a still earlier date: both have now disap-peared. As for other garments, I recollect the first minister who preached in long trowsers, and it was considered "a dangerous precedent" at the time: now, the short breeches have nearly *disappeared*. Nay, there are now some approved ministers who neither by hat, nor coat, nor neck-tie, can be known as Friends. Men's dress is not stereotyped amongst us, as the world supposes. It changes, as yours does, though less rapidly.

CHARLES. The abandonment of distinctive marks of "plainness" in dress is certainly good. Yet, if my memory does not deceive me, I have occasionally heard sermons directed against special items of dress.

JOSIAH. Some of our friends have laid a great stress on plainness of apparel, and have occasionally offered special advice on this point, generally in our meetings for discipline. When directed to peculiarity, and not to Christian simplicity of costume, these advices have always been painful to many amongst us.

CHARLES. You lament the fact, but do you not perceive the cause why you are so much disturbed? Is it not because you have accustomed yourselves to judge of the spiritual state of your members by the cut of their coats, or the shape or material of their bonnets? Are not these the thorns of which your hedge is made? No wonder then if they sometimes hurt your shins. Get rid of the notion that a man in a single-breasted coat is nearer heaven than one in a double-breasted, or that a silk and pasteboard bonnet is more spiritual than a bonnet of straw.

JOSIAH. I have no need to get rid of any such absurd notion. I should be ashamed to hold it for a moment.

CHARLES. Yes; *you*, Josiah, may not be so narrow-minded. But, my dear friend, the spirit of your sect is too clearly so. It is manifested on all occasions. As a young man "rises" in the Society his hat-brim grows *broader*, and so do the tails of his coat, while the collar grows narrower, and the buttons become fewer. So likewise the woman. Her satin bonnet changes to lutestring, the puckers become plaits, and the back frill disappears altogether. Cambric takes the place of net on her head and shoulders. In the last century she would have ended with a black skull cap and a green silk apron ; but these are no longer esteemed " plain. "

JOSIAH. This description is quite out of date, however applicable it might have been forty or fifty years ago. Nevertheless, thou wilt admit that when the mind becomes impressed with the importance of its eternal interests, it is likely that the change of feeling will affect the outward man. Such is the universal experience of Christians. Ornaments are laid aside. The whole deportment becomes graver and more staid.

CHARLES. True. Yet to my eye a plain straw bonnet is a much simpler article of dress than a " Friend's " silk bonnet: it does not cost a fourth of the price, and it is much more serviceable ; for the " Friend's" bonnet will not stand a shower of rain. I constantly hear complaints among my " Friend" acquaintances of the fair sex, of the inconvenience and cost of their "Friends'" bonnets, as compared with those made of straw,—and latterly I notice that many have abandoned the silk bonnet, whilst others wear it only when they go to meeting. These keep up this peculiar head-dress simply as a badge, and as far as they are concerned, "this ancient testimony " has degenerated into a mere form. Is it worth while retaining a form when the spirit that once warmed it is gone ? Depend upon it, you can never deal with this matter of dress but in one of two ways ; either let it regulate itself, as it does among *every other* class of the community ; or, if

2

you must have a costume different from other Christians, take example from the religious orders of the Church of Rome, and adopt a strict uniform, to be imperatively worn. At present you do neither. You have a half-and-half uniform, and, consequently, are as much troubled with changing fashions as other folk. Your thoughts are as much occupied with dress as theirs are, and in a much more pernicious way; for the changes of costume are watched among you as narrowly as if, like the rise and fall of the weather-glass, they indicated the weight or lightness of the wearer's Christianity. What is all this but a direct encouragement to those who make clean the outside, that they may appear spiritual before men? But perhaps I am speaking of a past day. Many of your Friends have, I perceive, already abandoned the *garb*, whilst retaining the *profession* of Quakerism. It is indeed becoming a rarity to see a young man in the peculiar coat of the sect. Will the backsliders long remain members, think you, after throwing off the dress?

JOSIAH. Thou seems to have studied this matter of dress very closely, but one might think that, like Rip Van Winkle, thou had been asleep for the last twenty years. The assertion, that the Society of Friends judges of the spiritual state of its members by the cut of their coats, or the shape of their bonnets, is a libel. Certainly, the subject of dress has had a very undue importance in the minds of many Friends, and there are still some who think too much about it; but this is passing away. Many of our most intelligent and influential Friends strongly feel the dangers of formalism, and while fully convinced that the true Christian is called on to renounce worldly vanities, *and* everything that nourishes pride in the heart, have yet contended that the whole question of dress and address ought to be left to the decision of the individual conscience. Thus our little Church is reforming itself, and I have strongly felt that this evidence of the power and of the willingness to reform is both a proof of present life and a ground for future hope.

CHARLES. You do not, then, despair of the future of your Society ?

JOSIAH. Certainly not. I have before said that the signs of revival are perceptible. We have discussed these miserable coats and hats and bonnets at greater length than they deserved. These are not the " peculiarities" of Quakerism. The real and important peculiarities of true Quakerism are of another character. It protests against all worship by proxy—against the notion that the presence of some one man previously appointed is necessary for the celebration of public worship. It protests against the unscriptural distinction of clergy and laity —the fruitful source of innumerable evils in the Church. Upholding the Holy Scriptures as the only standard of doctrine, it maintains the entire spirituality of Christianity as taught in the New Testament, accepting the realities of Baptism and the Lord's Supper, but rejecting the merely traditional encumbrances accumulated around them. It protests against slavery, war, and oaths, as unchristian, and condemned by the letter and spirit of the Gospel.

CHARLES. Your Society is certainly completely *protestant*. It began its career by protesting against every established ordinance of the Church, no matter how venerable, or on what authority based. Its founders claimed *immediate* inspiration, and a special commission

2*

to reform the Church and convert the world. How have they made good these claims? Is their little Society that stone " cut out without hands," which is to " become a great mountain, and fill the whole earth ?" To the world it has, for the last hundred years, been known chiefly by a peculiar garb and phraseology, by the active philanthropy of some of its members, and by the trading propensities and accumulative industry and sobriety of the majority. Internally it has been upheld by a strict discipline of forms and rules, which have too often been administered with dry formalism ; and now that the discipline is relaxed, and the garb and phraseology are passing away, it remains to be seen whether there be, in those " real and important peculiarities" of which you have just spoken, and which we may discuss in future conversations, sufficient stamina to keep your Society from melting away. Naturally enough, you take a hopeful view of your future. I, on the contrary, see nothing to prevent your members from becoming absorbed among other denominations, or joining the Church. But it is growing late; let us adjourn the discussion.

CONVERSATION II.

What! came the word of God out from you? or came it unto you only!—1 Cor. xiv. 36.

JOSIAH. In our last conversation I remember thou used the expression that "every one of our testimonies had in it a nucleus of truth;" words which I was pleased to hear from thy lips, although, at the time, it struck me as inconsistent that thou should quarrel with principles every one of which has a heart of truth. Now "a little leaven leavens the whole lump," and a plain man would naturally suppose that where the heart of a testimony is sound and healthy, it will send its life-pulse through every part of the body. What dost thou then object to in our fundamental doctrines?

CHARLES. That is a query which will afford us subject for many evenings' conversation. As to what you have just said about my admitting a "nucleus" of truth in each of your testimonies, had you ever looked at a comet through a telescope, you would know that the nucleus commonly forms a very small portion of the cometic haze. Now, to my mind, sects in general are very like comets— small bodies *cast off* from a great central body, round

which they revolve in orbits more or less extravagant.
They are furiously hot when near the luminous centre;
anon they fly off with a flaming tail, as if to set the world
in a blaze; and at last wander far away into the cold
regions of empty space, from which they may never return. I think many of your testimonies of a very cometic
nature.

JOSIAH. This is all very fine, no doubt; but let us
come back to *terra firma* and talk common sense. What
is the meaning of thy simile?

CHARLES. I mean that all sects, as it appears to me, rise
from taking one-sided views of truths; or from magnify-
ing one truth till it usurps more than its proper place in
the system. At first their founders burn with intense zeal.
They are mostly men gifted with much natural eloquence;
their preachings draw crowds who are captivated by the
eloquence of the preacher, or struck with the novel views
which he brings before them, and which they accept as a
new interpretation of truth. He collects a party. It at-
tracts notice from without; it is spoken against by some,
and lauded to the skies by others. It gradually takes shape
and becomes a sect, which separates from the general
body of the Church, and immediately afterwards fancies
itself to be "the true Israel," the "peculiar people" of
God. "Come out from among them and be ye separate:
touch not, taste not, handle not," is then the cry. The
sect so formed, like everything merely human, enjoys a
longer or a shorter career, according to the amount of
truth which its principles contain, and the numbers and
zeal of its members. But invariably, as all history proves,
it waxes feeble with age; the promises with which it
set out are unfulfilled, and gradually lost sight of; the

zeal of its members decays, or changes into a zeal, not for the supposed truth for which their founders originally struggled, but for the sect to which they have become traditionally attached. The sect is cut off from the body of the Church, round which it now revolves, but pride and prejudice forbid its again seeking shelter under the shadow of "the rock from whence it was hewn," or returning to "the hole of the pit whence it was digged." Now there is nothing in the early or later history of your Society different from this common case, except it be the greater boldness of dissent exhibited by George Fox and his coadjutors.

JOSIAH. The term "sect" in thy mind implies opprobrium. But I regard our Society not as a "sect," or something cut off, but as a *section* or integral part of the Church Universal. Thou would doubtless call the Baptists, Independents, and Presbyterians "sects" also, and yet they show no signs of waxing feeble with age.

CHARLES. They never diverged so widely as your founder, or advanced such extravagant pretensions ; and this perhaps may account for their greater vigour and longer life. Yet they have shown a marvellous aptitude for splitting and splintering : their attraction of cohesion will fail in good time.

JOSIAH. What are the pretensions which thou considers so extravagant ?

CHARLES. I allude to the commission from the Almighty, claimed by George Fox as boldly as if he had, like Moses, spoken with God face to face. St. Paul, when he tells the Galatians that he had not received the Gospel "of man, neither was taught it, but by the revelation of Jesus Christ," is scarcely more emphatic than was your founder. The "immediate inspiration" claimed by him is wholly unlike what the modern Friends pretend to. George Fox speaks " with authority ;" your modern preachers speak " as the Scribes." Now, as I cannot grant his authority to have been of the apostolic order, which his writings shew he believed it to be, I do not accept his exposition of Gospel truth.

JOSIAH. That language is too strong. No such claim was made by George Fox, who was accustomed constantly to refer to Scripture in proof of what he taught ; and who provided a Bible for the use of the preachers' gallery in the meeting-house at Swarthmore, where he resided. Like all other Christians, we receive the Holy Scriptures as the touchstone, by which the communications of our ministers and the principles of our Society are to be tried.

CHARLES. Yet the early followers of George Fox were frequently accused of setting their own inspiration above that of the Holy Scriptures.

JOSIAH. That calumny has been refuted over and over again, as thou ought to know very well. Hast thou forgotten what Barclay says ? " We do look upon them (the " Scriptures) as the only fit outward judge of controversies " among Christians ; and whatsoever doctrine is contrary " unto their testimony may therefore justly be rejected " as false : and, for our parts, we are very willing that " all our doctrines and practices be tried by them ; which " we never refused, nor ever shall, in all controver- " sies with our adversaries, as the judge and test. We " shall also be very willing to admit it as a positive cer- " tain maxim, *That whatsoever any do, pretending to the* " *Spirit, which is contrary to the Scriptures, be accounted* "*and reckoned a delusion of the devil.*" Does not this prove that our early Friends were constant in their appeal to Scripture, by which they were ready to stand or fall? They challenged their opponents to test their doctrines by this standard, and not by human creeds and glosses.

CHARLES. I agree with you that calumnious charges of this nature were brought against the early Friends, and were indignantly denied by them. I take it that the misapprehension of Friends' meaning arose from the vehemence with which they claimed immediate inspiration. They acknowledged the Scriptures, it is true, as dictated by the Holy Spirit; but they also believed that the same Holy Spirit spoke *immediately* (without the mediation of Scripture) through their founder and his fellow workers. They accepted the axiom that the Holy Spirit could not contradict Himself, and therefore agreed to submit their "testimonies" to be judged by Scripture. This sensible step alone kept the Society, as a body, from following the insane pretensions of such as James Nayler in early times, and of the "White Quakers"* in our own day.

---

* *White Quakers.* A name given to the adherents of one Joshua Jacob, who was expelled by the Quakers of Dublin about twenty-five years since, because he persisted in preaching in their meetings after repeated warning to be silent. He and his followers set up a community somewhat similar to the Agapemone of Mr. Prince. At one period they dressed themselves in undyed or white garments; hence the name. The community has long since been broken up, and Joshua Jacob, and some of his admirers, have become members of the Church of Rome. The collection of tracts published by the White Quakers under the title of "The Truth as it is in Jesus," is preserved in the library of Trinity College, Dublin.

JOSIAH. The fall of James Nayler is indeed a pitiable
story, but we are all liable to err. James Nayler was
disowned by Friends, yet, at the last, none was more sensible than he of the grievous error into which he had
fallen; and he died in the full acceptance of the truth
of our principles, and in full assurance of faith.

CHARLES. I know it; and yet 1 think his extravagant
errors the legitimate consequence of carrying out, to its
full length, your leading principle of immediate inspiration, as held by George Fox. The appeal to Scripture
in your case is, in itself, a lowering of the standard of
Quakerism; a departure from the first position taken up
by George Fox. With him, when he testifies, it is not,
such and such a text of Scripture forbids or enjoins such
and such a practice, but "The Lord showed me," "The
Lord opened to me," "The Lord commanded me," &c.
The use of such language is precisely like giving forth a
new law, as much as if he had said, "Thus saith the Lord;"
and the man who could in all sincerity use it must have
had a wonderfully exalted notion of his own commission,
and would be far more likely to make a refractory text of
Scripture bow to his requirements, than to bow in all humility to its authority. He might say, "The letter killeth,
"the spirit giveth life; and the Lord showed me that I
"was to take it in such and such a meaning," being whatever meaning was "impressed on his mind" at the
moment.

JOSIAH. As with Luther and some other eminent reformers, there was certainly much of enthusiasm about
George Fox. His expressions are strong, and often not
very lucid. By such expressions as thou refers to, we
must take him to mean that it was impressed on his mind

by the Holy Spirit. But, at any rate, we ought not to understand him as placing himself above the Scriptures, to which he always appealed. He was well versed in them, and I believe it was his practice frequently to preach with a Bible in his hand, and to quote from the written text.

CHARLES. A pity that he did not bequeath that practice to his followers ! He certainly does quote Scripture in his discourses and epistles, and not unfrequently gives a *peculiar* turn to the passages he quotes. Enthusiasts of every party are guilty of the same error ; but none are so liable to it as those who lay claim to spiritual illumination. No other Christian sect lays claim to such illumination so strongly as your Society ; hence the greater danger of error in which you stand. A sober minded interpreter of Scripture will compare one passage with another, so as to get, if possible, a comprehensive view of the subject before his mind, and will use every human means of understanding the true meaning of the words, whilst he prays that the Holy Spirit may be pleased to open to him the difficulty : but he will be very cautious of asserting that he knows "the mind of the Lord,"—as George Fox claims to do, unless my memory deceive me, both in his epistles and his journal.

JOSIAH. Thou speaks of the Holy Spirit opening the difficulty to the mind. Thou must therefore admit His *immediate* teaching. How does thy view differ from that held by Friends, or from George Fox saying that he was shown that he must take Scripture in such and such a meaning?

CHARLES. First let me state my own belief. I believe, what the Church in all ages has held, that " Every good

"gift and every perfect gift is from above, and cometh
"down from the Father of lights"; every pure spiritual
emotion is derived from that One Spirit who is the comforter and sanctifier of the Lord's people. This Holy
Spirit is shed abroad over all Christian hearts. "In
Him," as far as our spiritual life extends, "we live and
move and have our being." As in the natural world all
vivifying influence comes from the sun, so in the spiritual
world every pulsation of holy life comes directly from that
Holy Spirit who is "the Lord and Giver of Life."

JOSIAH. There may be nice shades of difference between
us, but it seems to me as if the great difference were in
the phrases used. The "universal saving light," or
"Christ within" of our early Friends, can only mean the
Holy Spirit. They believed that this Spirit influences the
soul of man *directly*, in accordance with the promise of
our Lord to His disciples, that the Holy Spirit should
"dwell with them and be in them;" should "bring all
things to their remembrance;" and "guide them into all
truth;" and further, that His teaching and guidance,
though gentle as "the still small voice" that spake to
Elijah, were perceptible to the mind of the true believer,
and would, if attended to, lead him into the paths of
peace. They accepted this teaching and guidance, not as
a theory, but as a practical truth.

CHARLES. If there be little difference between our theo-
ries, there is at least much difference in practice. You are
taught to wait in *silence*, like the impotent folk by the pool
of Bethesda, "waiting for the troubling of the waters."
We believe that God gives His Spirit to them that ask
Him; that He is ever more ready to hear than we to pray,
to give than we to receive; and that we must even use

importunity, (as appears by the parables of "the friend at midnight," and "the unjust judge") if we hope to receive the good gifts of the Spirit. The duty of instant prayer is clearly taught throughout the Scriptures.

JOSIAH. This is exactly our belief also : it is needful ₁ not only to wait and watch, but also to pray. George Fox pressed this duty very strongly upon Friends, and in one of his letters we find him supporting his exhortation by the passages thou hast just quoted, and by others of a similar character. He says, "Ask in faith, and whatsoever ye ask, believing, it will be given unto you ; it is Christ's promise." No one should be discouraged from the performance of this duty by a sense of his transgressions, but in humility and sincere repentance let him implore the forgiveness of God. Prayer is the first engagement of the awakened soul, and one of the greatest privileges a Christian can enjoy. But on all occasions when we venture to approach the Throne of Grace, we should remember the awful majesty of Him who fills heaven and earth, and our own unworthiness in His pure and holy sight.

CHARLES. I thought you considered that acceptable prayer could be offered only under the immediate impulse and direction of the Holy Spirit.

JOSIAH. The Apostle Peter desired Simon Magus to pray for forgiveness, while telling him that he was "in the gall of bitterness and the bond of iniquity :" yet certainly no true prayer can issue from the heart of the sinner, unless the Holy Spirit convince him of sin, and show the need of that for which he prays. The Christian believer requires no warrant for prayer, but the feeling of his *spiritual wants.* The Holy Spirit is promised to those who *ask,* and the sense of his spiritual wants is the work of that Holy Spirit in the Christian's heart.

> " Prayer is the soul's sincere desire,
> Uttered or unexpressed."

It must be uttered in faith, relying on Christ's promise, " If ye shall ask anything in my name, I will do it." ' Such is the teaching of our Society as respects individual prayer : we think a higher qualification, the special and impulsive influence of the Holy Spirit, is requisite to warrant any one engaging in congregational prayer. I fear, however, that many of our members have thought that the same degree of spiritual influence ought to be felt before engaging in private prayer, and thus have suffered loss ; but in this matter, as well as in others, I trust that the note of revival is heard amongst us.

CHARLES. Such mistakes are hardly avoidable so far as your more ignorant members are concerned. They have not been taught the *duty* of individual prayer, but have a general notion that all prayer and preaching are specially " inspired." They feel no special inspiration to pray, and hence they omit to do so. To the absence amongst you of all *direct* teaching on this subject I attribute much of that lack of spiritual growth which you deplore : I fear that too many Friends shut their eyes and ears to those passages of Scripture which enjoin, and, as strongly as language can do it, command us to pray to God. It is our duty at least to employ all the means that He has given us. And what are these? He has given us a *mind,* to conceive ; a *will,* to beget desire ; *language,* to utter our thoughts and petitions. These are all so many implements with which we are to dig in the soil of our own hearts. It is quite true that without His aid our labour will be in vain. But still it is our duty to labour. Show me a spot, throughout the universe, in which God does not habitually work through means. Show me an instance in which He expends a particle more of His great power than the occasion calls for. Boundless resources are at His command, yet there is nothing squandered ; to each several occasion is meted out exactly what aid is needed, and no more. I say then, let us use our privileges. He has told us to come freely to Him for help. And should our blindness be such that we know not what petition to put up, His Church supplies us with words like these :—" Almighty God, who knowest our necessities be-"fore we ask, and our ignorance in asking, we beseech " thee to have compassion upon our infirmities ; and those " things which for our unworthiness we dare not, and for " our blindness we cannot ask, vouchsafe to give us for the " worthiness of thy son, Jesus Christ our Lord. Amen."

JOSIAH. If our blindness be such that we have no feeling of want, the repetition of a formal prayer, however good, cannot avail us; for it is not a heart-prayer. If the Holy Spirit have convinced us of sin, have shown us the need of a Saviour, and raised in us desires after holiness, words will scarcely fail us. The prayer of the publican is still the true expression of the feelings of an awakened sinner. Set forms of prayer are at best dangerous. Men soon learn to " say their prayers," whilst forgetting to pray them : and thus the best set forms of prayer degenerate into those vain repetitions reproved by our Lord.

CHARLES. Still, my dear friend, this seems to me to be more of that one-sided view of which I accuse your Society. Our Lord does indeed warn us to avoid "vain repetitions," such as the heathen used; but immediately afterwards He supplies us with a *form* of prayer, in few words, but with fulness of meaning in every word. Now it seems to me that the Collects of our liturgy were framed as perfectly after this great model, as compositions, merely human, can be : their words are few but pertinent ; and the series of these short prayers embodies almost every want that the spirit of man can feel, even to those "groanings which cannot be uttered," and which we may consider comprised in the Collect I have just repeated. From first to last there is not a vain repetition; scarcely a redundant expression. To my ear they are perfect music. The "vain repetitions" of the heathen, which our Lord reproves, were such as the priests of Baal, in their contest with Elijah, uttered from morning to evening, "Oh Baal, hear us! Oh Baal, hear us! Oh Baal, hear us, &c."

JOSIAH. Our Lord's words are, "After this manner pray ye." The form He gave was an example of simplicity and fulness, in contrast with the long prayers of the Pharisees. It is a model for us in framing our petitions, not a form to be constantly repeated, as if the utterance of the words, although unfelt in the heart, were in itself an act of worship ; and we have no reason to believe that it was used as you use it, in the time of the Apostles, or of their immediate successors. The Collects of your liturgy are beautiful as compositions, reverent in expression and full of meaning, yet the daily use of them as they come in course, without reference to the spiritual or bodily wants of those who repeat them, must often be a " vain repetition." How often are they repeated without any thought or consciousness of their purport ! Holy words profaned by unholy hearts !

CHARLES. Our Lord's words, as recorded by St. Luke,

are, "When ye pray, say, &c." We do not prescribe the
constant repetition of the Lord's Prayer as a meritorious
act of worship. We use it and the collects as prayers,
expressing the daily wants of every Christian worshipper.
The Church supposes that those who come to the daily
service come with, at least, a desire to worship. She
endeavours therefore to teach them (as our Lord taught
his disciples) *how*, and *for what* they ought to pray.
Our bodies have their daily wants, one day with another, nearly of the same kind ; and so have our spirits.
Day by day we have need to confess our daily sins ; to
praise Him for His daily mercies towards us ; and to pray
for grace daily to do His will. Such, in brief, is the daily
public prayer of the Church ; but no restriction is put
on the private devotion of the closet, where every varying
want may be pleaded before God.

JOSIAH. It is well if those who put up the daily
prayers of the Church Service do *daily* feel the burden
of their sins, and their need of what they pray for. They
cannot feel thus except through the Holy Spirit, whose
aid is essential to all true prayer.

CHARLES. Undoubtedly : just as planted seeds will not
germinate without the warmth of the sun. We must use,
to the best of our ability, all the means at our disposal,
looking steadfastly for the blessing of Him " unto whom
all hearts be open, all desires known, and from whom no
secrets are hid." For this view of our duty there is ample
Scriptural warrant ; and as respects " repetitions," one of
the most solemn passages of our Lord's history shows
clearly (to my mind) the unscriptural character of your
scruple.

JOSIAH. *To what circumstance dost thou allude?*

3

CHARLES. I allude to the prayer in the garden, when His soul was "exceeding sorrowful, even unto death." The Omniscient Sufferer knew that "the determinate counsel and fore-knowledge" of the Father had appointed for Him the bitter "cup;" and that all things which were written of Him were about to be accomplished. And yet He prays that, if it be possible, the cup may pass from Him; nay, He thrice repeats the petition, "saying the same words." Will Friends dare to call this a vain re-petition? And was not this last prayer a heart prayer, full of faith, hoping against fore-knowledge, believing against despair? Is it not the agonised Humanity crying out from the very depths? And does it not teach us, under every circumstance to lift up our hearts in prayer? For though we may not obtain the petitions that our troubled hearts desire, we shall receive strength to bear our sorrow. But *we* ourselves must *ask;* the cry must proceed from that which is accountable within us; the effort must be our own.

JOSIAH. This certainly is no vain repetition. Friends object, not to the repeated asking, where the need is really felt, but to the repeating a set form of words, whether the need be felt or not, and calling such utterance a prayer. Still I apprehend there is no very irreconcilable difference between us. Friends hold that all true prayer is prompted by the Holy Spirit; and thou says that prayer originates with the mind that frames the peti-tion, but is not acceptable to God without the co-operation of His Spirit. We both hold the spiritual nature of prayer.

CHARLES. Prayer is the effort of the soul to realize communion with God, and therefore must necessarily

originate in the will ; but it is obvious that the distance
between the finite and the infinite can be annihilated only
by an infinite Being ;—hence the necessity for the aid of
the Holy Spirit " working with our spirits."

JOSIAH.   Well, let us resume this subject another time.
I am now desirous to ask thee what thou meant by saying,
a short while since, that the appeal to Scripture, in our
case, is " a lowering of the standard of Quakerism," as
first upheld by George Fox.

CHARLES.   My impression is that the early Friends
were fond of asserting that " the Spirit which gave forth
the Scriptures is superior to the Scriptures ;"—a mere
truism, needless to insist upon, if they only meant that
" he that hath built the house hath more honour than
the house ;"—but an assertion full of danger to the faith,
if they meant that the Spirit *speaking by them* had equal
authority with the written word.   Now, if I mistake not,
this latter is the meaning of the early Friends.   " Try our
" principles," they might say, " by the Scriptures if you
" will ; nevertheless we do not ground them upon the
" letter of the Scripture ; the Spirit which gave forth the
" Scriptures has given us this testimony to bear."   Surely
they claimed *supernatural* gifts, and grounded many of
their peculiarities *primarily* on immediate inspiration.*

---

* *Primary ground of doctrine.* Barclay in his " Apology" says,
" The principal rule of *Christians* under the Gospel is not an out-
" ward letter, nor law outwardly written and delivered, but an
" inward spiritual law ; *engraven in the heart, the law of the Spirit*
" *of life, the word that is nigh in the heart, and in the mouth.* But
" the letter of the Scripture is outward, of itself a dead thing, a
" mere declaration of good things, but not the things themselves :.

3*

Josiah. I deny that as a body they claimed any supernatural gifts ; but I do think that some of the early
Friends laid claim to the immediate teachings of the
Holy Spirit, to an extent that appears to me unwarrant-
able, and that certainly is not made now. Still they
constantly appealed to Scripture as the test of doctrine,
affirming "that no revelation coming from the Spirit
could ever contradict the Scripture's testimony."

Charles. I suppose you are now quoting Barclay, but
let us hear the whole passage. His words are, " We
" affirm, that no revelation coming from it [the Spirit] can
" ever contradict the Scripture's testimony nor right rea-
" son: *not as making this a more certain rule to ourselves,*
" but as *condescending* to such, who not discerning the
" revelations of the Spirit as they proceed purely from
" God, will try them by these mediums. Yet those that
" have their spiritual senses, and can savour the things
" of the Spirit, as it were *in prima instantia,* i. e., at the
" first blush, can *discern them without, or before they apply*
" *them either to Scripture or to reason.*"* If this doctrine
be admitted, a " condescending" appeal to Scripture will
not prevent " those that have their spiritual senses " from
making the written commands of God of none effect,
through their interpretations. I am, therefore, strongly
of opinion that George Fox and his immediate disciples

" therefore it is not, nor can be, the chief or principal rule of Chris-
" tians."—*Barcl. Apol. Prop. iii. s.* 2.

" That which of all things is most needful for him to know, to
" wit, whether he really be in the faith, and an heir of salvation,
" or not, the Scripture can give him no certainty in, neither can it
" be a rule to him."—*Ibid. Prop. iii. s.* 3.

* *Barcl. Apol. Prop. ii. s.* 15.

meant, by the "light within," the "Christ within," and similar expressions, something radically different from the influence of the Holy Spirit on the heart, as held by modern Friends. This is one point on which you have gradually left the early teaching of the sect, and gradually approached the parallel doctrine of the Church. Compare George Fox and Robert Barclay with Joseph John Gurney, and I think you will perceive the difference to which I refer.

JOSIAH. I fully admit that Barclay was one of those who laid claim to spiritual illumination in a manner that very few Friends would now do. I do not pretend to answer for all that either he or Gurney has written, nor even for George Fox himself. We may honour them as sincere and pious men without holding them to be infallible. Anglican "Doctors of Divinity" differ far more widely among themselves, and that upon the most important doctrines, than do our early and our later Friends. Still I feel confident that Fox and Barclay meant, by the "Light within," nothing else than the Holy Spirit, operating on the heart of the sinner to convince him of sin; or indwelling in a faithful heart, as the Comforter, the Spirit of Truth "who guides into all truth."* But if our doctrine herein has gradually approached yours, ought it not to please thee, instead of causing thee to reproach us?

---

* *The light within.* Different forms of expression were used by the early Friends, but evidently with the same meaning. William Penn, in his Address to Protestants, section v., writes as follows :—" For it cannot be denied, but that the great foun-" dation of our Protestant religion is, the divine authority of the " *Scriptures from without us,* and the testimony and illumination

CHARLES. It does indeed give me pleasure to see the
wearing out of unsound notions, and the substitution of
opinions nearer to the Catholic faith.   I do not object
to this, but to the claim made by George Fox and
his associates to something like a new effusion of the
Holy Ghost, as on the day of Pentecost ; or as some of
them expressed it, "a second coming of Christ in the
hearts of His people."   They spoke as if all spiritual
religion were confined to them and their system ; as
if none but they believed in the gifts of the Holy Ghost.
Hence they called themselves " the peculiar people,"
" the highly-favoured people," &c. and Quakerism was
termed " the truth :" while all other Christians were,
in their eyes, " professors," or " the world that lieth
in wickedness," &c.   These were high swelling words,
but where is the evidence to support them ?   St. Paul
would have desired to see "not the speech of these men,
but the power."   Where are the signs of an apostle
among them ?   Or must we take the very partial success
which attended their early preaching as evidence of a
divine mission ?   You have ceased to plume yourselves
on the dying words of Admiral Penn—"Son William, if
" your friends keep to their plain manner of living, and
" plain preaching, they will make an end of the priests,"
&c.   Where is the fulfilment of this prophecy ?   Far
from making an end of the priests, after a struggle of two
hundred years, you are now one of the least numerous of

" of the Holy Spirit within us."   And again :—" It is the general
" consent of all sound Protestant writers, that . . . . the
" *Scriptures only*, interpreted by the Holy Spirit in us, give the
" final determination in matters of religion ; and that only in the
" *conscience of every Christian to himself.*"

the earlier sectaries. If Quakerism has its thousands, Mormonism, the mushroom of yesterday, has its tens of thousands. So far as converting the world was a part of your mission, it has proved a complete failure.

JOSIAH. Truth is not to be judged by numbers. If it were, we and you should alike be condemned. The " broad way" will always have more travellers than " the narrow." Some of the principles for which our early friends contended are now much more generally recognised than they were then, and in particular the need of the Holy Spirit for the right performance of every religious duty—a truth on which they dwelt the more strongly, because it appeared to be forgotten by many professors of religion. If our numbers be few, thou must admit we have had some influence in the community, and that it has been often exercised for good.

CHARLES. I have already admitted it. Nor do I judge of truth by counting heads. But I deny that the Church has learned anything whatever from your Society respecting the need of the assistance of the Holy Spirit. If you take the trouble to consult the works of our early divines, the forerunners and contemporaries of George Fox, you will find the doctrine of the Spirit's teaching amply set forth, as it is also in all our formularies. Had George Fox been really sent by God, with a mission of the magnitude claimed by him and his followers, greater results should be looked for. He came preaching against " steeple houses," " man-made priests," " will-worship," and "hireling ministers," &c., and repudiating every established custom or ordinance of the Church. He and his followers believed they were commissioned to convert the world, and spent *their lives "going* to and fro in the earth," and endeavouring to do so. Well, two hundred years have since gone by ; and what has George Fox's Society done with "the talent" committed to its keeping ?

JOSIAH. I am glad to hear that your Church has always set forth the doctrine of the Holy Spirit's teaching ; but canst thou wonder that we doubted this, when her practice, at the time our Society arose, appeared so different ? Two hundred years is but a small space on the great dial-plate. The Christian Church has seen nearly nineteen centuries, and its work is still undone.

CHARLES. Let us, if you will, compare the progress of the Church with that of your Society. In the start you had all the advantage. At the death of George Fox, the Society had its many thousands of members, and its hundreds of meetings settled in Great Britain and Ireland, in North America, in the West Indies, and on the Continent of Europe. Such was the success of your early preaching, under the pressure of newly lighted zeal ; and this, one would think a fair promise of future greatness. The "grain of mustard seed" planted by our Lord, on the other hand, was "the least of all seeds that be in the earth." At the first meeting of His disciples, after His resurrection, "the names together were about a hundred and twenty." And was this then, His enemies may have said, the whole result of the example of His life, of His preaching, of His miracles, of His death and resurrection ? Was it for this that the Son of God was manifested and sent into the world ? To gain over a hundred and twenty converts from among the lowest of the people—the most illiterate classes ! We know the result. This little band quickly overmastered the greatest empire the world had *then seen, changing* the whole framework of society in the

-most polished nations. And, ever since those days, the Church's progress and the progress of civilization have gone hand in hand. Wherever Christianity has been corrupted or neglected, there civilization has declined ; and where its lamp burns clearest, there every object useful or ennobling to humanity advances. Opposition from the enemy without ; treachery and cold-heartedness within ; every device that could stay the progress of the Church militant has been tried against her. Her beauty has been marred by dissent ; her ranks thinned by heresy and schism ; her zeal cooled by internal disputes ; every human support has frequently failed, or, like a broken reed, treacherously wounded her ; and there have been times when the enemy rejoiced over her, as though she were slain. Thus far has her work been interrupted, and her mission arrested. But, notwithstanding all this, her branches extend wider and wider, and more and more children flock to her fold, to feed on her fruit, and rest under her shadow. And why ? Why, but because to *her* is the *promise* given ; hers is really that mission which every founder of a sect endeavours to appropriate.

JOSIAH. This is most true ; but I do not apply it, as thou seems to do, to any system of ecclesiastical polity, whether of Rome or of England, but to the Church Universal, comprising all those, of every name, " who love the Lord Jesus Christ in sincerity." To these is the promise given.

CHARLES. The promise is to the Church " built upon the foundation of the apostles and prophets ;" words which I take to imply the necessity of, at least, apostolic *order and doctrine.* Where can you show evidence of

growth like that of the apostolic Church in your *peculiar*
system of Christianity? Those principles, for the sake of
which George Fox and his followers dared to rend the
body of Christ, make no progress in your hands; and the
Society hangs together by its *esprit-de-corps*, and its
family associations.

JOSIAH. "Other foundation can no man lay than
that is laid, which is Jesus Christ." Every section of
Christendom that holds the fundamental doctrines of the
Gospel, as taught by the apostles, is a portion of the visible
Church, and is "built upon the foundation of the apostles
and prophets," that is, upon the foundation on which
the apostles and prophets built, "Jesus Christ himself
being the chief corner stone."

CHARLES. Every sect claims to be built on the one
foundation, and to uphold the fundamental doctrines
according to its own interpretation. We maintain that
everyone who deserts the apostolic *fellowship* (κοινωνία),
thereby cuts himself off from the visible Church, and if he
seek to draw others into secession, he further incurs the
guilt of schism.

JOSIAH. But what dost thou call " rending the body
of Christ"? Surely if ever men were sincerely devoted
to their Master, our early Friends were of the number.

CHARLES. I call the separation into sects, the wilful
withdrawal from the communion of the Church, and the
attempt to establish an independent society on different
principles, a rending of "the body of Christ," an expression applied by St. Paul to the Church.

JOSIAH. Thou takes it for granted that the Church of
England is "The Church," whilst I consider it to be only
a portion of that visible Church of which our Society

and other dissenting communities are also portions. But is there no cause sufficient to justify such a separation?

CHARLES. I regard the Church of England only as being one branch of the Catholic and Apostolic Church: but since, from the introduction of Christianity down to the middle of the sixteenth century, no other body in Britain called itself a "Church"—I do not think I assume much, if, in speaking to an Englishman, I call the Mother Church of England, "The Church." Schism I cannot justify; though circumstances may in great measure palliate the offence: but I do not think that such circumstances existed in your case.

JOSIAH. Thou art very bitter against dissent, and breach of unity. But what dost thou call the separation of what is called the Church of England from the Church of Rome? Was not this a rending, on your part, of the body of Christ, and establishing an independent society on different principles?

CHARLES. The separation was not on our part. The Church of Rome disowned the English Church, because the latter preferred the apostolic doctrines, originally delivered to her, in common with the Church Catholic, to the "developments" gradually invented in the middle ages, and attempted to be forged into a new creed by the Council of Trent. The English Church stands fast by the three ancient Catholic Creeds, to which she has added nothing, and from which she has taken nothing; and she can trace an unbroken descent from the ancient Church through which these Creeds have been handed down. So far she continues truly Catholic. She protests against additions to the creed and corruptions in the liturgy; and so far may be called Protestant. But she is no independ-

ent sect or society, starting aside from the main body of
Christians, and setting up for herself. Nay, notwithstanding her excision by Rome, she still acknowledges the
orders of the Church of Rome, nor does she withhold her
communion from any baptized person who seeks it faithfully. Every true churchman laments the estrangement
between the Churches, and, far from wishing to see the
Roman Church overthrown, he prays that, whilst there is
yet life in her body, the work of healing may go forward.
His hopes of reformation in her system may be very
feeble ; but all things are possible with God. And as all
extremes in time correct themselves, perhaps the very
extravagance of modern Ultramontanism and Mariolatry
may become, under God, instruments of good to those
true Roman *Catholics*, who prefer the immutable truths
of Christianity, "once delivered to the saints," to the fond
inventions of man, " developing" from age to age.

JOSIAH. It may as truly be said that the separation of
our early Friends from the Church of England was not on
their part. They sought to recall men to the ancient faith
as preached by the apostles, purified from the additions
and corruptions of after ages. The guilt of schism does
not necessarily belong to the seceding body. Those who
leave because they cannot profess creeds and adopt forms
which are unsanctioned by Scripture do not incur this
guilt: but the responsibility rests with the Church which
seeks to impose an unchristian yoke, rather than with those
who leave it. Some of the terms in which the two more
ancient Creeds are expressed are not free from objection,
while the Athanasian Creed offends many even of the
professed members of your Church. But you have added
to these Creeds the Book of Common Prayer and the

Thirty-nine Articles of Religion, some portions of which appear to me to be fairly open to objections, similar in character to those which you make to the other developments, by which the simple teaching of the apostles has been corrupted. Thou asserted that no sufficient cause existed to justify Friends in withdrawing from the established worship. Now they believed that the rites and ceremonies of your Church were not in accordance with Scripture. How then could they attend your worship? Besides, they differed from you in some matters of doctrine.

CHARLES. In minor matters they differed, and in "peculiar views" (which we may discuss in future conversations); but in those *essential* doctrines which constitute the faith of every Christian man, I trust, there is no irreconcilable difference between us.

JOSIAH. I should be sorry to think that there were. The same truth appears under different aspects to different minds; and two statements essentially the same may be made by skilful disputants to appear contradictory. Perhaps we agree more nearly than either of us may be willing to admit.

CHARLES. Making a noise about knotty points of doctrine and haggling about "conscientious scruples" are the peculiar vices of sectarianism, from the Pharisees downwards; and men become so enamoured of these trifles, that they finally quit what is essentially good, for the hope of attaining something which appears a little more plausible. George Fox was shocked at the corruptions of the times; and his writings would lead us to suppose that a deadness to religion and a depravity of manners were universal among churchmen, and that spirituality

and Gospel light were confined to his own sect. And yet
George Herbert, Bishop Jeremy Taylor, Bishop Bedell,
Archbishop Ussher, Archbishop Leighton, and a long, long
list of similar worthies were contemporaries of George
Fox ; men whose lives and conversation were exemplary, and whose writings will, to say the least, bear
comparison for spirituality with any that your Society
can show. Yet what were these men in the eyes of George
Fox ? They were " hirelings ;" " man-made priests ; "
" dumb dogs ;" " blind leaders of the blind," &c.   He
needed not to apply to such for advice or guidance. No :
that, in his eyes, would be " a consulting with flesh and
blood." So he founded a new sect, and became its acknowledged leader.

JOSIAH. George Fox and his associates did not seek
to found a new sect. They promulgated no new doctrines,
but, as I have already said, sought to recall men to the
pure Gospel faith, delivered to the saints 1600 years
before ; and this they did with the ability that God gave
them, believing the principles they advocated to be as old
as Christianity itself. Man is answerable to God alone in
matters of religion. All attempts to control the conscience lead either to dissimulation, or to the stake.
Surely the freedom of opinion which prevails in England
and America is one great element in the prosperity of
these nations. As " iron sharpeneth iron," so the continual rubbing together of opinions brings out the truth.

CHARLES. Yes ; freedom of will and freedom of opinion
are the indefeasible rights of man, who was created in
the image of his Maker, after His likeness, capable of
walking in all things erect. But it is one thing to vindi-
cate these rights, and another thing to set up a new sect,

(which in effect George Fox did, whether he designed to do so or not), in opposition to the Church of Christ. The Church speaks with an authority that can belong to no modern association ; an authority derived from the Great Head, confirmed to His Apostles, and by them transmitted from generation to generation. To her has been entrusted a message so full, so unchangeable, and so complete, that St. Paul invokes a curse on himself, or on "an angel from heaven," should he be found varying from what he had first preached. There can be no new phase in the verity which was "finished" when the great Sacrifice was accomplished. Hence the Church has no power to add to, or take from what she has received. The Catholic faith, like its Author, is immutable ; the same yesterday, to-day, and for ever. Hence St. Paul most earnestly "beseeches" the Corinthians that they should "all speak the same "thing, and that there be no divisions among them ; but "that they be perfectly joined together in the same mind "and in the same judgment." For he knew that curious questions in matters of faith spring from the sectarian spirit which saith, I am of Paul, and I of Apollos ; or, I am of George Fox, or of John Calvin, or of Joseph Priestley, or of John Wesley, or of any other leader of a sect or party. Now unless it can be shown that the Church of England in the sixteenth century had betrayed her Lord, by preaching " another gospel " than that she had received, the rebellion of the puritanical sects against her discipline and ordinances was unjustifiable.

JOSIAH. When our Society arose, the "rebellion of the puritanical sects" had already done its work, and George Fox "rebelled" quite as much against the Presbyterians and Independents who had ejected your bishops and clergy, as he did against episcopacy. But by what right dost thou call the Episcopal body "The Church," as if it alone could rightfully claim obedience? Are not the Presbyterians and the Independents equally entitled to call their communities Churches? Is not our religious Society quite as truly a Christian Church, as if its members were ten times more numerous? To assume that the Episcopal Church in England is "The Church," and identical with the Church of the apostolic days, is a mere begging of the question. All dissenters deny it. The Roman Church denies it.

CHARLES. The Church is represented to us in Holy Scripture as a society of believing and baptized persons, continuing steadfastly in the doctrine and fellowship of the apostles. This Church we find to have been visibly governed by the apostles during their life-time, through the instrumentality of presbyters and deacons. They also appointed bishops as their successors, through whom the government of the Church, under the same constitution, has been transmitted down to our own times. During a space of more than 1500 years this government by bishops, priests, and deacons continued unquestioned, with the solitary exception of Aerius* about the year 350. Aerius had no imitators, till certain of the communities which separated from Rome at the period of the Reformation, sought to defend the position which they assumed; and

---

* *Aerius.*—"Aerius, heretic, the intimate friend of Eustathius of Sebaste in Armenia, A.D. 360, and living when S. Epiphanius wrote his book against heresies, A.D. 374-6."—*See Smith's Dictionary of Greek and Roman Biography and Mythology*, for an account of his opinions.

then, but not till then, in the history of the Church, did any body of men devise another constitution, differing from that which the apostles once delivered to the early Christians. It has been the blessing of the Church of England to have retained in its integrity the apostolic polity no less than the apostolic doctrine and fellowship ; and consequently, whilst denying to no baptized Christian the title of a member of the Church Catholic, I cannot concede to any community which has abandoned the apostolic polity, the title which Scripture has conferred only on bodies formed after the apostolic model.

JOSIAH. I have already maintained that every Christian community that holds the fundamental doctrines of the Gospel, as taught by the apostles, is a portion of the visible Church : and all those, of every name, " who love the Lord Jesus Christ in sincerity," though known to Him alone, are living members of His true Church. As respects Church government, I know that Episcopacy has existed from an early age ; but there are many, besides us, who deny that it derives any support from the New Testament, or that it existed in apostolic times.

CHARLES. In the New Testament express mention is made of Titus, who was appointed bishop of Crete by St. Paul, and of Timothy, bishop of Ephesus, to whom the charge was given, " The things that thou hast heard of " me among many witnesses, the same commit thou to " faithful men, who shall be able to teach others also."

JOSIAH. Titus was left by the apostle in Crete that he should " set in order the things that were wanting, and " appoint (καταστήσης) elders in every city." It is evident that Timothy was left at Ephesus for a somewhat similar purpose. Whether this is proof sufficient that they were invested with the authority claimed by your bishops, and by those of the Church of Rome, I leave for others to discuss, as I do not care to enter into the controversy between Episcopacy and Presbyterianism. The notices in Scripture respecting Church government are few, but I think we may gather that *all* the members of the Church participated in the management of its affairs. The New Testament gives us no precise directions, we may therefore conclude that every community of Christians, or Church, as I should call it, has full power to arrange the mode of government which may appear best suited to its peculiar circumstances, and to alter its arrangements from time to time, as may appear necessary.

CHARLES. You admit, then, that Titus was left in Crete, and Timothy at Ephesus, with authority "to set in order the things that were wanting," and "to appoint elders in every city." Now these are the most important of the special functions of a bishop. But I have no wish further to argue this point with you. I am satisfied of the truth of what I have already maintained, and therefore I think that George Fox and his associates, if they believed they had a mission from Heaven for the restoration of Christianity to its primitive purity, ought to have endeavoured to promulgate their views *within* the Church, wherein the good providence of God had placed them. They should have sought to reform *it* rather than to set up a sect for themselves. If their views were true, one day or other they would prevail ; and they might have cleared their own consciences by promulgating what they believed to be " the truth," and, having done so, they should have left the result to the Great Head and Governor of the Church.

JOSIAH. And did they not bear their testimony openly, in market-places, in houses of worship—every where, in short, where they could get people to listen to them? But when they found that the ministers of religion, the appointed teachers of the people, were hardened against them, they were forced to separate, in order that they might in quietness profess the Gospel in its simplicity.

CHARLES. The duty of a reformer is always difficult, and requires a large measure of the Christian graces of faith and hope, and especially of charity, to enable him to perform it. The faith of your early Friends was sincere, their hope of converting the world was strong, but I fear their charity was somewhat deficient ; and hence faith and hope were misdirected.

JOSIAH. If their charity appeared deficient, it was only because it was eclipsed by their zeal.

CHARLES. The founding of a sect for the advocacy of special doctrines appears to me to have often originated in human pride, alarmed lest the work of the founders (devoted and pious men) should come to nought in the next generation : or it may be considered to indicate a want of faith in the good providence of God, as if the truth, which strikes with conviction the mind of a Fox or a Wesley, had been forgotten by Him with whom we have to do, and would be lost to the world unless we arranged a human organization for its maintenance.

JOSIAH. That is a new view of the subject.

CHARLES. Your early Friends might have refused to fight, or to swear, or to give flattering titles ; they might have enforced the advantage of silent worship by their example, and by open advocacy in words and in writing ; they *might have borne* their testimony to the necessity for inward purity, to the need of constantly renewed supplies of grace, and to the non-essential character of external or ceremonial ordinances; and all this without renouncing fellowship with the Church of their forefathers. If their views made way, well—and if not, they had done "what they could," and might leave the result to Providence. In such a course they would no doubt have had to bear persecution, but not more perhaps than they actually suffered, and they would not have added another to the schisms which are the reproach of Protestantism.

JOSIAH. How could they have carried out such a course in practice? Unless they had submitted to the rite of water-baptism for their children, the children would have been looked on by your clergy as outcasts, and treated as such; nor could they, with a safe conscience, have allowed your ministers to teach their children doctrines which they did not believe to be true. Would they not thus have been in a false position, retaining a nominal connection with a Church in the worship of which they could not conscientiously join? Would it not in reality have been equivalent to a separation?

CHARLES. It would certainly have been a position of great difficulty, requiring a large measure of faith, hope and charity. Still, if their course was a right one, I doubt not they would have been supported in it.

JOSIAH. But surely Luther and the German protestants were justified in separating from the Roman Church? Thou would not have recommended them to remain in connection with all the superstitions of Rome?

CHARLES. I cannot justify secession. However disposed to palliate their offence, I cannot but regard the separation from the visible Church as an "offence" still; and

" woe to him through whom the offence cometh." The
Reformers before Luther's time retained their connection
with the Church. They preached reformation of doctrine
and of morals, not a separation ; and the results of their
preaching, and of their devoted lives, and of the martyrdom of many, were felt in that ominous cry for reform
which, under the pontificate of Leo X., shook the Vatican
to its foundations. Erasmus contributed as much as any
one to the success of the Reformation, and he never left
the Church's communion. He disapproved of the secession, and of the violent proceedings of Luther, Zuinglius
and others ; and so do I. I think that the evil principle of
indefinite schism then introduced, and thenceforward justified and glorified under the specious name of " Protestantism," has borne bitter fruit ; and therefore it is that,
whilst I *sympathize* with the German and Swiss reformers,
I cannot *justify* their separation.

JOSIAH. If they had not separated, and formed another
Christian society, I fear their labours would have been
lost, and that in the next generation the Pope and his
priests would have recovered all their usurped authority.

CHARLES. The Pope and his priests did recover much
of what they had lost, in the re-action which naturally
ensued upon the anarchy created by the dissensions and
wild licentiousness of many of the separatists. We cannot
tell what would have happened, if the unity of the Church
had been preserved. The see of Utrecht may be cited as
an instance of a Church excommunicated by the Pope,
but refusing to separate herself by her own act from the
communion of the Church Catholic. In spite of the
excommunications thundered against them by Rome, from
Benedict XIII. to Pius IX., the members of the Jansenist

communion have lived and died in the unvarying desire of unity, and in the profession of the Catholic faith. Now I believe that if "the reformers" had maintained the true Christian ground of unity ; if they had not only " confessed Christ crucified," but "manfully fought under His banner," against the widespread corruption which had darkened but not defaced the sanctuary, they might have been made the blessed instruments in God's hand of bringing about a true reformation of that which was decayed : as it was, they pulled down the polished corners of the Temple, and tried, ineffectually, to build them up again ; but "even that which they build, if a fox go up, he shall even break down their stone wall."

JOSIAH. To have been the instruments of a thorough reformation would indeed have been a glorious mission. But is it not the duty of the Christian, whilst endeavouring to effect a reform, to separate himself from corruption? " Come out of her, my people, that ye be not partakers of " her sins, and that ye receive not of her plagues." After all, is it not a question of degree ? Some separations are justifiable—others are not.

CHARLES. He who seeks to reform a corrupted Church must indeed separate himself so as to be no partaker of the sins of the corrupters, but this does not necessarily imply secession from the Church's communion. It is a great evil of secession, even when, as in the case of Luther and the reformers, the seceders have strong doctrinal provocations to disunion, that all hope is lost of effecting a general reform in the Church. Those who desire reform withdraw ; their pure doctrine and example are lost to the body ; and the spirit of antagonism then drives those who remain still farther into error.

JOSIAH. The Roman Church has certainly gone still farther from the truth since the reformers left her communion; witness not only the decrees of Trent, and the creed of Pope Pius IV., but the latest papal stereotype,— the dogma of the Immaculate Conception. But will the principles thou maintains justify thee in leaving the Society of Friends, even if its founders were guilty of schism in leaving the Anglican Church? I find it laid down by Archbishop Whately that "the Church, what- " ever it is, in which each man was originally enrolled " a member, has the first claim to his allegiance, supposing " there is nothing in its doctrines or practice which he is " convinced is unscriptural and wrong;" and he further " says, even if a Church have originated in a rash separa- " tion from another Church, on insufficient grounds," that " for an individual to separate from it *merely for that* " *reason*, would be not escaping, but incurring the guilt " of schism."* Now thou hast admitted that we hold the essential doctrines of Christianity, though mixed with error. Why, then, didst thou not remain in the Church in which the good providence of God had placed thee, and endeavour to reform it? Who can tell what might not have been effected by thy exertions and exam- ple, and those of others who have left us on similar grounds?

CHARLES. I have already explained why I cannot allow that every sect is, as you maintain, equally entitled to call itself a Church; but if it were, I do not see how the guilt of schism could be incurred by an individual who passes over from one of these "churches" to another.

---

* *Whately's Kingdom of Christ, Essay* II., § 33.

Schism, as I understand it, implies secession for the purpose of drawing disciples after the seceder, thereby setting up a new focus of sectarianism. In my own case, I merely sought admission by baptism, into what I believe to be the visible Church on earth. This act of mine by no means necessarily implied separation from the Society of Friends. It was the stringency of your discipline which cut me off. But, to revert to what we were discussing, another evil which results from secession is, that the allegiance of its members to the seceding fraction becomes weaker and less fixed after the first breach of unity, and a slighter cause will induce another. Thus, most of the Protestant communities have had several divisions and subtractions, and many of the offsets have again been multiplied.

JOSIAH. Yet the variety of opposing sects has one good effect. Their conflicting opinions and watchfulness of each other's failings serve to elicit the truth, and to maintain zeal among those who might otherwise fall asleep.

CHARLES. Good is brought out of evil, but that does not justify the evil. Has not your Society had several divisions both here and in America?

JOSIAH. Yes. There was one in Ireland about sixty years ago, which was promoted by several ministers and elders. Their views were unsound as respects the inspiration and authority of the Scriptures, and as respects the divinity of our Lord, and the atonement. This schism was brought on by the preaching of a female minister from America, a woman of much ability, who had adopted Unitarian views. The same spirit afterwards broke out in America itself, under the leadership of Elias Hicks. Separations took place in almost all the

" yearly meetings*" in America; and in those of New
York, Philadelphia, and Baltimore, I believe the Hicksites were the majority. The aggregate numbers of both
parties now are nearly equal, being each about 80,000,
while in Great Britain and Ireland there may be some
25,000 persons who profess our principles.

CHARLES. I did not know there were so many Friends
in America; but have there not been other separations
there since the Hicksites left you?

JOSIAH. Yes. There have lately been separations in
New England and Ohio. The new separatists and their
abettors are seeking to narrow the precincts of Quakerism, by insisting on conformity to doctrines which *they*
deduce from the writings of George Fox, Robert Barclay,
and others of our early Friends; while the Yearly
Meeting of London, and the other Yearly Meetings in
connection with it, desire to bring all these writings to the
test of Scripture, and to be bound by this alone.

CHARLES. You will be bound by Scripture, that is, by
your own peculiar interpretation of Scripture. So also
say those who separate from you. Such splitting and re-
splitting illustrates the usual working of the old leaven,
whose end is confusion. Whatever pretence of superior
spirituality may clothe the leaders of a sectarian movement, sooner or later the spirit of Dathan and Abiram
reveals itself in the result. At starting, the promises are

---

* *Yearly Meetings.*—The larger provinces into which the Society
is divided for disciplinary purposes are called Yearly Meetings.
Besides the Yearly Meetings of London and Dublin, which
legislate for Friends in Great Britain and Ireland respectively,
there are in America eight yearly meetings of orthodox Friends,
and six of the Hicksites.

ever fair and plausible; but step by step every doctrine is frittered away to its ultimate thread, and no thread is too slender to hang a new sect on. But God ever brings good out of evil, and by the disobedient sects He chastens His Church, as He did the chosen people formerly by the nations among whom they dwelt, and who prevailed against them whenever they failed in their obedience to Him.

Josiah. Again and again the assumption that your body is " the Church," and that those who differ from you are only sectaries. We separated from you, believing that your Church practised rites and ceremonies which were the inventions of men, additions to genuine Christianity; you separated from Rome for a similar reason. You hold us as sectaries; they regard you as heretics, cut off from what they call "the Church," without whose pale there is no salvation. If we ought to return to your communion, why should not the same reasoning oblige you to go back to them? The tendency of thy high-church arguments is Romeward, and such they have proved to many of the clergy and other learned persons in your Church. I say then, my dear Charles, don't go to Rome, but return to us.

Charles. I do not claim for the Church of England that she is " the Church," in an absolute sense; but merely a true branch, which has never separated from the Catholic Church either in doctrine or in discipline. Her discipline and her doctrines, just as she maintains them, are older than the separation of the Greek and Roman communions, therefore most rightly does she claim to be derived *doctrinally* (as well as lineally) from the primitive, undivided church which descends to us from apostolic times. Rome cannot *truly* say so much. Her creed, as she holds it, is no older than the Council of Trent. No

Catholic is bound by that creed, though every *Papist* is. Let papal Rome therefore call us heretics, if she please. I do not think that the tendency of my argument is Romeward, for not until Rome shall return to the creed of apostolic times can my theory justify any Catholic in joining her communion.

JOSIAH. And I maintain that ours is also a true branch of the same Catholic Church, but it is too late to discuss this matter further at present. Let us meet again. Farewell.

CONVERSATION III.

Preach the word; be instant in season, out of season; reprove, rebuke, exhort with all longsuffering and doctrine. For the time will come that they will not endure sound doctrine.—2 Tim. iv. 2, 3.

CHARLES. I think that in our last conversation we did not fully consider the Quaker claims to direct or immediate inspiration. You make this, I believe, the *only* qualification necessary to constitute a minister of the Gospel? Do you not?

JOSIAH. Every operation of the Holy Spirit in the soul of man is *inspiration*, but this term is usually confined to that plenary direction and revelation which was vouchsafed to the Jewish prophets, and to the apostles and other inspired writers of the New Testament. Therefore we do not use this word; but we believe that there is no right appointment to the Christian ministry, except by the call of our Lord Jesus Christ, whose prerogative it is to send such as it pleases Him; and that the true qualification for this sacred office is the immediate and continued influence of the Holy Spirit. " As every man " hath received the gift, even so minister the same one " to another, as good stewards of the manifold grace of

" God: if any man speak, let him speak as the oracles of
" God : if any man minister, let him do it of the ability
" which God giveth." Learning is not essential, though
it is of great value, if seasoned by grace. The poor fishermen of Galilee were " unlearned and ignorant men," yet
the learning of Paul and the eloquence of Apollos were
made peculiarly useful in building up the Church.

CHARLES. You do not surely compare the inspiration
vouchsafed to the apostles of our Lord to the feeble mani-
festations which appear in your meetings. Nor ought
you to forget that both the poor fishermen of Galilee and
the learned Paul had received a *command* to preach, and
an *authority* to minister, directly from the lips of the
Master himself. Besides, the outpouring of the Spirit on
the day of Pentecost not only converted the hearts of the
Apostles, so that they never afterwards wavered in the
faith, but it actually enlightened their intellects. They
were no longer "ignorant" or uninstructed men, but
specially qualified for missionary teaching in all the
world. Was ever such an effect produced at a Quakers'
meeting ?

JOSIAH. The Sanhedrim, in its wisdom, looked on
Peter and John as " ignorant and unlearned," even after
they had received that special qualification. The degree
of qualification now bestowed is very different ; the
source from whence it comes is still the same. The
same Holy Spirit, which spake through the apostles,
" gently leads" the tender lambs of His flock in all ages ;
and as they submit to His guiding, He opens to them
the Scriptures, and makes them see clearly in spiritual
things. Some He leads in this way, through their life
long, in silence ; and such as these preach the Gospel

by their consistent walking in the sight of God and of men. Others destined to more conspicuous places in His vineyard receive higher spiritual gifts. To some is imparted the gift of teaching; to others that of prophecy —not the foretelling of future events, but that gift which the apostle Paul, when enumerating the gifts of the Spirit, describes as "speaking unto men to edification, and exhortation, and comfort." This is the highest gift which a Gospel minister can possess. Your Church, I believe, holds that the gift of prophecy ceased with the apostolic age, and therefore your ministers only assume to be pastors and teachers. Now, it appears to us that the gift of prophecy, as thus defined by the apostle, is needed in all ages, and we believe that it is the Lord's will to continue this gift to His Church.

CHARLES. Are you not predisposed to believe the gift of prophecy to be continued, *because* it appears to you to be needed in all ages of the Church? This is the very assumption by which the Romanists defend the useful and comfortable doctrines of infallibility and papal supremacy. But how do you judge of the commission of those that speak to you in Christ's name? When the apostles came preaching the Gospel by immediate inspiration, they proved the genuineness of their mission by healing the sick; raising the dead; casting out devils; striking gainsayers with blindness; and if they drank any deadly thing, or were bitten by serpents, it did not hurt them. When men come speaking in God's name, and vouching their doctrine by works like these, I shall believe in their supernatural commission to teach. But when no such apostolic or prophetic power is displayed, I may fairly question their title, and enquire whether they have not " taken that honour to themselves," instead of being " called, as was Aaron," who proved his call by the miracles which he wrought.

JOSIAH. Miraculous powers were granted to the first promulgators of Christianity to prove the divine authority of the new revelation which they preached : our ministers have no new Gospel to proclaim, and therefore do not need miracles to prove their commission. The plenary inspiration which the apostles possessed is no longer needed, because we have in the New Testament a permanent record of the doctrines which they preached : but the gifts of the Spirit necessary for the conversion of sinners, and the edifying of the body in love, are the permanent inheritance of the Church, according to our Lord's promise, " Lo ! I am with you alway, even unto the end of the world." Our ministers claim no more supernatural commission than *appears* to be claimed by the candidate for deacon's orders in your Church, when he declares that he is " inwardly moved by the Holy Ghost to take this office upon him."

CHARLES. It is to me a new view of Quakerism to be told that your ministers claim no more than the candidate for deacon's orders professes to do. If this be so, and if the candidate-deacon and the Quaker minister stand only on the same footing as respects "inspiration," then our candidate has, in most cases, a decided advantage over yours. For we require ours to be well learned men ; you do not ; and consequently, very few indeed of your appointed ministers can so much as read the New Testament in the language in which it was written. I do not dispute the value of an inward call to the ministry. But, both in the Jewish and the Christian Church, there has always been an *outward*, as well as an inward call and appointment; and accordingly our Church, by her XXIIIrd Article, declares that "those we ought to judge lawfully "called and sent, which be chosen and called to this "work by men who have public authority given unto "them in the congregation for this purpose."

JOSIAH.   Thou admits the *value* of an inward call to the ministry : we believe in its *necessity ;* and do not admit the claim, unless we believe this call has been received : but whilst in theory you admit the value of an inward call, in practice you ignore it altogether.   I agree with thee that ministers should be regularly appointed.   They receive their qualification from the great Head of the Church, but it is right that their call should be recognised by their brethren, according to stated rules ; and I am not afraid to compare our mode of procedure with that of the Episcopal Church.   "Do you trust that you are in- "wardly moved by the Holy Ghost to take upon you "this office and ministration to serve God for the pro- "moting of His glory, and the edifying of His people ?" Such is the question of the bishop to the candidate for the office of a deacon ; to which he solemnly replies, "I trust so."   And such is the virtual declaration of every Friend who exercises the office of a minister of the Gospel.   His brethren judge of the evidence of his gift, and if it appear good, they recognize it.   This mode of procedure appears to me to be in accordance with the practice of the primitive Church, and I do not believe that so many mistakes are made in this assumption and recognition, even in proportion to our numbers, as are made in the "ordinations" of the Episcopal Church.   Not needless was the exhortation of the poet—

From such apostles, O ye mitred heads,
Preserve the Church, and lay not careless hands
On skulls that cannot teach, and will not learn.

CHARLES. I have no wish to defend undue appointments to the ministry. Nay, I freely grant that bishops, in unduly ordaining to holy orders, sin far more grievously than your " brethren" can possibly do.

JOSIAH. What then may be thy notion of a regularly appointed ministry?

CHARLES. That question is easily answered by referring you to the New Testament history, and thence downwards to the history of the Church in succeeding ages. Christ *personally* commissioned His apostles. They *personally* called others, " ordaining elders in every city," and gave authority to others, as Timothy and Titus, *personally* to ordain others, as the necessity for more labourers in the vineyard increased; and so forward, from that day to this, there has ever been preserved a succession of men duly commissioned to minister in holy things, and to whom the promise of Christ is more especially applicable, " Lo! I am with you alway, even unto the end of the world."

JOSIAH. Many of those whom thou calls " duly commissioned " have been very ill suited " to minister in holy things." Even now men are appointed who have given no evidence of their fitness, except their studies at college, and who, it may be, only desire the office as a means of livelihood. This may be what you call apostolical succession, but it does not appear to me to have been the apostolical practice. I cannot call such men, ministers of the Gospel. The qualification for the Lord's work must come from the Lord himself.

s

CHARLES. I grant the necessity for a divine appointment; but it would appear from Scripture that God has been pleased, at times, to make use of unworthy instruments. You cannot question the apostles' commission, as they were chosen by our Lord, who "knew from the "beginning who they were that believed not, and who "should betray him;" and yet, knowing this, he selected and appointed Judas Iscariot.

JOSIAH. Our Lord's foreknowledge of what Judas would become is no proof that he was unworthy at the time he was chosen : although he afterwards fell away, I see no reason to doubt that his motives were sincere when he first became a disciple. When the first seven were appointed, the apostles left the choice to the whole body of the Church at Jerusalem. Paul and Barnabas ordained or appointed the presbyters whom the churches elected.

CHARLES. Many things may have been done in the infancy of the Church, which are not necessarily binding on all after ages. The organisation of the discipline was gradual. On the particular occasion of the appointment of deacons it was very desirable that the wishes of the multitude should be consulted. I do not find that the churches had previously elected those presbyters whom Paul and Barnabas appointed ; but even if they did, the act of ordination was vested in men set apart for the purpose.

JOSIAH. I have stated it as regards Paul and Barnabas on Dean Alford's authority, using his very words.* Timothy certainly received his appointment at the "hands of the presbytery," not of a bishop. Now you consider that

* *Alford's Notes on Acts,* xiv. 23.

no one but a bishop can appoint to the ministry, and the congregation have no voice in the matter.

CHARLES. In early times greater power was given to the laity in the choice of bishops and curates, but owing to the abuses that occurred it has been discontinued. It is clear from 2 Tim. i. 6, that St. Paul, on the occasion of Timothy's ordination, acted not as a mere presbyter, but in a special and superior manner. The preposition here used is διὰ, denoting *instrumental cause*, and is a proof for episcopal power : that used in reference to the hands of the presbytery is μετὰ, *along with*, and this authorizes the practice of the presbyters laying on their hands also. By our ritual it is ordered that the bishop, with the priests present, shall " lay their hands severally upon the head " of each candidate.

JOSIAH. I was not aware that any one took part in the ceremony except the bishop. With you no man is permitted to preach Christ unless he have received ordination, however holy his life, and however much his heart may yearn to declare to others that gospel of salvation which is so precious to himself.* Yet you give the title of minis-

---

* Lord Macaulay, in his essay on Ranke's History of the Popes, points out, in his own graphic manner, the loss which the Church of England has suffered by placing such a bar before the man who feels himself called to the ministry, but who has not received a collegiate education. Of such a man, impelled by a desire " to impart to others the thoughts of which his own heart is " full," Lord Macaulay says, " Zeal for God, love for his fellow-" creatures, pleasure in the exercise of his newly discovered " powers, impel him to become a preacher. He has no quarrel " with the establishment, no objection to its formularies, its go-" vernment, or its vestments. He would gladly be admitted " among its humblest ministers. But, admitted or rejected, he

ter without scruple to men of vicious lives, if a bishop have laid his hands on them. Can this have been intended by the great Founder of Christianity? No! It is a mere mockery of sacred things to acknowledge the "orders" of such men; or to hold that the apostles' commission could have been transmitted through their unhallowed hands. Why it is notorious that enthroned bishops, and even popes, have been open infidels, as well as men of the most corrupt lives. Yet, according to thy theory, these are links in that golden chain which connects your modern ministry with the Great Head of the Church, and which cannot be broken without endangering the authority of what you term the Christian priesthood. This is a strange doctrine.

CHARLES. It would indeed be a strange view of the Gospel ministry to assert that those "sinners against their own souls," who so grievously betrayed the trust com-

---

"feels that his vocation is determined. Nor will he, for lack
"of human credentials, fail to deliver the glorious message with
"which he [believes himself] charged by the true Head of the
"Church. For a man thus minded, there is within the pale of
"the establishment no place. He has been at no college : he
"cannot construe a Greek author or write a Latin theme : and
"he is told that, if he remain in the communion of the Church,
"he must do so as a hearer, and, that, if he is resolved to be a
"teacher, he must begin by being a schismatic. His choice is
"soon made. He harangues on Tower Hill or Smithfield. A
"congregation is formed. A licence is obtained. A plain brick
"building, with a desk and benches, is run up, and named
"Ebenezer or Bethel. In a few weeks the Church has lost for
"ever a hundred families, not one of which entertained the least
"scruple about her articles, her liturgy, her government, or her
"*ceremonies.*"

mitted to them, are *necessary* links in any chain except a
chain of regular episcopal succession. As such I admit
them. They received a lawful commission in the church
from the lawful officer, acting in the name and by the
authority of Christ ; just as Judas received his commission directly from the Master himself. Therefore, as I
must allow Judas to have been an apostle, so I allow
Alexander VI. to have been a bishop of Rome, and so of
all other cases of unworthy ministers. At no time has the
Church been free from these tares. Even in apostolic
times were found men " speaking perverse things." Our
Lord ordinarily works through human means, and does
not leave himself without a witness, be mankind never
so corrupt. In his house are vessels of honour and of
dishonour ; and vessels of wrath, too, fitted to destruction.
We cannot narrowly enquire into His mode of governing
either the Church or the world. We know that out of
what seems unmixed evil there constantly springs forth
good. Even under your own system there is nothing to
prevent the intrusion of unworthy ministers, concealed
by the mask of hypocrisy.

JOSIAH. When we discover our ministers to be unworthy, we no longer recognise them as such, and they
have no power to appoint others : but your prelates and
those of Rome, although unworthy, are authorized to
ordain ministers " in behalf of Christ."

CHARLES. A bishop of the Anglican Church, if duly
convicted of unworthiness, ought to be, and would be
deprived of episcopal authority. It is clear from Scripture that the Gospel was commanded to be preached
to all nations by messengers sent by the apostles.

JOSIAH. *Not quite so* clear that it was by the apos-

tles that the messengers were sent. " The Holy Ghost
" said, Separate me Barnabas and Saul for the work
" whereunto I have called them." Were not all in fact
sent by the same divine authority ?

CHARLES. Read a little further : "And when they had
" fasted and prayed, and *laid their hands on them, they*
" sent them away." These, and indeed St. Paul himself,
(Acts, ix. 17,) notwithstanding his miraculous call to the
apostleship, were duly appointed by the laying on of
hands. If then imposition of hands were required for
men called directly by the Holy Ghost, much more it
should be insisted on in all other cases. Some were faithful to their trust, and others betrayed it. St. Paul tells
us that by some Christ was preached "of envy and strife,"
and by some " of love "—and adds, " What then ? not-
" withstanding, every way, whether in pretence or in
" truth, Christ is preached, and I therein do rejoice, yea,
" and will rejoice."

JOSIAH. This laying on of hands on men already commissioned by the Holy Spirit would not surely have
conveyed any spiritual gift. Neither was it an appointment to the office of minister, but the acknowledgment
of their divine call on that particular occasion. If you
are to follow this example, you should ordain for every
distinct service by the imposition of hands. So far as
appears from Scripture it was not the hands of bishops
which were laid on Paul and Barnabas, nor on Paul himself when he received his sight and was filled with the
Holy Ghost.

CHARLES. The laying on of hands on men called
specially by the Holy Ghost was not in mere *acknowledgment* of a previous call, but an attestation of the fact of

the call, and as such the church has always used it. The cases of the apostles were peculiar; yet Ananias was *specially* deputed to lay hands on St. Paul, and there were prophets at Antioch (Acts, xiii. 1) when Paul and Barnabas were sent forth.

JOSIAH. I do not see much difference between the acknowledgment and the attestation of a call, but I think your Church goes much beyond either; for I find in the " Form of ordering of priests," that the bishop and priests present lay their hands on the head of the candidate, and the bishop says, " Receive the Holy Ghost for the office and " work of a priest in the Church of God, now committed " unto thee by the imposition of our hands." And then follows a declaration that the newly appointed priest is possessed of the power to forgive or retain sins. This is no attestation of a fact, but the assumption of the power of conferring the Holy Ghost. We know that the apostles did possess the power of conferring the gifts of the Spirit, and in so doing were accustomed to use the form of laying on of hands, but the miraculous powers they possessed are not continued to the Church. Why then continue the form when the power no longer exists?

CHARLES. The discontinuance of the miraculous powers which the apostles possessed, is no reason why we should alter a positive institution handed down to us by the authority of ancient and general practice. The charter that gives a bishop power to ordain empowers him likewise to do it by the imposition of hands, and the practice of the Catholic Church, from the apostles' time to this day, confirms the use of this ceremony.

JOSIAH. Well! to revert to what thou said a short time since, I must say that I little thought to hear thee defending a corrupt ministry as thou hast done. And, as if Judas Iscariot was not enough, thou must bring forward Alexander VI. too, one of the vilest monsters that ever disgraced humanity. How can such bad men be ministers of Christ? If not His ministers, how could they transmit His authority?

CHARLES. I defend neither Judas nor Alexander. You mistake my statement—which is, that unfaithful ministers are still ministers, though bad ones. To their Master they stand or fall. It is His prerogative, not mine, to displace them. Alexander VI. is nothing to me but an unworthy bishop; and even had the Church of England received her orders through him, which, thank God, she does not, they would not be invalidated by his unworthiness. The authority to transmit the commission is in the office, not in the individual who fills it. The line of the priesthood was continued through Phinehas, notwithstanding his vileness. The blessing delivered by Balaam lost nothing through the iniquity of the prophet.

JOSIAH. Then these bad ministers form links in the chain of apostolical succession; and yet surely they are not members of Christ's Church, for which Christ died?

CHARLES. I am compelled to see Christ in the office he has himself instituted. To me the minister is no more than an instrument in the hands of Christ. His office I "reverence;" but he who fills it is only "reverend" by courtesy, unless he fill it worthily. Then indeed he shall be "counted worthy of double honour." The very name of "minister" shows the subordination of the man to Him who has promised to be with His ministers "even unto the end of the world."

JOSIAH. Aye, with His *faithful* ministers, and with

His faithful people too : but not with those who take up
the ministry from ambition, lust of power, love of money,
or other unworthy motives. These have neither part nor
lot in His ministry.

CHARLES. I have as yet taken only the black side
of the question. You asked me what was a *regularly*
appointed ministry ; and a sufficient reply would have
been, one appointed by a rule sanctioned and confirmed by
the practice of the apostles, and of the Church since their
days. So far for mere regularity. But if you had asked
me what I consider a *fitly* appointed ministry to be, I
should have added to the regular appointment, the qualifi-
cations of faith, zeal, charity, aptness of speech, knowledge, and such other graces as will make him useful to
the Church. Now I think you must allow that, if we
have to deplore the existence of unfaithful ministers, we
can also show (and that from generation to generation), a
goodly array of faithful men who have loved their Lord
and his gospel above every other object.

JOSIAH. I fully admit it ; but to return to the subject
we were discussing, I wish to state more fully our views
as respects true Gospel ministry. They depend upon this
leading principle, that the Lord Jesus Christ is the Head
of His Church upon earth ; that He is not only " the High
Priest of our profession," our advocate and mediator with
the Father, but that, through His Spirit dwelling in the
hearts of the faithful, He rules and directs the members
of His Church, feeds them with " the bread of life," and
administers those spiritual gifts which are needful for the
edifying of the body. " One is your master, even Christ—
" all ye are brethren," or, as Dean Alford explains it,
" All are substantially equal—none by office or precedence

" nearer to God than another ; none standing between his
" brethren and God." It is the prerogative of Christ to
call those whom He pleases to labour in His service, and
He qualifies them for the work by the immediate and
continued influence of the Holy Spirit. The true Gospel
minister is not only " inwardly moved by the Holy
Ghost to take upon him this office and ministration,"
but he also receives assistance whenever it is right for
him to exercise his gift. He does not claim that plenary
inspiration which gives language to the tongue and
knowledge to the understanding, but he does feel that
his Divine Guide strengthens and instructs him for the
work, and at times leads him to address himself particularly to those subjects which are specially suited to
the condition of his auditors. Thus may we describe
that gift of prophecy which we believe is still continued
to the Church.

CHARLES. Some of your ministers have gone much
beyond that, and have claimed something nearly approaching to the inspiration of apostolic times. I think Barclay
says that " every evangelist and Christian pastor ought
" to be led and ordered " by the Holy Spirit, " both as to
" the place where, as to the persons to whom, and as to
" the time wherein he is to minister."*

JOSIAH. Robert Barclay does maintain this, and there
are records of many ministers who do appear to have been
so watchful of the gentle intimations of the Holy Spirit in
their hearts, that they may be said, in the exercise of their
ministry, to have walked by faith and not by sight. Still I
believe that many are truly called who do not receive more

---

* *Barc. Apol. Prop. X. Argument.*

than the general call to labour in the Gospel. Those of
our ministers who have themselves stamped their authority
so very high as some have certainly done, have gone against
the express advice of the Church, which directs ministers
to "beware of laying stress on the authority of their minis-
" try ; the baptising power of the Spirit of Truth accom-
" panying the words being the true evidence."*

CHARLES. Such exaggerated claims to divine direction
must have deprived you of the services of many a sober-
minded, intelligent man. The result has been that several
of your congregations have no minister at all, and have
not had for many years.

JOSIAH. There are certainly several congregations in
which the voice of ministry is rarely heard, except when
they receive visits from those who come from a distance.

CHARLES. You consider that the discourses of your
ministers ought to be wholly unpremeditated ?

JOSIAH. To fix beforehand on a particular subject with
the determination of preaching on it at a particular time, is
certainly inconsistent with a belief in that guidance by the
Holy Spirit which is involved in the idea of the gift of
prophecy : but this does not apply to the exercise of the
gift of teaching in the Church.

CHARLES. You do not then consider that learning, or,
as Friends designate it, " head knowledge " is altogether
useless ?

JOSIAH. The study of divine things by unassisted
human reason, or, as it has sometimes been termed, " head
knowledge," will never make a minister of the Gospel.
Still I must say that many Friends have unnecessarily

---

* *Advices to Ministers and Elders.*

disparaged intellectual attainments, as though they interfered with the work of the Spirit. It is one thing to assert that such knowledge is essential, and another, and quite a different matter, to assert its great usefulness when sanctified by the presence of the Holy Spirit. Christianity claims for its service *all* the faculties of man.

CHARLES. True.

JOSIAH. In a document lately issued by a quarterly meeting in England, we find it stated as their opinion that a disposition to look "for extraordinary revelations, has " led to a disregard of that all-pervading influence by " which the natural powers of the mind might have been " sanctified to the Lord's service, and that they believe " it has, in some instances, produced a discouraging effect " on those who might otherwise have been engaged in the " work of the ministry."

CHARLES. In other words, the doctrine of the "immediate influence of the Spirit," or "immediate revelation," as taught by Fox and Barclay and their earlier and later disciples, has had the effect deplored by this quarterly meeting. I am not surprised at the result.

JOSIAH. The result has arisen from perverted views of that doctrine ; but this does not invalidate the truth of the doctrine itself. Among you but one minister is usually appointed to each congregation, I believe ?

CHARLES. One minister is specially appointed to the charge of each parish or district, but where there is need of more help, he has subordinates to assist him.

JOSIAH. Yet in apostolic times there were evidently several ministers in each congregation, as we find from Paul's epistles to the Corinthians. "The manifestation of the Spirit was given to every man to profit withal ;" that is, to every living member of the Church. Whoever felt an inward impulse might speak in the assembly, but no one was to wish to be the sole speaker, and no one was to interrupt another. " Let the prophets speak, two or three, " and let the others judge. If anything be revealed to " another that sitteth by, let the first hold his peace. For " ye may all prophesy one by one, that all may learn and " all may be comforted."

CHARLES. In the passage you quote respecting " the manifestation of the Spirit" being given to every man to profit withal, the apostle does not mean to say that such manifestation is given equally to every member of the Church ; but that to whomsoever a " manifestation " is given, it is given that it may be useful to the Church.

JOSIAH. Certainly the manifestation is not given *equally* to every member. The apostle has just stated that " there are diversities of gifts," and after affirming that the manifestation of the Spirit is given to each individual (ἑκάστῳ) he proceeds to enumerate the various ways in which the Spirit works, " dividing to each (ἑκάστῳ) severally as He will," and then, comparing the Church to the natural body, he shows that " all the members of that one body" have a part to perform in its service.

CHARLES. The practice of allowing several speakers may have been very proper in the early days of the Church, while the gift of prophecy was continued, but when it ceased, a different mode of conducting public worship became necessary. And undoubtedly the Church has power, from time to time, to alter the arrangements for the public services.

JOSIAH. I cannot admit that the gift of prophecy has ceased ; that is, the ministry of the word under the quickening influence of the Holy Spirit. See how the Apostle Paul speaks of it in 1 Cor., chap. xiv. " Desire [or strive for] spiritual gifts, but rather that ye may prophesy," and he goes on to shew that prophecy, which he describes as " speaking unto men to edification and exhortation and " comfort," edifies more than speaking with tongues ; and that while profitable for those who have not yet believed, it is eminently intended for believers. He speaks as if this gift had been conferred on several persons in the congregation, and ends as he began by desiring the Corinthians to " covet [or strive] to prophesy." Can we believe that this gift, thus freely bestowed on the early believers, and which the apostle so strongly enjoins the Corinthians to strive after as being peculiarly valuable, has been wholly withdrawn from the Church? There is nothing in its nature, or in the object for which it was bestowed, that should lead us to think that it would be confined to the apostolic age.

CHARLES. " Speaking unto men to edification and exhortation and comfort" is doubtless as necessary now as ever it was ; nor can this or any other ministerial function be worthily performed but by and through the Holy Spirit. Yet the grace vouchsafed to the Christian ministry now is surely very unlike that spiritual outpouring which marked " the gift of prophecy" in the apostolic age. But is prophecy the *only* gift you allow to remain ? Have you forgotten the gift of teaching—surely a permanent inheritance of the Church? Where are your teachers? Our ministers, besides speaking to " exhortation and comfort," assume to be teachers ; and they teach not only by sermons, but by orally catechising children and young persons, who are not brought to be confirmed by the bishop till they have been taught, at least, the chief heads of Christian doctrine. How is it with you? I fear that whilst vainly looking for instruction through miraculous gifts, you neglect that most important duty, for the performance of which you have ample promise of Divine assistance. The ignorance not only on religious subjects generally, but on the broad principles of Christianity, which prevails, (or which did prevail within my memory,) among your younger members, justifies what I say.

JOSIAH. The charge is too sweeping, though certainly there is ground for it. I might almost say that the gift of teaching has been practically ignored amongst us. Our deficiency in this respect has been a great loss to us, and it is, I believe, the principal cause of our present lukewarmness. It ought not to have been so, for teaching is clearly distinguished from prophecy by the writers of the New Testament, and its necessity is amply shown. There were "diversities of gifts" in apostolic days, and it is the same now. The apostle Paul, when enumerating the gifts of the Lord to His Church, says, " He gave some, apostles ; " and some prophets ; and some, evangelists ; and some, " pastors and teachers ; for the perfecting of the saints, for " the work of the ministry, for the edifying of the body of " Christ." The same Holy Spirit must qualify *all* the labourers whom the Lord sends forth, but the qualification differs according to the purpose which it is intended to serve. The gift required for teaching, or for the work of an evangelist or missionary, is different from that of prophecy. Yet do these gifts merge into each other : it is not so much a question of kind as of degree ; the Holy Spirit's aid will be given in proportion as it is needed.

CHARLES. The prophecy spoken of in the New Testament

was uttered under the direct inspiration of the Holy Spirit. Independently of this, there were those who " preached " or proclaimed to unbelievers the glad tidings of salvation, and those, in every congregation, who instructed believers in the doctrine and practice of Christianity. You have merged all these gifts into one, and that one a creation of your own imagination.

JOSIAH. To proclaim the glad tidings of salvation to the unenlightened, or to the heathen, and to instruct the young and ignorant in the truths of the Gospel, are duties requiring the aid of the Holy Spirit; but this assistance is generally afforded by enlightening and directing the human understanding, in its prayerful efforts after the knowledge of divine things, rather than by the more special guidance which is conferred in the gift of prophecy. Yet we cannot attempt to define the limits between prophecy and teaching; both gifts may be bestowed on the same persons, and may even be combined in the same discourse; and I believe that the gift of prophecy has often been conferred on, and exercised by ministers of other religious communities as well as ours, who have, however, only assumed to be pastors or teachers.*   If

---

* The ministers of other religious communities not unfrequently claim both *special assistance and immediate guidance* in terms very similar to those used by Friends. The private memoranda of David Brainerd, whose success as a missionary among the North American Indians is so well known, contains many such expressions as the following :—" Lord's Day, October 17th, 1742. " Had a considerable sense of my helplessness and inability, so " that I must be dependant on God for all I want, and especially " when I went to public worship. I found I could not speak a " word for God without His special help and assistance. I went

the gift of teaching had been more clearly recognised, and more fully practised amongst us in time past, many might have found that, in making use of the one talent confided to them, they would have been considered worthy of more, and thus, as in the early church, teaching would frequently have been combined with the higher gift of prophecy. I think, also, that the recognition of teaching as a distinct office in the Church would have induced a more careful and intelligent study of Scripture, and thus have freed us from the reproach thou brought against us a short time since, that " very few of our ministers could read the New Testament in Greek."

CHARLES. This is wholly inconsistent with the views of George Fox and the early Friends.

" into the assembly trembling, as I frequently do, under a sense " of my insufficiency to do anything in the cause of God as I " ought to do. But it pleased God to afford me much assistance, " and there seemed to be a considerable effect on the hearers." . . " October 26th. I shall certainly 'daub with untempered mortar,' " if God do not grant me special help. . . . . God afforded me " some life and power, both in prayer and sermon. He was pleased " to lift me up, and show me that He could enable me to preach." " March 9th, 1743. Had some assistance, and I trust something " of the Divine presence was among us." . . . "July 1st, 1744. " In the forenoon preached to the Indians without any heart : " in the afternoon still barren, when I began to preach ; but soon " I found in myself a spirit of love, and warmth, and power to " address the poor Indians ; and God helped me to plead with " them. I am persuaded also that the Lord touched their con- " sciences, for I never saw such attention raised in them before."

Similar expressions, denoting a belief in the *special* help and guidance of the Holy Spirit, are to be found in the letters or other writings of pious men of all communions. The following are taken from the *letters* of Henry Watson Fox, a missionary in

JOSIAH. I cannot admit that it is inconsistent with their *principles*, though our practical neglect, as respects religious teaching, may naturally lead thee to think so. Considerable improvement, however, has taken place of late years. The children at our public schools are now carefully instructed ; our deficiency towards those of riper years is acknowledged ; and the duty of the Church towards all its members is fully recognized. This subject has received the close attention of the Yearly Meeting of London, and, at its last annual meeting, minutes of advice were adopted, recognising " the diversities of gifts, " intellectual as well as spiritual, which the Lord, in His " care for the Church, is pleased to confer upon its several " members ;" and in the belief that " every living mem-

---

India under the Church Missionary Society :—"August 2nd, 1840. " I believe, from the bottom of my heart, with that strong sense " of certainty and assurance which is only given to us on import- " ant points, that the missionary career of life, on which I am " about to enter, is my peculiar mission and work, for which I " was brought into this world; . . . and were I now to resist the " light I have, or had I neglected to follow where the light (once " not so clear) led me, it would have been in no wise inconsistent " with God's providence and mode of dealing with us, to have " taken me away from all work, either by lingering disease, by " death, or other means. For every soul born into this world has " its own peculiar mission ; and to the soul that strives to know, " the knowledge of its mission is given, which, if it refuse to " follow, woe be to it !" . . . . "April 3rd, 1843. Will you " make it one of your prayers for us, that we may be guided to " know what is God's will regarding us?" . . . "January 13th, " 1848. God does not always make our distant plans clear to us; " only, if we have sought His guidance, he will make the next " step to be taken clear to us."

" ber has a place of service, the manifestation of the spirit
" having been given to such to profit withal," exhorting
them to " a freer exercise of the various gifts bestowed
upon them." We are, indeed, slow in making changes,
yet I trust that before long, our body will not be so liable
to the charge of neglecting the gift of teaching.

CHARLES. It is well to be improving. Meanwhile,
many of your young people are deserting you, and seeking
instruction in other communions; and unless your new
arrangements are quickly completed, there is some danger
that your teachers, when appointed, may preach to empty
benches. You quoted just now from the epistle to the
Corinthians; pray read the chapter to the end. What
is this about " women keeping silence in the Church?"
Is that like the practice of your meetings?

JOSIAH. That prohibition to women has no reference
to their exercising the gift of the ministry, but to their
" asking questions" in the church. It is written that "in
Christ Jesus there is neither male nor female;" " all are
one." Priscilla joined with Aquila in "expounding the
way of God more perfectly" to the neophyte Apollos. We
also find that Paul refers to those women who laboured
with him in the Gospel, and that Philip had four daughters,
" virgins, which did prophesy," showing that women's
preaching prevailed in apostolic times. Paul, moreover,
gives directions that a woman praying or prophesying
should not uncover her head.

CHARLES. I know that Friends are very apt to apply
everything that is said of prophets and prophesying in the
New Testament to Gospel ministry, as if prophesying and
preaching were the same thing, and as if there were no
other ministration in the early church. The word prophe-

6*

sying is indeed sometimes used in the sense of preaching the Gospel, to designate a discourse flowing from the direct revelation and impulse of the Holy Spirit. In the seed-time of the Church supernatural gifts of many kinds were freely bestowed, and, amongst others, the gift of prophecy was frequently given. Had such continued to be God's dealing with the Church; were such communications from the Holy Spirit still continued, and partaken of by women as well as men, something might be said in favour of women exercising their gifts in public. But as it is, I do not think the case of Philip's daughters makes any thing for women's preaching.

JOSIAH. You consider the gift of prophecy to have ceased, and that your ministers are only pastors and teachers. Now if this office is to be confined to a single person, that person certainly ought not to be a woman; because to undertake its duties would be " to usurp authority over the man." Your ministers also assume to be priests, and as such to have the exclusive right to perform certain "holy functions," as you call them, without which you can have no public worship, or, as some say, no salvation. To be eligible for this "office" a man must obtain a university degree; he must study theology, and undergo examinations as to his proficiency in his studies before he is admitted to the lowest grade. You can hardly quote Scripture for this course of study, which is more like the training for some worldly calling. Our practice, on the other hand, has ample warrant. "The wind bloweth where it listeth;" and the Holy Spirit sheds his gifts alike on learned and unlearned.

CHARLES. We shall discuss the question of the priesthood hereafter. By the theory of Quakerism there can be no *ministry* amongst you; at least no pastoral ministry. Preachers or "prophets" you may have, but none to obey as those "that have the rule over you," "that watch for your souls as they that must give account." Such pastors and teachers the apostles were careful to appoint in every congregation settled by them; but you have set aside their example.

JOSIAH. We are certainly not without pastoral care, though it may be less complete than it should be. This is the purpose for which our overseers and elders are appointed, and, allowing for human imperfection and weakness, they perform their duties faithfully and often zealously. Perhaps George Fox was more thought of by his contemporaries as an "elder ruling well," and "feeding the flock," than even as a minister of the word.

CHARLES. As to the degree of education required in those who are destined to be pastors and teachers in the Church, remember that none but a polished shaft is fitted for the Lord's temple; that the best gifts are improved by culture; and that one who is to be "apt to teach" cannot himself be too well learned. A university degree is not indispensable, though usually required as a guarantee of a good education. If the Church do nothing more unscriptural than insist that those who enter her service shall first be instructed in learning and sound doctrine, she may be forgiven; for you will hardly say, as Festus said unto Paul, "Much learning doth make thee mad." On the contrary, you allow that both Paul and Apollos owed much of their usefulness, humanly speaking, to their learning.

St. Paul was chosen, we cannot doubt, on account of his profound learning ; and Apollos is said to have helped, by his scriptural learning, "those who had believed through grace."

JOSIAH. It is by the graces of the Holy Spirit that the shaft is polished for the Lord's temple. The qualification recorded of Barnabas is, that " he was a good man, and full of the Holy Ghost, and of faith." I have already admitted the great advantage of human learning, though I deny its necessity.

CHARLES. Nor do we insist on its absolute necessity. You said just now that your ministers speak under the immediate influence of the Holy Spirit. Do you really believe that all you hear from your preachers' gallery is uttered under the immediate guidance of the *infallible* Spirit of God ?

JOSIAH. The Holy Spirit is indeed infallible, but the human instrument is weak and liable to err. Hence the necessity for the appointment of elders.

CHARLES. The elders are, I suppose, appointed to watch the ministry of those who speak in your meetings ?

JOSIAH. It is one of their principal duties to guard against the encroachments of unsound doctrine, to encourage the feeble and diffident, and to restrain the forward and hasty. For the proper performance of their important duties, they require a measure of that gift which the apostle Paul designates as " discerning of spirits," in order that they may be qualified to distinguish between the operation of the Holy Spirit and the workings of the human mind. "Let the prophets speak two or three, " and let the others judge." If anything be revealed to

" another that sitteth by, let the first hold his peace. For
" ye may all prophesy one by one, that all may learn and
" all may be comforted. And the spirits of the prophets
" are subject to the prophets." That is, the prophet can
control his own spiritual emotions, so that he may be
silent for a time, and wait his turn to speak. " For God
is not the author of confusion but of peace."

CHARLES. Then I presume we may receive all we hear
from the mouths of "acknowledged ministers," in their
prophesying, if sanctioned by the discerners of spirits who
are present, as being delivered *ex cathedrâ;* spoken scripture, so to say.

JOSIAH. Certainly not. The plenary inspiration granted
to the apostles is not continued to the Church, nor, as
I said before, is it needed; because we have in the Holy
Scriptures a complete record of Christian doctrine. I
may cite the opinion of Neander, respecting the prophets in the early Christian Church, that "although
" illuminated in a high degree by the Divine Spirit, they
" were still liable to err," and that they " did not pretend to
be infallible." How then could we claim infallibility for
either our elders or our ministers? Even those who have
received a true call may sometimes be deceived by the
working of their own imaginations, or by " him who can
transform himself into an angel of light." They may become careless or unfaithful; they may grow lukewarm
through love of the world, or lose themselves by spiritual
pride. They have "this treasure in earthen vessels;"
therefore that which is of God has, mingled with it, much
that gives proof of the weakness of the man. Yet, if
always humble and watchful unto prayer, they would

know the voice of the true Shepherd, and would not be suffered to go astray.*　　　·

CHARLES. It is not very easy for the uninitiated to follow your doctrine, or to see what it is you gain by this "immediate guidance of the Holy Spirit" to which your ministers lay claim. You·tell me that "the true gospel minister is qualified by the immediate and continued influence of the Holy Spirit ;" you profess to believe that such exist among you ; and then you leave me and the unlearned of your congregations to judge whether what is spoken by your inspired minister is to be received or

---

* *Liability of ministers to err.* Neander, in his *History of the Planting of Christianity, vol.* 1, *p.* 138, in reference to 1 Cor. xiv., 29-33, says,—" If Paul considered such injunctions to be neces-
" sary, it is apparent that he by no means recognised, in the
" prophets of the Church, pure organs of the Divine Spirit, in
" whom the divine and human might not easily be confounded.
" On the contrary the churches were to be guarded against the
" delusions which prevailed, . . . by exercising a trial of spirits,
" for which a special gift was granted to individuals. . . . . The
" design of this gift was certainly not merely to decide who was
" a prophet, and who was not ; but chiefly for the purpose of dis-
" tinguishing, in the addresses of those who stood up as inspired
" speakers in the Christian assemblies—between what proceeded
" from the Divine Spirit, and what did not proceed from that
" source ; so Paul, on this point, recommended the Church to try
" every thing communicated by the prophets, and required them
" to separate the good from the bad. 1 Thess. v. 21. And as
" the prophets did not pretend to be infallible, but were conscious
" of their liability to error, they submitted themselves to the
" judgment of the Church, or of their organs appointed for the
' purpose, and thus were preserved from the self-delusion of pride,
" that fruitful source of enthusiasm."

rejected. Your mode of dealing with this subject seems to me to be identical with the neological method of treating the inspiration of Holy Scripture. Do you then apply the same rule to the written word?

JOSIAH. By no means. We receive all the canonical books of the Bible as fully as the Church of England does. The Holy Scriptures contain the revelation of the Divine will, and are the divinely appointed means for preserving the truths of Christianity undefiled. We receive them as the authorized standard of doctrine, believing that whatsoever any one advances which is contrary thereto, falsely pretending to be moved by the Spirit, must be deemed a delusion of the devil.

CHARLES. This does not appear to me to be a consistent course. According to your theory, Holy Scripture and "true gospel ministry" spring from "the same source." However different in volume the stream that flows to each may be, as they come from one Fountain Head, I suppose them to be intrinsically of the same nature. But the written word of prophecy you receive in faith; and the spoken word of your ministers, whom you believe to be endowed with the spirit of prophecy, you criticise just as if it were a human composition. I think that formerly your belief was much less discriminatory. I well remember the reverential awe with which, as a boy, I looked up to a "travelling Friend,"* and how firmly I believed in the inspiration of what he uttered. Nor was my belief singular, nor merely the unhesitating confidence of a child. But latterly the halo of rays seems fast departing from the

---

* A name commonly given to a Quaker preacher when travelling *away from home* in the exercise of his ministry.

preachers' gallery. Children hear their parents talking over what has been preached in meeting, and perhaps criticising the sermons. Naturally they become critics too, and, as I take it, criticism and scepticism in such a case are one. They will soon cease to believe even your modified view of their "ministers'" inspiration. If you wish to preserve the faith of your young people in this leading doctrine of Quakerism, you must beware of the schoolmaster now abroad, and keep your children to the old-fashioned, narrow education of the original sect.

JOSIAH. The criticism will not always be unfavourable. Parents will often speak of the discourse they have heard, so as to recommend it to their children's minds. If in a right spirit, criticism will do good and not harm.

CHARLES. I cannot be surprised that your more intelligent members should criticise, and that severely too, much that they are compelled to listen to. My surprise is that any intelligent person continues to put faith in your doctrine of immediate influence. Sometimes they hear a long, rambling discourse, which runs hither and thither, so that it is difficult to follow the sense; sometimes a string of texts, often incorrectly quoted, tagged to a few words; and occasionally the relation of a personal history, or a commentary on a remarkable dream. It is impossible that well educated young persons can believe in the immediate inspiration of such addresses. Give me in preference the well studied, well put together, and comprehensive sermon of an educated and pious man, although his appointment come through the hands of a bishop. I shall then know what I have to deal with; but I cannot tell whether what I hear in your meetings is given forth by the true or by a false inspiration.

JOSIAH. I fear that on such occasions these Friends exceed the measure of their gift, if they have one. Your preachers also sometimes deliver sermons which are not acceptable to the congregation. Our advices to ministers recommend them "to be frequent in reading the Holy "Scriptures, diligent in meditating upon them, and care- "ful not to misquote or misapply them." I have often heard discourses which, for logical clearness and purity of doctrine, would compare favourably with the sermons of your college-taught preachers, and which, in earnestness and pathos, possess the advantage which a discourse that is spoken always has over that which is read. Even as respects the weakest of those who minister amongst us, I have often thought of the lines of George Herbert :

> Judge not the preacher ; for he is thy judge.
> If thou mislike him, thou conceivest him not.
> God calleth preaching folly. Do not grudge
> To pick out treasures from an earthen pot.
> The worst speak something good : if all want sense,
> God takes a text, and preacheth patience.

CHARLES. I do not suppose that *all* the professedly inspired discourses of your ministers are feeble or confused. "A good man out of the good treasure of his heart "bringeth forth good things." Many a man of fervid temperament, whose heart has been renewed by the Holy Spirit, is also gifted with natural eloquence and a logical head. Such an one may become a powerful preacher, whether he believe in immediate revelation in the Quaker sense, or not ; and such, surely, are to be met with among Christians of all denominations. I remain of the opinion, therefore, that your theory of immediate guidance is unproven.

JOSIAH. It rather rests with thee to show that this guidance of the Holy Spirit is not still continued to the Church : the apostle Paul gives no indication that he considered it to be temporary. Thou wholly ignores the evils of your system, whilst thou exaggerates those of ours ; we believe it to be in accordance with Scripture, and see no cause to change it.

CHARLES. Surely "the gold has become dim." Two centuries ago your preachers were Boanerges, sons of thunder. Latterly the majority of your preachers have been women ; a sure sign of weakness in the body.

JOSIAH. In things spiritual the woman is often the stronger vessel, her faith and love deeper, her zeal more abounding, her knowledge as clear. Hast thou forgotten the lines,

> No tongue of hers her suffering Lord betrayed ;
> She, while apostles shrank, could danger brave,
> Last at His cross, and earliest at His grave.

CHARLES. They are true and beautiful lines. Yet I cannot think the prevalence of women's preaching a sign of health in your body. Surely at least it proves a deficiency on the part of the men ; a decay in their faith, love, zeal, and knowledge. It shows that they have left the post on the watch tower to those who had better be employed by the fireside, in the care of their children and servants. I fancy St. Paul had some such thoughts when he says, "I " suffer not a woman *to teach*, nor to usurp authority over " the man, but to be in silence."

JOSIAH. I do not think he had any such idea in his mind when he wrote these words : yet it certainly is a proof of lukewarmness or worldly-mindedness on the part

of the men, that more of them are not called to the work
of the ministry : but in this respect, also, there are signs
of improvement.

CHARLES. Woman's highest mission is in her family.
How many celebrated men have had highly gifted and
careful mothers. It is a rare thing to see a distinguished
father have an equally distinguished son ; but nothing is
more common than to find the germs of a great man's mind
in that of his mother. Depend upon it, a woman who
brings up a family of Christian children, to whom her
daily life is a practical sermon, is not only far more useful
in her day and generation, but a more faithful servant of
her Lord, than if she had left her family to the care of
others, and gone preaching up and down the world.

JOSIAH. I feel the great importance of maternal care.
It is a woman's first duty ; yet we are encouraged to leave
" father and mother, son and daughter, for Christ's sake
and the Gospel's. "

CHARLES. Doubtless there are cases in which it becomes
a duty to give up all for Christ's sake. The right hand
and the right eye may be called for, and should be given
up.

JOSIAH. And doubtless so our women friends feel
when first they are called on to undertake this duty.

CHARLES. I do not doubt that they feel it, and that it
is a sore trial and giving-up to many of them. My doubt
is, whether this sacrifice be called for by the Holy Spirit,
or by a spirit of enthusiasm transformed into an angel of
light. Can any ministerial call authorise a woman to
neglect her own peculiar duty ? He who ordained marriage laid woman's highest and holiest duties on the
mother's shoulder. It must be indeed a " weighty con-

cern," which would justify a woman in deserting her own family to travel in this "ministry." I think you very frequently see the children of women-preachers ill brought up. They are often allowed to take care of themselves, because their mother's thoughts are engrossed with the care of the Church.

JOSIAH. I have heard as much of the children of clergymen.

CHARLES. But it must needs be still more true of the children of *clergywomen.* The mother's influence in guiding the dispositions of young children, at the age when dispositions are often determined for life, is much greater than that of the father. When she is so taken up with the outer world that she cannot attend to home duties, she incurs a heavy responsibility. Some mothers give themselves up to fashion, and some to preaching; and no wonder if the lambs of their flock are lost to the fold.

JOSIAH. Yet, surely the proportion of good mothers is as large in our Society as in any religious community. Whether it be the domestic habits consequent on the seclusion from a life of gaiety, or the responsibility thrown on them by being employed in the service of the Church, there is, I think, no body of Christians in which women are more conspicuous for sound good sense, more exemplary in the discharge of all the duties of home, or more desirous, both by the silent influence of their example and the wisdom of their precepts, to train up their children " in the nurture and admonition of the Lord."

CHARLES. It may be so; but this makes nothing in favour of women's preaching.

JOSIAH. On the other hand, can the arrangement of your Church be right, which totally refuses the services of women? It seems to me to place them in a very different position from that which they held in the time of the apostles. The Church of Rome is wiser, and avails itself largely of woman's piety and devotion.*

CHARLES. The Church does not refuse the legitimate services of women. It is notorious that ministering church-women are actively employed in every parish, and most gratefully are their labours among the poor, the sick and the ignorant, appreciated by clergy and laity. There is a strong desire among the more earnest clergy to increase the field of woman's usefulness, large as that already is. All that our Church " refuses " to women is clerical status and licence to preach.

JOSIAH. Let us return to our subject. Thou hast already given me thy notions of a regularly appointed ministry, but hast said nothing about a regularly paid one.

CHARLES. I despise the man whose only end in preaching the gospel is to put money in his pocket. You will find me as bitter as yourself against " hireling ministers."

---

* Lord Macaulay, in the essay on Ranke's History of the Popes before referred to, speaking of the Church of Rome says, " Even for female agency there is a place in her system. To " devout women she assigns spiritual functions, dignities and " magistracies. In our country, if a noble lady is moved by more " than ordinary zeal for the propagation of religion, the chance " is that, though she may disapprove of no doctrine or ceremony " of the Established Church, she will end by giving her name to " a new schism. If a pious and benevolent woman enter the cells " of a prison to pray with the most unhappy and degraded of her " own sex, she does so without any authority from the Church. " No line of action is traced out for her ; and it is well if the " ordinary does not complain of her intrusion, and if the bishop " does not shake his head at such irregular benevolence."

JOSIAH. Then thou must agree in our interpretation of
" Freely you have received, freely give," as implying that
the Gospel should be preached without fee or reward ;—
that the minister should have neither tithe nor stipend,
but should earn his bread, like other folk, by the labour
of his hands and the sweat of his brow. Paul was a
tent-maker, and wrought at his trade ; Peter and John
were fishermen ; and Luke was a physician. Just as, with
us, one may be a banker, another a lawyer, and others
either merchants or shopkeepers.

CHARLES. You mistake me. It is one thing to preach
for hire, hire being the motive, and another, " to live of
the Gospel," to receive a stipend from the congregation to
whose spiritual wants you minister. The passages in the
New Testament where this is enjoined are numerous,
especially in the writings of St. Paul. I need however
only instance 1 Cor., ix. 7-14, ending with these words :
" Even so hath the Lord ordained that they which preach
" the gospel should live of the gospel." Observe, it is
the Lord who has ordained this : the same Lord who said,
" The labourer is worthy of his hire."

JOSIAH. Yet Paul immediately afterwards repudiates
such a provision for himself, and it is abundantly clear
that both at Corinth and elsewhere he refused a maintenance, and wrought at his trade. He appeals to the
Ephesians : " Ye yourselves know that these hands have
" ministered to my necessities, and to them that were
" with me."

CHARLES. Yes. This is true enough. But it is also
very clear, from many passages of his writings besides
what I have already quoted, that St. Paul regarded his
own case as an exceptional one. He is very particular to

establish by argument the *right* of the labourer to his hire. That settles the question between us, for you deny the *right.* He tells the Corinthians that he " had not been burdensome" unto them, but had "taken wages of other churches to do them service ;" and he asks them to " forgive him this wrong." Here is a case in which the spirit speaking by George Fox contradicts the Spirit speaking by an apostle. Which are we to believe ?

JOSIAH. There is no such contradiction. The apostles left their homes and ordinary avocations, and therefore could not support themselves, unless when, as in the case of Paul just now referred to, they remained for a considerable time in one place. Their whole time was occupied in their mission, and it was therefore right that they should be supported by those for whom they laboured. " If we " have sown unto you spiritual things, is it a great thing " if we shall reap your carnal things ?" When any of our ministers leave home in the performance of their duty, they also receive support and all that they require. But where do we find any example, in Scripture, of the support of the teachers or pastors or prophets of any particular congregation, while living at their own homes ? Or where do we find any warrant for the continuation of the Jewish system of tithes ? Your legalized system fixes a stipend " for the cure of souls" in each particular locality, and therefore, in many cases, men " enter the Church," and undertake the holiest of duties, not for Christ's sake, but as a means of livelihood ; or they are induced to choose this profession by the respectability which it confers on those who engage in it. Such an establishment inevitably produces this result. Hence many neglect the *sheep*, but look very carefully after the shearing. The system of lay impropriation exemplifies this disgracefully. The right of presentation to livings is openly bought and sold, and numbers are induced to take "holy orders" solely for pecuniary reasons, without feeling any call to the ministry.

CHARLES. Lay impropriations are indeed a monstrous abuse of power, under the name of "law." There are abuses in every system, but these cannot set aside a rightful claim. It is as much a part of the duty of the Church now to instruct the young and the ignorant, as it was in the apostles' days to proclaim the glad tidings of the Gospel far and wide, through all lands. For this purpose, as well as for the celebration of the appointed ordinances, and the orderly conducting of public worship, it is necessary to set apart a body of men ; and it is but reasonable to supply them with food and raiment, or with an annual income to provide things decent.

JOSIAH. "Provide things honest in the sight of all men," was the exhortation of the apostle Paul to his Roman brethren, while he recognised them as being "many members," having different offices in the same body. But though speaking of prophecy, ministering and teaching, &c. being the several duties of different "members," he gives no indication of the division of the Church into laymen and clerks. Such a division produces evil results, leading people to imagine that a different rule of Christian morality is to be applied to either class. And, in practice, the laity too often seem to imagine that the whole work of religion is to be done by the clergy, and that laymen may neglect it with impunity. Where do you find Scripture warrant for a division into clergy and laity ? The apostolic *practice is* against you in this matter.

CHARLES. Let us first settle what is a "cleric," and what is a "layman." Both ought to be Christians in reality, and not in name only. The "layman" is an individual member of a congregation, and his public duty is fulfilled, if he "does unto all men as he would they should do to him." The "cleric," besides owing all obligations which the layman owes, has the oversight and teaching of a community of laymen committed to his charge; he is the shepherd, they the sheep. A short while ago you spoke of George Fox as having been "an elder ruling well;" you therefore recognised him as a *ruler;* and surely by the appointment of elders and overseers, and by the recognition of executive power in "the meeting of ministers and elders," your Society virtually acknowledges a clerical order. Yours is indeed a "clergy" of the very lowest type; but a clergy, of one kind or other, is indispensable in a Christian *society*, although a *community* may exist without it; a society implies order and government; in a community all things are in common, and every man may do what is right in his own eyes.

JOSIAH. Our elders and overseers, whose appointment thou considers "a virtual acknowledgment of a clerical order," have pastoral duties committed to them, and also executive power over the members of their own body; but whatever executive power they possess is subject to the authority of the congregation by which they have been appointed, and which is assembled monthly to transact the affairs of the Church; so that our elders and overseers are the servants of the Church instead of "ruling over" it. Perhaps I was wrong in speaking of George Fox as "ruling." I find no such term applied in the Greek *Testament to* Christian ministers. They are

7*

spoken of as presiding, (προϊστάμενοι, Rom. xii. 8) ; leading, (ἡγούμενοι, Heb. xiii. 17) but never as ruling, (κυριεύοντες.)

CHARLES. I am content with the words προϊστάμενοι and ἡγούμενοι, as used in the passages you quote, though I cannot quite agree with your attenuated translation. The word ἡγούμενος, which you say means not "ruling" but "leading," is the same word which is applied to Christ in Matt. ii. 6, "out of thee shall come a *Governor* that shall rule my people Israel." It is also the word in Acts, vii. 10, applied to Joseph ; "He made him *Governor* over Egypt." Finally, 'Ηγεμών, a cognate noun, is the word used for "governor" in speaking of Pontius Pilate and Felix. Manifestly, they who preside over or "lead" others in spiritual things, and to whom the apostle (Heb. xiii. 17) enjoins obedience, do exercise that clerical authority which I maintain has existed in the Church from the very first.

JOSIAH. I might object to the word "obey," by which πείθεσθε is translated in Heb. xiii. 17, although in most other places where the verb πείθω occurs, it is rendered by "trust" or "be persuaded," as in Luke xvi. 31. I admit that the word ὑπείκετε (submit), which occurs just afterwards, would be looked upon by many as defining the meaning ; but it appears to me that the obedience ought not to be the submission to authority, but the willing obedience which results from being persuaded. In saying, a short time since, that the "layman fulfils his public "duty, if he do to all men as he would they should do to "him," thou seems to me to place the laity in a very low position indeed ; so that, instead of its being their duty to endeavour to promote the kingdom of their Lord, it *would* seem as if any action on their part would be an improper interference with the business committed to the clergy.

CHARLES. If you wish to know the "position" of gifted laymen in our Church, I recommend you to study the writings of Alexander Knox,* the confidential adviser of the saintly Bishop Jebb, and to read the recently published life of Joshua Watson.† You will there see how faithful laymen may be eminently useful in promoting the kingdom of their Lord, without interfering with ministerial functions.

JOSIAH. Ought not every true believer to endeavour to promote the good cause, as he may have opportunity? We may remember that, in the great persecution which arose after the martyrdom of Stephen, "*all* were scattered " abroad throughout the regions of Judæa and Samaria, " except the apostles," and " they went every where preaching the word :" we are also told that "the hand " of the Lord was with them ; and a great number be- " lieved and turned to the Lord." Dost thou think these preachers had received any ordination, or any outward commission other than the original command addressed to the apostles ; " Go ye into all the world and preach the Gospel"? Wherever they went they told of that with which their own hearts were filled ; and thus the Gospel was proclaimed in these regions apparently for the first time.

CHARLES. I certainly cannot tell whether *all* who were

---

* *Remains of Alexander Knox. London,* 1834-7. *Thirty years correspondence with Bishop Jebb. London,* 1834.

† *Memoir of Joshua Watson, by Archdeacon Churton. Oxford and London,* 1861.

scattered abroad were ordained; but I do not think it likely. Neither do I find myself compelled, by the text you quote, to believe that " all" means every single Christian that then dwelt in Judæa; nor that " every where" means every part of the world. That *many* were dispersed, who went preaching to the Gentiles, is certain; but I cannot see that this fact at all affects the subject we were discussing. We have no objection to lay preaching. It is common on shipboard and in camp for the captain or officer in command, not only to read the Church prayers, but often also a sermon to the sailors or soldiers. Nor is there any necessity that the sermon should be a written one.

JOSIAH. The context shews clearly that the expression " everywhere" means " every where throughout Judæa and Samaria;" and I think it is implied, that *all* who " were scattered abroad," proclaimed that Gospel for the sake of which they had been driven from their homes in Jerusalem. What warrant does Scripture afford for the appointment of the clergy as a distinct order among Christians?

CHARLES. You have quoted St. Paul speaking to the Romans. The same apostle says to the Ephesians: "And " he gave some apostles, and some prophets, and some " evangelists, and some pastors and teachers; for the per- " fecting of the saints, for the work of the ministry, for " the edifying [building up] of the body of Christ: till we " all come in the unity of the faith and of the knowledge " of the Son of God, unto a perfect man," &c. He enlarges on the same topic to the Corinthians (1 Cor. xii.), illustrating his subject by comparing different *ministrations to* the different members of the human body, each one having its appointed office ; and often, in his other epistles, he sends special messages to the appointed and subordinate ministers or clergy ; as to Archippus (Col. iv. 17) ; and more particularly to Timothy : "Let no " man despise thy youth, but be thou an example," &c. " Neglect not the gift that is in thee, which was given " thee by prophecy, *with the laying on of the hands of* " *the presbytery.*" Who were the presbytery that joined in giving his commission to Timothy ? Were they not members of the clerical body ?

JOSIAH. Thy quotations show the variety of gifts conferred on the Church, but offer no proof that those who exercised them constituted a distinct order. Surely it is not the clergy alone, but the whole Church, which the apostle Paul compares to the human body, and he describes a great variety of gifts as existing in the different members of that one body, which is very different from your single pastor with "his flock." But how dost thou deduce the formation of what thou calls " the clerical body"?

CHARLES. The clergy, at the first, consisted simply of the apostles, chosen and commissioned by our Lord for the performance of certain specific duties (Matt. xxviii. 19, 20). By their apostleship they were as distinct from mere laymen, or "the disciples," as a general of an army is from a private soldier. When the Church began to spread from city to city, it became necessary to increase its ministers proportionally. The apostles could not impart apostolic power indefinitely, for all could not be generals, but they did appoint other officers—the overseers or bishops, or angels as St. John styles them, who, like Titus and Timothy, were commissioned to "ordain elders in every city," and to superintend public worship generally. As the Church still grew wider, various other ranks of church-officers were appointed, and the aggregate began to be distinguished—it could hardly have been otherwise —as a select few, set apart to minister about holy things. Thus the Christian priesthood, or clerical order, was of gradual growth. The seed was of the Lord's planting ; the young plant was tended and watered by the apostles ; God gave the increase, and His providence has preserved, from the apostles' days downwards, a clear line of distinction between those who minister at the Lord's table, and those whose privilege it is to be ministered unto, but who are not thereby discharged from religious obligation.

JOSIAH. Whatever may have been the case in later times, it cannot be shown that, in the apostles' days, any distinction existed separating those who ministered in the congregation from the other members of the Church.

CHARLES. But it can be shown that the apostles themselves were the nucleus of a clerical order, and that a clerical order was, from the very first, established in all churches founded by them. Who were the "angels" of the Seven Churches of Asia?

JOSIAH. Thou hast told me already that they were bishops, and I am aware that many commentators take this view. Dean Alford thinks they were really angels— the guardian angels of the Seven Churches, and cites the authority of Origen, Jerome, and others in support of his opinion.

CHARLES. When St. Paul sent for the elders [or presbyters] of the Church at Ephesus (Acts, xx.), he addressed them as a bishop might charge his clergy, thus :—" Take

heed to *yourselves*" (ye presbyters), "and to all the flock,
" *over* the which the Holy Ghost hath made you overseers,
" to feed the Church of God," &c. Here, and throughout
the whole chapter, there is a marked distinction between
" the flock " or laity, and the " presbyters or overseers,"
whose divinely appointed duty it was "to feed " the flock ;
and also "to watch for (their) souls, as they that must
give account." (Heb., xiii. 17.) If then the presbyters
were responsible to God for the souls of those committed
to their care by the Holy Ghost, how say you that they
were not, as presbyters, members of a body segregated
from the flock *over* which they were appointed to watch ?

JOSIAH. I fully recognise the duty of those who are
placed as " overseers over the flock," to " feed it," and to
" watch for their souls as they that must give account ; "
but what I deny is, that these " overseers or elders" were
constituted into a distinct order, having greater privileges
or powers than the other members of the Church. They
were not to *rule* as being "lords over God's heritage," but
to *lead* and *guide* as being " ensamples to the flock." If
we read the whole address of the apostle Paul to the
elders of Ephesus, I think it will be evident that, whilst
exhorting them to the faithful discharge of their duties,
he also addresses the whole body of the Church through
them as its representatives. He speaks of having "taught
them publicly, and from house to house ; " and adds, " I
" take you to record this day, that I am pure from the
" blood of *all* men, for I have not shunned to declare.
unto *you* all the counsel of God."

CHARLES. You truly say that St. Paul speaks to the
elders as " representatives of the whole body." Do you
not know that *the English word parson* (derived from

persona,) means one who personates or represents the
body of the parish ? This is what I contend for.

JOSIAH.　I have already maintained that the advancement of their Lord's kingdom was not to be the duty
of one select class alone, but that all the living members
of the Church have a part to perform in its service.

CHARLES.　True ; but "all have not the *same* office."

JOSIAH.　Certainly not : some receive higher gifts than
others, but, to use Dean Alford's words, " All are sub-
" stantially equal—none standing between his brethren
" and God." If this view be correct, it appears to me to
exclude the idea of a clerical order, distinct and separated
from the other members of the Church ; and I think that
such distinction has had injurious effects on both classes ;
because it has led to the idea that the clergy are, by their
office, peculiarly " holy," and bound by a stricter rule of
life than the other members of the Church.

CHARLES.　I have already maintained that the apostles
themselves were the nucleus of a clerical order.　Prove to
me from Scripture, rather than from " Dean Alford," that
the apostles never exercised clerical authority, and I am
content.

JOSIAH.　I think I have already said enough on this
subject, although more might be brought forward, if it
were well to prolong the discussion.　But thou spoke just
now of a Christian " priesthood."　Why do you call your
ministers " priests," who have no sacrifice to offer ?　The
term is not applied in the New Testament to any officers
of the Church, but Peter addresses the whole body of
believers as a " royal priesthood, a holy nation, a peculiar
people."　There is but one " High Priest over the household of God," and His is an unchanging priesthood, in

whose fulness all other priestly offering and ministration have been absorbed, who offered the once-offered sacrifice for sin, and who ever liveth to make intercession for us.

CHARLES. The English word "priest," as well as the French "*prêtre*," is etymologically contracted from "presbyter," which means "an elder ;" "Presbyter," to use Milton's words, being but "priest writ large." Is not this a sufficient reply to your objection to the word on scriptural grounds, without adverting to your irrelevant introduction of the question of sacrifice? But indeed, the fact that St. Peter addresses the whole body of Christian believers as "a royal priesthood," no more proves the non-existence of a distinct priesthood, properly so called, than the fact that Moses applied the term "kingdom of priests" to the whole body of Israelites, proves the non-existence of a distinct order of priests in the congregation or Church of Israel. St. John, in the Apocalypse, represents Christian believers as "kings and priests :" would you from this object to the use of the term "king," as distinctively applied to a Christian sovereign? At the same time we maintain no less strongly than you, that there is only one High Priest in the Christian Church, in whose name all our religious rites are performed, and from whom alone all their power and efficacy are derived.

JOSIAH. It is the present meaning, not the derivation, which is in question ; and certainly the word "priest" does convey the idea of a man who offers sacrifices, and who holds a position which authorises him to act, in some degree, as a medium between God and man. If you only mean "presbyter" or "elder," it is to be regretted that you still make use of a term which, to the uninitiated, conveys a false impression. I know that Wiclif, in several cases, translated the word πρεσβύτερος by " priest ;" but in the authorized version it is never so rendered; while the Jewish ministers of religion are always called by this name.   But it is time to conclude.   Farewell.

CONVERSATION IV.

I exhort therefore, that, first of all, supplications, prayers,
intercessions, and giving of thanks, be made for all men; for
kings, and for all that are in authority; that we may lead a quiet
and peaceable life in all godliness and honesty.—1 *Tim.* ii. 1–2.

CHARLES. We have as yet but incidentally con-
versed on the mode of conducting public worship. My
recollection of your silent meetings is not favourable. As
a boy I found them insufferably wearisome to sit through,
and usually occupied myself in idle dreams. As I grew
up, and began to appreciate the purpose for which your
meetings are held, my attendance was more voluntary,
and my time, I hope, not altogether mis-spent. But the
system never pleased me ; circumstances removed me to a
distance from a meeting-house; I began to frequent the
Church service, and finding therein what I had never
found in your assemblies, I gradually became weaned from
Quakerism. It is now many years since I attended a
Friends' meeting, and, though unconscious of hostile feelings, I have no wish ever to enter one again.

JOSIAH. I am sorry to hear thee say so. Thou knows
how highly I regard our mode of conducting congregational worship. We do not copy the forms of any

Church, but, finding no explicit instruction in the New Testament, we meet, as we believe the early Christians did, without pre-arranged form of service, depending on Him who has promised to be with the "two or three" who are gathered in His name. Therefore we sit down in silence, thinking it the best preparation for the spiritual worship, enjoined by our Divine Master himself, in His conversation with the woman of Samaria. I might quote the experience of other young persons in opposition to what thou hast said of thy boyhood, but I forbear. There are two classes which have their representatives among the attenders on every form of worship, whether it be the gorgeous ritual of Rome, or your cathedral service with the excitements of its full choir and pealing organ; or in the quiet country church, or the modest chapel of the dissenter; and these two classes are also found in our meetings, whether held in unbroken silence, or occupied with vocal prayer and the ministry of the word.

CHARLES. I spoke of my own experience as a boy, before I had put away childish things. That the thoughts of some young persons are better occupied I have no doubt, and I willingly grant that the experience of older persons may be different. I do not doubt that many of those who go to meeting for the purpose of inward retirement and waiting upon God, do enjoy that communion with the Great Head of the Church which He has promised to all who sincerely seek Him; and I can fully understand how refreshing and invigorating it must be to such persons, to leave the outward world and come taste these living waters. My doubt is, whether this silent method be the best mode of conducting public worship, in a community which must needs consist of a

great variety of dispositions, and of different degrees of
spiritual enlightenment and devotion. The object of coming together congregationally is "that *all* may learn,
and *all* may be comforted." Now the spiritually minded
carry their comfort with them ; no man can deprive
them of it, and it is just as much theirs, while travelling
up and down in the world, as it is in the meeting-house.
These may go to meetings to watch and pray ; but with
the ignorant and the empty it is not so. They have
much to learn which they cannot teach themselves, and
they do not understand or appreciate the comfort which
the spiritually minded enjoy. What is to be done with
these, who may not be the minority in some of your
assemblies ? How are they to be taught and comforted ?
Ah, Josiah, you have made a great mistake, in your neglect of all outward means in your assemblies for public
worship.

JOSIAH. I have already admitted our deficiency as
respects public teaching in the Church. The Society, as
a body, has not heretofore made sufficient provision for
scriptural instruction. It seems to have been expected
that parents would instruct their children, and the duty
of doing so has been often and urgently pressed upon
them. George Fox strongly calls on all Friends to
" exhort their families, whether they be servants or
" children, that they may be informed in the truth;" and
many have been the addresses, in the pastoral epistles
which the Yearly Meeting of London has issued annually
since 1681, calling on parents to " watch over the con-
" duct and behaviour of their children," and to " take
" particular care to acquaint them with the Holy Scrip-
" tures," " instructing them in the great love of God to

" mankind through Jesus Christ, the work of salvation by
" Him, and sanctification through His blessed Spirit."

CHARLES. And do parents generally act on this advice?

JOSIAH. Many do. Some are lamentably deficient.
Unless parents have themselves been taught in the school
of Christ, they are badly qualified to instruct others. I .
may ask thee, dost thou suppose the proportion of parents
who train their children in a religious life and conversation, is greater in your Church than in ours?

CHARLES. Careless and unfaithful parents are to be
found in all communities. Yet it is very general for
parents amongst us to teach their children the catechism,
the Lord's prayer, the commandments, and, especially,
the collects. The mother who commences her task in
weakness and fear, finds, in this treasury of prayer
which the Church offers to her use, a " schoolmaster" to
bring to Christ, not only the little ones under her teaching, but herself also. Her children are accustomed from
infancy to kneel at their bedside evening and morning,
and in a simple form of prayer, to ask forgiveness of their
Heavenly Father for what they have done amiss, to thank
Him for His goodness, and to implore His continued protection.

JOSIAH. In many cases the form will be beyond the
comprehension of the child, and the repetition, as a prayer,
of words which he does not understand, is, to say the least
of it, of very doubtful propriety. Archbishop Whately, in
his " Errors of Romanism," classes among superstitions,
the teaching forms of prayer to children unless they are
quite capable of understanding them. He says, " Every
" one who knows what it is (not merely to say his prayers,
" but) really to pray, must be conscious that a continual

" effort is requisite to prevent a form of words with
" which he is very familiar, from sliding over the ear or
" the tongue, without being properly attended to, and
" accompanied by the heart and the understanding." And
he considers this difficulty to be increased by the practice
of teaching such forms to children, if beyond their comprehension.[*]

CHARLES. The form ought to be short and simple. A
child will, under a mother's careful teaching, soon learn to
attach a reality to it. Many a man can trace to the habit
of daily prayer, acquired almost in infancy, the religious
course of his after life : and many also can bear witness
to the loss sustained by those who have never acquired
the habit of daily prayer.

JOSIAH. Thou speaks of " a mother's careful teaching."
This is what has worked on the child's mind for good, not
the formal prayers.

CHARLES. A form of prayer is a great assistance, even
to private devotion : it serves to remind us of our daily
need. Is it not the practical result of your Society's
repudiation of stated prayers, that many of your members
do not pray at all, and that some appear to have scarcely
a thought of religion above the formal attendance of your
silent meeting once in the week ?

JOSIAH. This charge is applicable to all communities.
Are there not many in your Church also who appear
to think little about religion ; who " merely say their
prayers," but do not " really pray ?" It is right to have
regular stated times for public worship and for private
devotion, but this is very different from a stated form of

---

[*] *Whately's Errors of Romanism, Essay* I., § 6.

prayer, to be used irrespectively of the circumstances, or of the state of mind of the worshipper. The appointed times for public worship have, as thou knows, been always carefully observed by our Society. There are few families who are not assembled once or twice a-day for the reading of the Scriptures; and in the solemn pause which succeeds there is time and opportunity for silent prayer. In some houses the voice of prayer or praise is, at times, heard aloud, and is not the less fervent because the prayer is not read from a book, and is not the stated observance on every such occasion. Private devotion, for the most part, shrinks from observation; we can judge of it only from its fruits; but I cannot doubt that the retirement of the closet, morning and evening, is appreciated by many, both young and old, who highly value and enjoy the privilege of pouring out their hearts in prayer in their Saviour's name. Still, as respects children, I must admit the difficulty of supplying the place of the short and simple form of prayer, night and morning, and the value of the habit thus created when these forms are used in a really devotional spirit. With us, while much deficiency still exists, there is reason to hope that considerable improvement has taken place of late years. I do not like to speak strongly, but I believe I may assert that in the families of many Friends, and in our public schools, the children are carefully instructed in the great truths of Christianity, by those who seek to recur in prayer to the true Fountain of living waters, to Christ himself—that His Spirit's influence may apply the truths of Holy Scripture to the hearts and consciences of those under their care.

CHARLES. I am glad to hear it, for I feel confident that

the intelligent study of Holy Scripture will show many of them how much they lose by excluding themselves from the communion of the Church, whose liturgy, to a very large extent, is almost in the very words of Scripture.*

JOSIAH. Let them judge for themselves. I think some of the fruits of this improved teaching are to be seen in an increased desire for the improvement of others, and especially in the attention to Sunday Schools, of which there are now more than fifty under the care of members of our Society, attended to by about seven hundred teachers, chiefly young men. I regard this movement as among the most encouraging signs of the revival I have before alluded to.

CHARLES. I am glad to hear that you have established Sunday Schools. You say that in many families of Friends the children are carefully instructed, but admit also that many parents are very remiss in the religious teaching of their children. With us, if the parents neglect this duty, the Church, by its pastoral teaching, strives to occupy their place.

JOSIAH. If parents neglect their duty it is not easy for any one to perform it for them. Example is stronger than precept, and the instruction of the minister is often counteracted by the evil influences of home. Our members, young and old, are not left without instruction. They are exhorted (to quote the words of the " Annual Advices")†

---

* See *The Liturgy compared with the Bible,* among the publications of the Society for Promoting Christian Knowledge.

† *Annual Advices.* A series of Advices, so called because they are directed to be read, at least once a year, in all the meetings for discipline held by Friends, and also *after* the close of their meetings for worship.

" to take heed to the convictions of the Holy Spirit, who
" leads, through unfeigned repentance and living faith in
" the Son of God, to reconciliation with our Heavenly
" Father, and to the blessed hope of eternal life, purchased
" for us by the one offering of our Lord and Saviour Jesus
" Christ ;" and " in religious meetings reverently to pre-
" sent themselves before the Lord, and seek, by the help
" of the Holy Spirit to worship God, through Jesus
" Christ."

CHARLES. Your quotation is very good, though I do
not think an *annual* advice is any improvement on the
Church's teaching through her *daily* and *weekly* services.
Pardon me, but you seem to me to have turned your backs
upon an abundant fountain of living waters, refusing to
irrigate your crops through its streams ; and to be
patiently waiting for the dew of Heaven to fall upon
your tender seedlings which are fainting for lack of
moisture.

JOSIAH. Thou seems to claim something like inspiration for the compilers of your liturgy, in speaking of it as
" an abundant fountain of living waters."

CHARLES. Perhaps I should have said " cistern," instead of fountain, although the perfect accordance of
the liturgy with Holy Scripture would justify that title.
Your system of private and public worship may succeed
with the spiritually disposed, but it seems to offer no
machinery for the instruction of the young and the ignorant, for arousing the thoughtless, or for converting the
sinner.

JOSIAH. There may be some grounds for this charge,
but I cannot admit it in the unqualified way in which
thou puts it. The deficiency, whatever it may be, does

not arise from the principles we profess, but from the mode of carrying them out in practice. Even as it is, if we look to the results, I think thou wilt find that our system, where thou says there is " no machinery for arousing the careless or converting the sinner," works as well as your complicated arrangements. With you, also, there are many who attend only one service in the week, and some whose attendance is still less frequent. Is there, among even the educated attenders on your ritual, more of vital religion, in proportion to numbers, than exists with us ? Then, as respects the poor and the less educated classes, your regularly-appointed pastors have allowed the sheep to run wild without care. Some have been attended to by volunteers, but by far the larger number are straying on the mountains without any shepherd to care for them, or any fold to enter. In England, thousands of the poorer parishioners never enter a place of worship: in Ireland, while you work hard to make a few proselytes, you allow the poorer members of your flock to stray towards Rome from sheer want of pastoral care. Your system is not suited to the poor : it is too exclusive. Your churches have comfortable pews for the rich, and but little accommodation for others ; and this in that house which is appropriated to the worship of Him with whom " there is no distinction of persons." Can you be surprised that so many of the lower classes of society flock to dissenting ministers ?

CHARLES. You are so occupied in contemplating the Quaker revival, that you appear to be ignorant of ·a far deeper and wider revival which is stirring up the Church of England. What you say of the neglect of the poor is just ; but it applies to a time now happily passing away.

The Church is looking after her poor in good earnest, even in Ireland. The pew system—a relic of the pharisaical times that marred the Reformation—is losing favour, and I trust the time will come when every seat in God's house shall be free. In England, the more earnest of the clergy are striving to substitute the free-will offerings of the congregation for pew-rents ; and I have hope that the Church will yet free herself from all the trammels which a corrupt age has bequeathed to her.

JOSIAH. I hope so too; and am pleased with the acknowledgment that other churches want a little improving as well as ours.

CHARLES. I think you suffer loss by your neglect of stated family worship, other than the formal reading of a chapter from the Bible.

JOSIAH. There is something more amongst us than the mere "formal reading" of the Bible : there is the solemn pause after the reading, affording opportunity for religious reflection, for individual mental prayer, and, at times, for more public approaches to the throne of grace. Still I must acknowledge our deficiency in respect of family worship, and that the fear—perhaps an undue fear—of wanting a true preparation of heart, deters many from uttering, in the presence even of their children, the petitions which arise in their hearts. This is, I believe, much the safest side to err on ; still I think there is, in some cases, "a withholding more than is meet," and that "it tendeth to poverty."

CHARLES. Surely this is a case in which the Quaker theory of immediate guidance shows its faultiness. Except from an "acknowledged minister," I do not recollect ever to have heard a vocal prayer, and but rarely even a word of exhortation or comfort uttered in your family gatherings.

JOSIAH. Vocal prayer on such occasions is somewhat more frequent amongst us of late years, and that it is not still more frequent arises no doubt from the cause I have just mentioned, combined with that lukewarmness, in many, which is the canker of all Christian churches. It was not so in the early days of our Society.

CHARLES. Your early members, who joined the Society from other communities, were probably brought up in the habit of family prayer ; a habit lost by their descendants, as the practice of silent meetings grew common.

JOSIAH. I may remark that our practice of a silent pause before meals is to me much more solemn than the customary saying of " grace," as it is termed ; and I think that pause, though short, is not unfrequently a time of thankfulness for mercies received, and of prayer for ability to use them aright.

CHARLES. The short pause may be, and often is, as formal as the carelessly spoken " grace." Perhaps an expression of thanks, followed by a short pause, would be better than either separately.

JOSIAH. Both may be mere forms, but thy suggestion induces me to say, that the rapidity with which I have sometimes seen persons turn from the reading of the Scriptures, or from other religious acts, to common conversation or gossip, has often been to me very painful.

CHARLES. Such irreverence is always painful. But, to resume our subject. The design of having fixed times set apart for public worship, involves something more than affording opportunity for that individual waiting upon God in silence, into which Friends resolve all worship.

JOSIAH. Worship, whether private or public, must be, as regards each of the worshippers, an individual act, for it is the engagement of the individual mind. The listening to preaching, however good, is not worship, though it may be an excellent incentive and preparation for it ; and some time of silence seems absolutely necessary to enable those who hear to worship, which they cannot do while their faculties are fully occupied with that to which they are listening. Worship is the communion of the soul with its Maker, and it appears to me to consist of confession, prayer, thanksgiving and praise, or of that state of adoration in which all these are blended together. Yes, Charles, though worship may be united, and the whole congregation may be "of one heart and of one soul," yet must it be for each an individual act. Therefore we desire reverently to present ourselves before the Lord in silence, and to pray for the help of His Holy Spirit to enable us to worship Him. But this silence is only a preparation, to afford opportunity—it may be for individual self-examination and confession—for silent prayer and praise : or it may be for vocal supplication, or the public ministration of the word and the calling sinners to repentance.

CHARLES. I never supposed that listening to preaching or to prayers was worship, or that worship was not an individual act : nor do I find fault with your definition. But I think that the liturgy supplies the elements of worship to all attentive hearers, and that a hearer may appropriate to himself, by faith, the prayers and praises of the Church, and make them his own : and that thus may be performed worship as spiritual as by the most abstracted person in your silent meeting.

Josiah. Though listening to preaching is not worship, yet many appear to care for nothing else. They go to hear a favourite preacher, and if there were not to be a sermon, they would often not go at all. I have sometimes thought that this, at least, might be alleged in favour of our meetings, silent as they often are, that we cannot deceive ourselves in thinking we have been worshipping, when our thoughts have not been properly engaged. But with you I fear it not unfrequently happens, that he who joins in repeating the prayers, though with indifferent or averted mind, thinks that, in so doing, he is fulfilling the great duty of worship; and that he who hangs enraptured on the words of a favourite preacher imagines that he is worshipping God, when, in reality, he is only idolizing the genius of His creature.

Charles. The undue exaltation of preaching and of preachers is very much more common among dissenters, and semi-dissenting frequenters of fashionable proprietary chapels, than among churchmen. It is but too true, however, that many go to church to please their itching ears, and apparently for little else. My objection is not to silent worship in the abstract, but to the adoption of this as the form of congregational worship. Prayer in secret is, I believe, enjoined among all Christians; it certainly is so enjoined by the Church, and practised by churchmen.

Josiah. Our meetings are not always held in silence. We highly value the preaching of the Gospel, but, if we are right in believing that no one can properly minister to the wants of the congregation, unless called and qualified by the Great Head of the Church, it is evident that public worship *must* be in silence, unless some one be present who believes himself to be thus called. Even if the public ministry of the word be not vouchsafed to us, we are not thereby prevented from offering acceptable worship in our assemblies. With you public worship cannot take place without the assistance of an ordained minister : but with us even the two or three meet together in the Lord's name. In the early days of our Society, meetings were rarely held in silence ; and if the word is now less frequently heard in many of our meetings, I am disposed to attribute the change to the causes we discussed a short time since. We trust that the " Lord of the harvest" will, in His own time, " send forth more labourers into His harvest."

CHARLES. Let us turn for a while from your prac- tice to ours. When we unite together in public wor- ship, we are enjoined "to confess our manifold sins " and wickedness ; to render thanks for the great benefits " we have received" from the Almighty ; "to set forth " His most worthy praise, to hear His most holy word, " and to ask those things which are requisite and neces- " sary as well for the body as the soul."

JOSIAH. That is, I believe, a quotation from the intro- ductory address in the service of your Church.

CHARLES. Yes. And to my mind it forcibly expresses the train of thought in which we should enter a house of prayer, and the duties to which we should especially give heed therein. I grant that it is often heard without being attended to, too many heads being busy with other thoughts, or looking around to see who has entered or is entering the church.

JOSIAH. A few minutes ago, thou objected to our silent meetings, that they allowed scope for wandering thoughts and worldly or idle cogitations. It seems that your forms are no protection from similar temptation.

CHARLES. I did. But every congregation that I have seen, whether of Church people or Meeting-house frequenters, contains a larger or smaller proportion of thoughtless, careless, or worldly minded persons; and even among the more spiritually disposed present, wandering thoughts will too often intrude. The legend of St. Anthony is no unreality, for something like it is acted, at times, in most of our hearts. The prayers which one day•fill the heart, every petition striking a responsive chord, fall heavy on the ear on another occasion, and pass away from memory as soon as the voice that utters them is passed. Every one's experience will, I suppose, tell this tale.

JOSIAH. Yes. Human nature is the same in every age and climate, and under every form of discipline. It is easy to make the body go through its appointed exercise, but impossible to ensure the co-operation of the mind. This being so, I do not see how our meetings, even when held in silence, are inferior to yours. The spiritual amongst us are refreshed by their silent prayers and pious meditations, as the spiritual among you are by the words they hear; the careless and indifferent, in both cases, are alike. Our silence is not more irksome to them than is your formal ritual; through both they carry on the current of their worldly thoughts; but which incurs the greatest responsibility, the man who uses words of prayer which he does not care to feel, or he who does not attempt to pray at all?

CHARLES. I think, however, that there is a material difference in favour of our system as a mental school, and as leading to a more diffused spirit of worship in a mixed congregation. Thus, with you, everything is left to *individual* exercise. If all present be so far advanced in Christian life as to need no outward admonition or teaching, it is very well. Silent worship will then become all that you can claim for it. But, as we have just agreed, there is no such thing as a congregation composed of such members. Therefore the Church, knowing that her net gathers of every kind, and that the good and bad will be permitted to be together until the end, wisely regards all her children as, at all times, having need of milk ; that is, of oral teaching, even concerning "what be the first principles of the oracles of God." Thus there is no one present, however ignorant, who can justly complain that he has not, in the Church service, something, at least, which is capable of giving him spiritual knowledge ; for all have daily set before them an epitome of Christian life and doctrine, and all may join in prayers that speak the language of the weakest as well as of the most "advanced" Christian soul ;—prayers that meet every case, and sound the depths of every human want ; that unite together all that the wisest and best can conceive or desire, and all that the need of the sinner or the castaway cries out for. These prayers often remind me of the manna that fell round about the camp of the Israelites, which every one must gather for himself according to his own eating, and of which no one could lay up a superfluity ;—"for he that gathered little had no lack, and he that gathered much had nothing over."

JOSIAH. The knowledge of religious truth is of little value, unless it be sealed on our hearts by the Spirit. I have read over the daily prayers ; and I admit that as compositions they are very beautiful, and contain holy desires expressed in scriptural language. But it seems

to me that the language of many of them can only be truly
uttered by the holiest and most devout and fervent spirit,
and that, in the mouth of an ordinary frequenter of the
service, they are little better than unmeaning phrases, if
they be not a taking of God's name in vain : and coming
from the mouth of a careless or worldly minister, they are
more like a solemn mockery of worship than any thing
else. Has not this ever occurred to thee? Hast thou
never said in thy mind, What right has that man at the
reading desk, whom I know to be worldly minded, to
utter such petitions as these?

CHARLES. In this you fall into an error natural enough
to one brought up among dissenters. Look at Article
XXVI. of our Church. The prayers of the liturgy
are neither the prayers of the minister individually,
nor of any individual present : but of the Church, the
Lamb's wife. She prepares a spiritual banquet for her
children. She sets before them the bread and the water
of life. She stands here on earth, the witness for Him
who is her husband and Lord ; and as such she is bound
to dispense His graces in all their fulness and purity, and
to teach her children to utter the fullest, the most earnest,
the holiest prayers. She is bound by the model which
her Lord has left her, to "hallow his name" by fervid
praises ; and in order that "His kingdom may come,
and His will be done on earth as it is in heaven," she
is further bound to frame the holiest petitions ;—and
this is the "daily bread" she sets before her children.
As I said before, all cannot partake alike ;—but there
is much for ALL nevertheless ; and the more the attention is turned to each petition, the more the capacity
to embrace it is vouchsafed. Thus the daily prayers

are never out of date; they are never hackneyed to
the attentive ear, for they have life in themselves, and
apply to every age and circumstance. They are like the
beams of the Sun of Righteousness, falling round about
us, and bringing light and warmth and healing; and it
is wholly our own fault if they fall around us in vain.

JOSIAH. It seems to me very inconsistent to use such
forms, unless at the same time the mind go fully with
them. Look, for example, even at the opening "con-
" fession of sins." There is certainly nothing in it but
what is most true, and it truly expresses the utterance of
a contrite heart, but it sounds very anomalous (as I take
it) out of the mouths of worldly persons, who, without
any feeling of repentance, confess themselves " miserable
sinners," and yet habitually " do those things which they
ought not to have done," and " leave undone those things
which they ought to have done."

CHARLES. Our services regard *all* as sinners needing
grace, but the degree of sin in each is not prejudged.
How are the unholy to become sanctified if they do not,
at least, strive to pray. Would you leave them, as the
extreme Calvinist does, to a divine election irrespective of
human efforts ? Unfortunately careless worshippers are of
old date. " They honour me with their lips, but their heart
is far from me," was a complaint made thousands of years
ago. The Church service is framed for those who *desire*
to worship God ; not for those who go to hear some
" favourite preacher," or because they have nothing better
to do to kill time on a Sunday, or because they have some
new article of finery to show off in public, or for any other
such reason. In the mouth of such as these, the prayers
are indeed little better than solemn mockery. But we

cannot turn them out of doors. The tares must grow with the wheat till the time of the harvest.

JOSIAH. If the prayers be fitted for the faithful only what are the unconverted to do? Are they to stand idly by, or would thou have them join in prayers and praises in which their hearts have no concern?

CHARLES. The book of Common Prayer is, as I have said, adapted to every need of the sinner and the cast-away. It embodies the experience of every Christian generation from the very dawn of our holy religion. It is no modern compilation, reflecting the caprice or the taste of any single age, but it sums up, in language of touching eloquence, retaining at the same time the most intimate dependence on the very words of Scripture, all the hopes and feelings that every Christian heart has breathed, throughout each period in the history of the Church of God.

JOSIAH. But dost thou not think it still capable of improvement? Thou wilt not let me speak of "vain repetitions," I suppose; but has it never struck thee that there is too frequent a repetition of the Lord's prayer, and of prayers for the Queen in the same service?

CHARLES. That is a very common objection, both with dissenters and with churchmen; and the American Episcopal Church, since their revolution, has curtailed many of the repetitions to which you object. In some places I think the American Church has perhaps gone too far, and has thereby marred the beauty of the service, chiefly in omitting several of the ejaculatory prayers and responses. She has also left to the discretion of the officiating minister the omission of several prayers, and among the rest, this repetition of the Lord's prayer.

JOSIAH. And is not this generally considered an improvement?

CHARLES. I believe many so regard it, but I do not think this the best kind of improvement.

JOSIAH. Then what would thou do?

CHARLES. I would restore the distinct services, as originally contemplated by the framers of our present liturgy. If you look into the Prayer Book, you may see that the Morning Prayers, the Litany and the Communion service, which are now all repeated one after the other on Sundays, are in themselves perfect and distinct forms, and were intended to be separately celebrated. The Morning Prayers were to be said every morning, as the first-fruit of the lips; the Litany, thrice in the week, at a later hour; and the Communion Office, on Sundays and Holydays. The amalgamation of these forms was, I believe, a compromise between the Churchmen and the Puritans in the troubled times, and is certainly to be condemned. The three forms, as they now stand, are too long to be consecutively uttered by most persons with profit; a part must either be less dwelt on than the rest, or be heard in heedlessness, as I fear it often is. With the very imperfect discipline at present in action in the English Church, it will be difficult to alter a practice which has so long been tolerated, but I trust we may live to see the day when distinct services may be restored.

JOSIAH. I should think it would be a great improvement on your present system, and would do away with many of the repetitions now complained of. It may perhaps be the union of these three distinct forms which makes the usual service so long, that it is frequently hurried through, with, what appears to me, indecent haste. I have rarely been at the worship of your Church, but when I have been, I have longed for a little breathing time—an interval of silence, however short, between one portion of the service and another. The minister has not had time to close the book before he says hurriedly, " Let us pray."

CHARLES. I, too, have often been pained with irreverent reading, as if the reader were anxious to have the Church prayers over, and to be at work upon his own flowery composition. The division of the services would be a great boon both to priest and people. Yet, strange to say, if you suggest this easy and orthodox method of shortening the Sunday-morning service, to the very persons who now complain of its length, they will either tell you that no one would come to hear the morning prayers separately, and so the congregation would lose all the benefit of the Scripture lessons read therewith ; or they will call you " Puseyite" for making such a proposition, and, of course, that is reason sufficient for turning a deaf ear to you. Daily morning prayers in public have been so long neglected by both clergy and people, that even clergymen object to " the experiment" of restoring them on Sundays, on the plea that no one could be found to attend the two services. If this be really so, it argues something far more " rotten" in the state of England than Englishmen generally think, when they compare themselves with their neighbours.

JOSIAH. There is great force in habit. The evening service, at least in towns, is generally well attended, and a morning service might also again become so, if the custom were restored of having it at the proper hour.

9

CHARLES. At any rate, I think the noon service would be better appreciated by those who heard it, if they heard it separately ; and though only half as many words were directed to the ear, these would be listened to with greater profit, than the whole compound service.

JOSIAH. Yes ; and many persons in weak health who might desire to be present either at the morning or the noon service, but who are physically unable to sit out both, would thus be accommodated. But remember that even if you separate the forms of prayer, as thou proposes, you do not quite get rid of repetitions. The Lord's prayer is repeated twice in the form for morning prayer. Might not this repetition be omitted ?

CHARLES. I am not surprised that a person unaccustomed to the liturgy, and particularly one educated among Friends, should think this repetition objectionable. I suppose few persons will question the appropriateness of this prayer where it first occurs, immediately after the General Absolution. It seems then the most natural expression of the first breathings of the accepted soul—the " Abba, Father," from which it is about to arise to the duties of thanksgiving and praise, before listening to the lessons from Scripture. And if you take notice of the place where it is next repeated, you will find that it introduces, in like manner, a distinct period of the service. The Psalms, the Lessons, the two hymns and the Creed, have consecutively passed before the mind of the worshipper, who is now to be called on to join in the collects and closing prayers. His attention has just been occupied with a variety of duties, ending with a profession of the articles of the Christian faith, and his mind requires to be allowed to settle down again into that solemn communion in which prayer becomes the language of the soul, before it can answer to the petitions of the first collect. Hence the framers of the liturgy have wisely interposed the Lord's prayer, with the sentences and responses that precede and follow it, as being the best and most natural prelude to what is to follow. As far as my own experience is a test, I may say that I have often found it the best preparation for a fuller appreciation of the petitions of the collects.

JOSIAH. Well, I know so little of the action of these forms, that I shall not dispute with thee in this matter. But what canst thou say for the repetitions in the opening sentences of the litany, where the Persons of the Godhead are separately and then collectively addressed, with the same petition, "Have mercy upon us?" This grates harshly on my spiritual ear, as being a needless repetition, inconsistent with the general simplicity of tone which, I allow, pervades much of your liturgy. Surely it is needless to address separately to the Son and to the Holy Ghost, and then collectively to the "Holy, blessed and glorious Trinity," that prayer which has just been put up to the "Father of heaven." It sounds very like a vain repetition.

CHARLES. I cannot admit that the repetition is unmeaning. Without this distinct invocation of the Persons of the Godhead, specifying the peculiar office of each, and His part in the work of redemption, the litany, as a general supplication, would be very incomplete. We ought to be grateful for the benefits which this and other forms of prayer dispense. But for such we should be at the mercy of that "exercise" which is commonly called

9*

"extempore prayer," and which, in my opinion, is often both irksome and painful to listen to.

JOSIAH. Thou knows I am no advocate for extempore prayer, unless it come from. a heart enlightened by the Holy Spirit, and be prompted by Him.

CHARLES. Yes : and I must do Friends the justice to say that if the prayers, which are publicly offered in their meetings, be fewer and farther between than the "extempore" offerings of other dissenters, they are usually greatly superior to those effusions. There is generally a solemnity, a fulness, a brevity in the public prayers of your ministers such as we rarely find in the prayers heard at other dissenting places of worship.

JOSIAH. It is painful to listen to a man who seems to be endeavouring to spin out, what purports to be an address to the Almighty, so as to occupy a certain space of time ; and which is sometimes as like a sermon as a prayer.

CHARLES. I have never been partial to dissenting meetings, and have latterly altogether avoided them ; and I can truly say that it was the "extempore" prayers, and not the preaching, that drove me away. I have heard many excellent and well arranged sermons from dissenters. But rarely have I been able to sit out their prayers without an inward feeling of something like pain, mingled with wonder that any one should think such addresses to the Almighty were more "spiritual," or more acceptable to Him, than the prayers of the liturgy. You follow the extempore leader, not knowing whither he may take you ; you have heard his last petition ; you are on the watch for the next ; and so, from step to step throughout, *you know* not where you are travelling. You are entirely at his mercy, unless you turn a deaf ear to him. But when joining in the prayers of the liturgy, you know the ground and every step of the way. The minister may mumble the words, or the building may be so large, and his voice so feeble that only a word or two here and there may be heard. No matter; you know the prayer, you know that it contains all you need, put in the noblest, yet shortest and simplest language, and all you are asked to do is to "lift up your heart," and join with the brethren. The "extempore" prayer, at best, is but the prayer of the officiating minister; the liturgy is "common prayer," the united aspiration of all the faithful present,— a petition which they have met together for the express purpose of presenting to God,— a petition, therefore, not got up in "extempore" haste, on the spur of the moment, but carefully considered and prepared by wise and good men, and embodying all the wants of the petitioners ;—well fitted too "to revive the spirit of the humble, and to revive the heart of the contrite ones." Besides, the form supplies a guard against false doctrine from the preacher; thus serving to detect and remedy any deviation from the truth.

JOSIAH. The public prayers of our ministers claim to be prompted by the Holy Spirit, and to give expression to the wants felt by a large part, at least, of the congregation. They may, therefore, when uttered under right direction, be regarded as "common prayer." But dost thou suppose that all the public prayers heard at dissenting meetings are "got up in haste, on the spur of the moment?" Are they not, sometimes at least, carefully considered by a "wise and good man," of whom there are surely many to be found in all denominations?

CHARLES. I put the matter on its broad basis, that of

principle. The dissenters object to *forms* of prayer, because they are prepared, and studied, and written down
beforehand, and then read. Their *vivâ voce* prayers are
preferred, because they are supposed to be *spontaneous.*
I believe, however, that the spontaneity is often more in
appearance than in reality, and that young ministers frequently prepare their public prayers, and get them by
heart beforehand, so that they may appear to pray extempore, and yet may be certain that they shall not break
down. " Prayer meetings " too, seem, at least sometimes,
to be associations got up for teaching the art of vocal
prayer. I never was present at more than one prayer
meeting, and that was by accident, whilst travelling in
the United States. I had been travelling one Sunday,
on a railroad, and arrived late in the afternoon at my
quarters for the night. After the evening *table d'hote* I
strolled out into the streets, and hearing bells, I followed
the sound, and came to a building resembling a church,
the lower story, or crypt, of which was lighted up. Seeing a congregation entering, I went in and sat down, without knowing amongst what sect I had alighted. It proved
to be a congregation of Baptists, met in prayer meeting.
A man at the head of the meeting gave out hymns, read
extracts from reports, and addressed us; and, in the inter-
vals, he called aloud to Brother This—and Brother That—
to " offer a prayer." The persons called on were scattered
about the meeting, and each, as he was called on, immediately knelt down at his seat, and " offered a prayer," the
congregation meanwhile standing up. Whether there
were a previous agreement between the minister and the
brethren addressed by name I know not, but to a stranger
it had the appearance of a school exercise, where one

pupil after another is called up for examination. I cannot say that I was much edified by the "exercises" that were so got up.

JOSIAH. I do not wonder at it; and were I to admit into our religious meetings any vocal prayer, other than what I have already spoken of as being prompted by the Holy Spirit, I believe I should prefer, with thee, to follow the prayers of a well ordered liturgy rather than the uncertain extemporizations of the speaker. But my mind revolts from either, and I return to our quiet meetings with renewed zest, and with thankfulness that I am not forced to entertain the question.

CHARLES. I cannot hope to wean you from your quiet meetings. Some minds are so constituted as to find, in assemblies like yours, all that they need. They enjoy communion with the Shepherd and Bishop of souls, and truly have "meat to eat" that the carnal "know not of." But on the other hand, a form of prayers, with stated Scripture lessons, psalms, and hymns, as in our liturgy, is, by the mass of mankind, not only needed "for instruction in righteousness," but is the best and most efficacious human agent for calling forth spiritual religion in the soul.

CONVERSATION V.

Ye are my friends, if ye do whatsoever I command you.—
St. John, xv. 14.

With my whole heart have I sought thee: O let me not wander from thy commandments.—*Ps.* cxix. 10.

CHARLES. One of the Friends appointed by the monthly meeting to visit me, at the time when I joined the Church, drew my attention to a little book, called, if I remember correctly, " The History and Mystery of those called Sacraments." I just glanced through it, and from what I read, it appeared to me that the author was either very ignorant of the facts of the " history," or so mystified by the " mystery " in which his prejudices had involved the subject, that he had concocted a history very likely to mislead a young and uninformed mind, though . such as could only raise a smile from a person acquainted with the subject of the treatise. Have you ever seen the book, and do you know anything of the writer ?

JOSIAH. I have seen the little book thou refers to, but have never read it carefully. I was not personally acquainted with the writer, but have heard much in his *favour* from those who knew him intimately. He appears to have been a worthy, good man, much esteemed and respected in his own circle; but not one whom I should have chosen as an advocate on such subjects.

CHARLES. I am sorry that such a man should not have rested content with the esteem and respect of his own circle; for certainly he appears to have been little fitted to handle the subject of which he treats.

JOSIAH. Why dost thou think so?

CHARLES. I think he has either suppressed or misstated leading facts of the "history," and, if this be so, it is a sufficient answer to your question. But is there not something pitiable in the flippancy with which he endeavours, in the first page, to find fault with the very word "sacrament," because as he says, and as every one knows, it is derived from the name of the oath taken by the Roman soldiery? He would also infer that a word, so derived and associated, is only profanely applied to any "mystery" connected with the worship of the Prince of Peace. On similar grounds he ought to quarrel with St. Paul, who continually uses imagery taken from warfare, in enforcing obedience to "the Captain of our salvation."

JOSIAH. Your church defines a sacrament as being "an "outward and visible sign of an inward and spiritual grace "given unto us, ordained by Christ himself, as a means "whereby we receive the same, and a pledge to assure us "thereof." The term therefore purports to designate an intimate connexion between an outward and bodily action and the work of the Holy Spirit. Now we do not believe this connexion to exist, or that any such rite as a sacrament was instituted by our Lord, and therefore we object to the use of the word, not on account of its derivation, but of its present meaning.

CHARLES. Yet your friend, as a Quaker, was doubtless more consistent in cavilling at the word, for his objection is exactly similar to George Fox's scruple about the names of the days of the week and of the months.

JOSIAH. We have already discussed that subject.

CHARLES. Well, passing from the origin of the word, your friend next takes offence at the number of "those called sacraments," and in his second page passes on to the Council of Trent, as if that assembly were the earliest that recognised sacramental observances, because it had issued a canon respecting the seven sacraments of the Church of Rome. With this Council of Trent I have nothing to do, for its sayings and doings are a very modern fungus-growth on the Catholic doctrine; nor ought a fair historian (as your friend professes to be) to have started his history at such a late period. He knew very well that the two chief sacraments, baptism and the eucharist, which the Catholic Church has ever acknowledged to be obligatory on all Christians, were not introduced by the Council of Trent, or by any human authority, but had been orally delivered by our Lord Himself to His apostles, and invariably administered by them; and that they continued to be celebrated uninterruptedly for sixteen hundred years, until George Fox, in his superior wisdom, thought fit to set them aside as "carnal ordinances."

JOSIAH. Thou hast given me a long analysis of the arguments of this little book, of which I had previously known scarcely anything. But thou hast not offered any proof that the rites which you call "sacraments" were ever instituted, as such, by our Lord, or that they were intended to be of perpetual obligation on the members of His Church.

CHARLES. When we come to discuss each sacrament separately I shall endeavour to state the grounds on which the Church upholds it.

JOSIAH. I know that the two rites to which thou confines the name of sacrament, have been observed, in some form or other, by nearly all Christian communities up to the present time, the Society of Friends being almost the only exception ; but this does not prove thy case.

CHARLES. And we hold that the two rites of baptism and the Lord's supper have been used in the Christian church from the very earliest period : nay, that they are among the marks which essentially constitute the visibility of the Church of Christ.

JOSIAH. This is the very point for discussion. I have nothing to do with the Council of Trent and its seven sacraments, yet certainly the doctrines to which it gave the sanction of a council were not inventions of *that* day, but had gradually grown up under the shelter of a Church for which thou claims the authority derived from the apostolical succession, and which, according to thy theory, must have been the true visible Church of Christ. You reject five " sacraments," it is true, but the two rites which you have retained are founded, at least as respects the mode of administering them, upon the authority of that Church. We cannot recognize that authority, and do not find warrant for these rites in Scripture, and therefore we reject these two also.

CHARLES. Stop a moment. I cannot allow you to confound the *authority* on which we uphold sacramental rites with that on which the mere " mode of administering " may rest. The outward rites of baptism and the eucharist, we, in common with most professors of Christianity, maintain to have been unquestionably "ordained by Christ himself." The mode of administering has varied in different places and at different times, and I need hardly tell you that our mode is widely different from that in use in the Roman Church, as theirs differs from that practised by the Greeks.

JOSIAH. I said we reject these rites because we do not find warrant for them in Scripture. But, while rejecting the "outward and visible signs," none can more highly value the "inward and spiritual graces" with which you consider them to be connected, but which we believe to be independent of these outward ceremonies. The true Christian baptism is that " of the Holy Ghost and of fire." Jesus Christ himself is the bread of life. The true supper of the Lord is to feed by faith on that " bread of life "—" the bread which came down from heaven "— " His flesh, which He gave for the life of the world."

CHARLES. The surest way of disconnecting " inward and spiritual grace" from an outward rite is by unbelief. You do not believe in the connection. The surest way of deriving spiritual benefit from an outward religious act is by faith. We are told that if, when we pray, we believe that we receive our petitions, we shall have them. In like manner, we believe that the faithful recipients of baptism and of the Lord's supper do indeed participate in the spiritual benefits conveyed to such persons by the outward administration. But, how is it that you find no Scripture warrant for the " outward signs"? Are there not our Lord's commands: "Go, and teach, baptizing"— " Do this in remembrance of me"?

JOSIAH. Our Lord does indeed promise that the prayer of faith shall be answered, but I have yet to learn that He ever promised that spiritual graces should be conferred by either of these rites. We fully acknowledge the authority of the commands thou refers to; but the question is, do they refer to Jewish observances previously in use, and intended to be temporary, or was it our Lord's intention to institute rites of perpetual obligation? And, again, do these commands, or anything to be found in the New Testament, warrant the idea which your Church attaches to what it calls a sacrament, namely, that it is a means of conveying grace to the recipient?

CHARLES. We receive those commands in the sense in which they were understood by the apostles, in which the apostles practised them, as we read in the book of Acts, and in which they have continued to be understood by all branches of the apostolic Church, and by almost all professors of Christianity except your Society. What reasons do you offer for rejecting the universal interpretation of Christendom?

JOSIAH. I cannot admit that these commands were understood by the apostles as you now hold them; but let that pass for the present. The first reason which induces us to doubt the institution of any ceremonial ordinance binding on Christians is this, that Christianity is a religion of spiritual realities, in contradistinction to the material types of the Jewish ritual. When our Lord bowed his head on the cross, and said, "It is finished," and when "the veil of the temple was rent in twain," He put an end to a religion of types and figures, and carnal ordinances, and introduced one of a purely spiritual nature. The shadow was to be exchanged for the substance, the types and figures for the great truths which they typified. There is therefore an antecedent improba-

bility that new types would be instituted ; and on a careful examination of those passages of the New Testament
which are generally regarded as pointing to the institution
of outward rites, we have been led to the conclusion that
no such institution was intended.

CHARLES.   Your doctrine as to the sacraments looks
very like an hypothesis sought to be defended by Scripture weapons against the plain evidence of Scripture history.   In contravention of your hypothesis there is the
practice of the apostles and of the apostolic churches ; in
your favour you can adduce only your own conception of
what constitutes " an antecedent improbability" and "a
religion of spiritual realities."   Scripture, thus translated,
may be made to prove any doctrine, however wild.   But
what is your next reason ?

JOSIAH.   Again, when we look to the institution of the
Jewish rites and ceremonies, we find the most minute
instructions as to the mode in which, the time when, and
the persons by whom they were to be celebrated ; and
analogy would certainly lead us to expect that, if our
Lord intended to institute ordinances of such importance
as these rites are considered by your Church, He would
have left precise directions respecting the mode of celebrating them, and would not have left us in any doubt as
to their value and the effect on the recipient.

CHARLES.   Analogy is a very uncertain guide.   No doctrine can ever be securely built upon it, but any wild opinion may most easily be defended by it.   Have you no
better reason for your " peculiar" interpretation of our
Lord's words ?

JOSIAH.   We are well aware that the early Christians
—following the Jewish usage on the reception of prose-

lytes—baptized their converts, and that they also partook
of bread and wine together as a token of brotherly love,
and in commemoration of their Lord's death; but we
cannot see that their practice in these respects had in it
anything of the character of a sacrament. There is no
indication of a rite to be performed only by "ordained
ministers," much less of the blessing of the water and the
consecration of the elements, leading to the mystery with
which these ceremonies soon became invested, and finally
to the dogma of transubstantiation.

CHARLES. It was not in compliance with any Jewish
usage that St. Paul said, "As many as are baptized into
"Christ are baptised into His death;" or, "As often as ye
"eat this bread and drink this cup, ye do shew the Lord's
"death till he come." As to the persons administering;
in a fully organised church good order would, I think,
require that religious rites should be administered by
authorised persons. And there is clear intimation that
ministers were "ordained" in every church founded by
the apostles. We are not answerable for the superstitious observances and beliefs of other branches of the
Church.

JOSIAH. They are superstitions to which the sacramental idea naturally led, and which arose very early in
the Church. To quote the words of Dr. Arnold of Rugby:
"It seems historically certain that the Judaism which
"upheld circumcision and insisted on the difference of
"meats, after having vainly endeavoured to sap the Gos-
"pel, under its proper Judaic form, did, even within the
"first century, transfuse itself into a Christian form; and,
"substituting baptism for circumcision, and the mystic
"influence of the bread and wine of the communion, for

" the doctrine of purifying and defiling meats, did thereby
" pervert Christianity to a fatal extent."

CHARLES. Did Dr. Arnold therefore propose to abolish
the sacraments of baptism and the Lord's supper? If not,
your quotation goes for nothing. He is arguing against
the *abuse*, not the *use* of these ordinances.

JOSIAH. I think Dr. Arnold's authority on this subject
is more valuable than it would have been if he had proposed to abolish them.

CHARLES. Your Society, in repudiating the sacraments altogether, presumes to be more spiritual than
the apostles of our Lord, if not than the Master Himself
who appointed the observance of these outward forms
which you think unnecessary.

JOSIAH. Some of the apostles, at first, desired to maintain Judaism, and expected that all Christian believers
would adopt its forms : all Christians now consider that
they have clearer and more correct views, on this point,
than these apostles had then. We do not say that the
early Christians were wrong in baptizing their converts,
or in holding those " feasts of charity" at which what
was termed " the Lord's supper" was distributed. These
forms had their use in that day, as a public acknowledgment of the profession of Christianity, and as a token of
mutual love, and of a common allegiance to Him whose
blood had been shed, and whose body had been broken
for them; but we deny that these observances were sacraments conveying Christian graces to the recipient, or that
they were intended to be of perpetual obligation.

CHARLES. You say that "some of the apostles desired
" to maintain Judaism." Have you never read the fifteenth
chapter of the Acts, or is this your rendering of its sense ?

It is there written that "*certain men* which came down from Judea" had taught Judaism ; that "the apostles and elders came together to consider of this matter ;" the result was an apostolic condemnation of the Judaizing doctrine. Our Church does not pretend to have clearer views than the apostles had when they gave forth that judgment on the case at issue, and which had no reference to sacramental rites, which were *invariably* observed by all the apostles of whom we have any record, and have been as *invariably* maintained by apostolic churches to the present day.

JOSIAH. The calling of that council is proof that there had been a difference of opinion previously, and I think it is evident, from the apostle Paul's rebuke to Peter as told in the epistle to the Galatians, that Peter and James, and probably others of the apostles, partook of this Judaizing tendency. But as thou refers to this council, let me call thy attention to its explicit command, "to abstain from things strangled and from blood." This command, we are told by Luke, was not merely an injunction of the apostles, but that it "seemed good to the Holy Ghost ;" and yet neither of us considers it of perpetual obligation, but as intended only to serve a temporary purpose?

CHARLES. Was it George Fox who discovered the temporary obligation of this apostolic precept? Doctor Adam Clarke, the learned Wesleyan, held that it was sinful to eat black puddings. I quarrel with no man who holds so innocent an opinion ; though I should object to a sophist who, because "pollutions of idols and fornication" are coupled in the same sentence of the apostolic letter with the " things strangled and blood," should seek to prove that these four *subjects* of reprobation were all equally sinful, and the command to abstain from each of *equal* stringency.

JOSIAH. Thou might well object to such sophistry, seeing that one of the things so prohibited was an infringement of the moral law.

CHARLES. The real cause for George Fox's rejection of the sacraments was, I doubt not, the idolatrous corruptions of them which grew up in the middle ages.

JOSIAH. Certainly the simple forms used by the early Christians became corrupted very soon, but I deny that the idolatrous corruption of these ceremonies was the reason for our Society's rejecting them. Nevertheless, the extent to which they have been perverted gives strength to our belief, that the practices in question were never intended to become rites of perpetual obligation, because the perversion has evidently been a natural consequence of their having been regarded as sacraments.

CHARLES. One extreme leads to another, and I cannot but think that the idolatrous corruption of the sacraments in the mediæval Church, now stereotyped by the new creed of Rome, must have been largely the cause why George Fox rejected all sacramental observances, though he may not himself have been aware of it. But observe his inconsistency. It is impossible, whilst we have bodies, to dispense altogether with outward forms and ministrations. Why did George Fox sanction the uncovering of the head and kneeling of the body in prayer, when it cannot be questioned that prayer may be, and often is, as devoutly uttered with the head covered, and with the body either sitting or standing or lying down? The *form* of kneeling with uncovered head is as much an "outward or carnal observance" as the use of material water in baptism.

JOSIAH. Kneeling is certainly an outward form, but one that the universal instinct of mankind has recognised from time immemorial, and which the example of our Lord and His apostles fully sanctions. In prayer we most fully realize our own nothingness and the supremacy of the Almighty, and hence it is a natural impulse of the devout spirit to express our relation to Him by a voluntary humbleness of posture; as natural almost as it is to laugh in pleasure, or to cry out in pain. I do not think this natural act of body-worship at all analogous to a ritual such as that of baptism, in which it is asserted that God has "sanctified water to the mystical washing away of sin."

CHARLES. This posture in prayer seems to you to be an act of natural piety, yet, if I remember rightly, some of the early Friends, at one time, viewed it in the light in which I have now placed it—namely, as a carnal observance incompatible with the simplicity of spiritual worship. I think Thomas Ellwood tells us, in his journal, that at one time he felt "moved" to keep his head covered, and to remain sitting during public prayer, but that afterwards he became sensible that this spiritual impulse was a delusion of the devil, and he condemns it accordingly.

JOSIAH. In which condemnation the Society has ever heartily concurred.

CHARLES. This only shows that the Society, as a body, was careful not to adopt the errors of every enthusiast; but, on the Quaker theory, Thomas Ellwood was abstractedly right. The theory of Quakerism sets forth that *all* outward forms are to be disused, as being carnal and not spiritual. You have carried this notion to the extent of setting aside *all* stated prayers, such as were enjoined by

10*

the apostle (1 Tim. ii., 1-2); all congregational reading
of the Scriptures, such as was sanctioned by our Lord
(Luke iv. 16-20); and all hymns of praise, such as were
sung in all ages, from the days of Miriam and of David
to those of Him who with His disciples " sung an hymn,"
in that night in which He was betrayed; and as if this
were not enough, you have abolished the formal observance of His sacraments : and having reduced the service of the sanctuary to your silent meeting, you cannot
see that the very customs of that meeting are forms
still ! If the disuse of forms be the test of spirituality,
doubtless the more complete is the disuse, the more
refined ought to be the spiritual idealisation. Why
should you rise and uncover your heads, and why should
your ministers kneel when engaged in vocal prayer?
Or why do you go to your meeting at all ? Is not this a
form also ?

JOSIAH. We do not object to any useful and seemly
practice because it is a form. Forms might possibly be
dispensed with by spiritual essences, but are necessary for
beings of the compound nature of man, in whom the spirit
acts through bodily organs. No religious body could exist
without forms, and we only object to those which are
superstitious, which interfere with the freedom of spiritual worship, which are not warranted by Holy Scripture,
or which tend to make men "honour their Creator with
their lips, while their hearts are far from Him." Yet,
as there is a natural tendency in the human mind to fall
into forms, constant watchfulness is necessary ; for the
whole history of the Church proves, that as the human
element increases, the divine diminishes. The mind relies
on these forms as a means of procuring spiritual benefit,

and the substance is lost sight of, while looking to the shadow. I see no proof that the apostle Paul, in exhorting that prayers should be offered for all men, meant a stated form of prayer, and I have already, in a previous conversation, explained our reasons for objecting to such forms, whilst we fully maintain the great importance of public prayer. The same reasons apply also to the singing of hymns as a part of congregational worship, seeing that, in every congregation, there will probably be many persons, who, if they join in the singing, will utter with the lips sentiments which do not spring from the heart.

CHARLES. You admit, then, that some forms are indispensable even in " a religion of spiritual realities ;" this is one of St. Chrysostom's arguments in favour of the outward observance of sacraments. Your objection to stated prayers and hymns seems to me to apply with equal force to the vocal prayers of your ministers, and, especially, to your long silences which are utterly unsuited to many in your assemblies, and which must be specially unfit for children and young persons. Yet whilst well aware of the advantage of some external aid to keep alive the devotional feelings, you refuse to read, for the edification of the congregation, what you esteem to be the unquestionably inspired words of Scripture, at the same time that you allow any of your members present to address you, under the plea of immediate inspiration ; a plea which you yourselves allow is frequently made without sufficient warrant. Is this justifiable ? Why do you not read the Holy Scriptures in your meetings ? Is it because such reading would " interfere with the freedom of *spiritual worship* ? "

JOSIAH. We feel that we cannot estimate too highly the value of that gift which has been granted to the Church, in the possession of the inspired words of Holy Writ. We strongly press on all our members the duty and the advantage of making themselves well acquainted with the contents of the sacred volume, by frequent and regular study; and I believe there are few families amongst us, in which it is not the practice to assemble for the reading of the Scriptures at stated times, and at least once every day. Meetings for religious instruction have, of late years, been set up in several places, in which the Scriptures are read and commented on : and I trust the practice will, ere long, become general amongst us. The reading of the Scriptures cannot be considered as an act of worship, though of great importance as a means of grace ; and now, that almost every one possesses the sacred volume, and is able to read it, there is not the same necessity as formerly for its being read in the public assemblies of the Church. But the communications of our ministers abound in Scripture quotations, and I see nothing in our principles to prevent any Friend, if he feel it to be his religious duty to do so, from reading, out of the Bible itself, such portions as he may consider applicable to the congregation, as was done formerly, on more than one occasion, by George Fox, and also by Samuel Bownas.* Neither

---

* *The Bible used in preaching.*—George Fox, in his Journal, relates his having preached, on several occasions, with a Bible in his hand, to which he referred for the texts he quoted ; and the autobiography of Samuel Bownas, who lived in the early part of the last century, contains the following account of his use of the Bible, when preaching at the funeral of a friend in Dorsetshire :— " I pulled my Bible out of my pocket, and opened it ; upon

do I see anything to prevent the exercise of such a liberty, on the part of any one who may feel that the silent perusal of the sacred volume would assist him to maintain a devotional spirit.

CHARLES. I was not aware that the Scripture meetings you have referred to had become a part of the recognized order of your Society. You do well to enjoin the reading of the Scriptures in private, and I hope your members generally follow the injunction. Our Church, besides encouraging the private study of the sacred volume, takes care that all who outwardly profess their faith by joining in the public worship, shall hear some portions of the text when they assemble congregationally, whilst our whole liturgy is an echo of its words. Thus, if the privilege of reading at home be neglected or despised, the Church, so far as it can act, assists the infirmities of the weak, and tries to counteract the slothfulness of the slothful. Such is one of the many uses of the stated observances which you do not think needful. But why is it needful to go to meeting? Can you not worship in silence by your own firesides?

JOSIAH. As respects the attendance of meetings for worship, it seems scarcely needful to reply. It is a pub-

---

" which the people gave more attention than they had done be-
" fore, and I had a very acceptable time, often in the course of
" my matter referring to the text for proof, and giving an ample
" testimony of the value we put upon the Scriptures ; earnestly
" pressing the careful reading of them, and advising to consider
" what they read, and to seek the Lord, by prayer, for assistance
" and power, that they might practise what they read, which
" was the ultimate end of reading, as well as [of] the hearing of
" preaching, for without practice it would avail but little."

lic acknowledgment of our Christian profession, and of
our dependence upon God for all the blessings, whether
spiritual or temporal, that we enjoy. It was an apostolic
injunction to " consider one another to provoke unto love
" and to good works ; not forsaking the assembling of
" ourselves together, as the manner of some is ;" and
our Lord's gracious promise to those who should gather
together in His name, is a clear indication of His purpose
that His followers should thus unite from time to time.
We know that it is in accordance with the constitution of
man, that the outward senses should be made use of as a
means of conveying spiritual life, by the preaching of the
word and by prayer ; and we believe that it is our Lord's
will that this spiritual life should be more fully felt,
when Christian believers assemble themselves in dependence upon Him, looking for His help to worship aright;
and that these times should be occasions for the exercise
of the gifts entrusted to His servants.

CHARLES. Well, I certainly do not mean to object to
the few forms you have retained. I only wanted, by
pushing the argument to an absurdity, to show your error
in rejecting those you have rejected. But, to return to
the ordinances which we were discussing ; you deny that
the corruptions of these ordinances were the cause of
your rejecting them. I do not wish to charge you
with any want of candour in this matter ; but the
causes which influence our opinions are often so remote
and hidden that we are not ourselves aware of them, and
I think these corruptions, which have been so displeas-
ing to all Protestants, must have had this effect with you.
The abuse of anything good is no argument against the
right use of it. What good thing is there in the wide

compass of creation, over which the "trail of the serpent" has not passed? Meat and wine in their places are both good gifts, fitted for the healthful nourishment of the body, and to be used as not abusing them; but because the Son of Man came "eating and drinking," the self-righteous objectors of that day said of Him, "Behold a gluttonous man and a winebibber," just as if that Holy One had prostituted His Father's gifts to the dishonour of His Father's image. And thus has it happened to His Church. She has been accused of superstition and idolatry, because superstition and idolatry have sometimes been practised in her name; and you have set aside her sacred ordinances altogether, because unfaithful stewards have perverted their meaning. And all this you do complacently, without regarding by whose authority these ordinances were first appointed, and by whose example and exhortation they have ever since been enforced.

JOSIAH. This is assuming the whole question in dispute.

CHARLES. How can you say so? You talk much about the purity of the Church in the apostolic times, compared to its degeneracy in later ages; and one would therefore suppose that apostolic practice and exhortation would have weight with you. Yet you either ignore all the passages of the New Testament, (and there are many,) which refer to the administration of the sacraments or else you speak of them as referring to "relics of Judaism," from which, forsooth, the apostles, educated as they had been under a law of types and shadows, could not divest themselves! Take care lest in so doing you cast an imputation on the Master Himself, as if He too had His "Jewish prejudices!"

JOSIAH. We neither "ignore" nor overlook the passages which speak of the breaking of bread and the drinking of wine, nor yet those which speak of baptism by water; but we maintain that these passages refer to practices very different in character from the rites observed by the Anglican Church. Hitherto we have dealt only in assertion and denial; no proof has been offered that it was intended by our Lord to institute ceremonies of perpetual obligation, much less sacraments conveying grace to the recipient. Let us discuss each of these observances separately, taking baptism as the subject of our next conversation.

CHARLES. Agreed. Let us adjourn for this evening.

CONVERSATION VI.

But as many as received him, to them gave he power to become
the sons of God, even to them that believe on his name; which
were born, not of blood, nor of the will of the flesh, nor of the
will of man, but of God.—*St. John* i., 12, 13.

CHARLES. At our last meeting we discussed the
general subject of sacramental rites. I suppose the sacrament of baptism will afford us a sufficient subject for this
evening. Shall it be so?

JOSIAH. I am quite ready. And first, what Scripture
proof canst thou give of the institution of the outward
ceremony as a rite perpetually binding on Christians, and
as a sacrament conveying grace to the recipient?

CHARLES. The proofs of the institution of baptism
and of its perpetual obligation appear to me to be plain
enough. St. Matthew relates that our Lord, shortly before
His ascension, thus addressed His apostles : " All power is
" given unto Me in heaven and in earth. Go ye therefore
" and teach (or make disciples of) all nations, baptizing
" them in the name of the Father, and of the Son, and of
" the Holy Ghost; teaching them to observe all things
" whatsoever I have commanded you, and lo, I am with
" you alway, even unto the end of the world." I under-

stand by these words, that our Lord commissioned His apostles to convert all nations to the faith, and, as a sign and seal of discipleship, to administer baptism to each and every convert : and I infer the perpetual obligation of the rite more especially from the words, "teaching them" (that is, the converts from age to age, for the apostles could not possibly have taught "all nations") "to observe all "things whatsoever I have commandèd you, and lo, I am "with you alway, even unto the end of the world." At what period of their ministry were the apostles to cease "teaching their converts to observe *all things* whatsoever" they had been themselves commanded to observe and do? Plainly, not until Christ should cease to be with them and their disciples ; that is, not "until the end of the world." We know that *they* so understood the command, and followed it ; and we know that the Christian Church, for fifteen centuries, taught, as an indisputable and undisputed article of the faith, that baptism is a covenanted means of grace, of which material water is "the outward and visible sign," and " a death unto sin and a new birth unto righteousness " the benefit imparted ; and that, to ensure the spiritual blessing, the sacrament should be duly administered "in the name of the Father, and of Son, and of the Holy Ghost," according to our Lord's command.

JOSIAH. I cannot see, in these words, anything like a command to administer a sacrament "in the name," &c. ; neither can they be understood as instituting a new rite, because baptism had already been in use, and was well known among the Jews. The parallel passage in Mark contains only the command to "preach the gospel," baptism being referred to as the form usual on the admission of converts ; and I see no more reason for supposing that this particular mode of admission was of perpetual obligation, than that the signs which were " to follow them that believed" were to be witnessed in all ages of the church. The evangelist Luke relates our Lord's words, "that re-" pentance and remission of sins should be preached in His " name among all nations ;" and again, in Acts, chap. i., he records our Lord's promise of the baptism of the Holy Ghost, and that the disciples should be witnesses for Him, " unto the uttermost part of the earth;" but in neither place does he make any allusion to the outward ceremony.

CHARLES. This is not a different account of the same transaction. The. discourse recorded by St. Mathew is stated to have been delivered on a mountain in Galilee, but St. Luke relates what took place at Jerusalem just before our Lord's ascension.

JOSIAH. I am aware of the difference as to time, but on both occasions our Lord commanded His disciples to preach the good tidings of salvation " among all nations," and it was on the first occasion only that he mentioned the outward ceremony. Many have maintained that His words, as given by Mathew and Mark, as well as the discourse recorded by Luke, refer only to spiritual baptism, and the arguments they have brought forward have certainly much force. Amongst those who hold this opinion are Robert Barclay and J. J. Gurney, and a recent writer, not belonging to our Society, who has proved the sincerity of his convictions by relinquishing a living which he held in Scotland. I have thoughtfully considered the reasons they have advanced, but it appears to me that the reference must have been to the well known Jewish cere-

mony which His disciples had already practised, no doubt
with His permission; and which, as Jews, they would
naturally continue to practise on the reception of a new
proselyte: yet afterwards our Lord carefully points their
attention to the true spiritual baptism. His words are
memorable, "John truly baptized with water, but ye shall
"be baptized with the Holy Ghost not many days hence."
It is the same baptism of which John had before spoken
in similar words, "I indeed baptize you with water unto
"repentance, but"—"He shall baptize you with the Holy
Ghost and with fire." The Jewish rite then was with
water. The Christian baptism is that of the Holy Ghost.

CHARLES. I am glad to find you dissenting from the
reasonings of Barclay and Gurney, and admitting that
our Lord's words referred to the outward rite. Surely
He *commands* His apostles to baptize as fully as He commands them to teach or to convert. He does not commission them to baptize "with the Holy Ghost;" that is
His own especial prerogative; but they are to baptize in
faith, trusting that He will add spiritual grace to their
outward act. You quote the promise of the newly risen
Saviour, foretelling to His bereaved disciples the miracle
of Pentecost. The words, "not many days hence," clearly
define the time when the promise should be fulfilled. And
it was literally fulfilled, and the disciples were "all filled
with the Holy Ghost." They all, on that occasion, collectively received an inspiration which you have already
admitted to be fuller and greater than the "spiritual
guidance" vouchsafed to your ministers, or to George
Fox. Yet the apostles never set aside "the outward
and visible form" of baptism, though far more super-

eminently gifted " with inward and spiritual grace" than any of your teachers. Christian baptism includes both the sign and the thing signified.

JOSIAH. The New Testament contains no code of rules, either of morals or for the direction of the Church. There are principles laid down, and the continued assistance of the Holy Spirit is promised, to " guide into all truth." Neither our Lord himself nor his apostles attempted directly to controvert or set aside the existing institutions or the prevalent customs of society ; but He inculcated principles which, when received into the heart, would gradually work a complete change, by purifying the springs of action. I may not refer to war, on which we should differ; but I will refer to the system of slavery, to the gladiatorial and theatrical exhibitions, and, as a case particularly in point, to the fact that He nowhere states that the rites and ceremonies of the Jewish ritual were to cease; so that, even many years after His death, his disciples, the apostles included, were in doubt on this matter. Now this appears to me to afford some explanation, why our Lord permitted His disciples to continue this Jewish rite to which they had been accustomed, and which every Jew considered essential on the admission of a proselyte into the Church.

CHARLES. Surely it was not a mere permission ; it was a command.

JOSIAH. Our Lord's words are, " Go ye and make disciples of all nations, baptising them in"—or, as it should be rendered, *into*—" the name," &c. It was a command to convert the world from heathenism to Christianity : the apostles obeyed it, and preached the glad tidings everywhere. The command was to make converts, baptizing them *into* the name of the Father, and of the Son, and of the Holy Ghost. That is, those to whom this baptism should be administered would be thus introduced into the profession of the faith in the Father, and in the Son, and in the Holy Ghost as preached by the apostles, instead of into the profession of faith in the Father only, as in the case of converts to Judaism; and he who received this doctrine into a faithful heart had the promise of the indwelling of the Holy Spirit, by which he would be regenerated or born again, a new direction would be given to his thoughts and aspirations, and he would be enabled to obey the commands of his Lord. The baptism thus wrought in the soul by the power of the Holy Spirit is, indeed, "a death unto sin, and a new birth unto righteousness;" and is certainly of enduring necessity. Does not the apostle Paul refer to this spiritual baptism when he writes to the Galatians, "As many of you as have been baptized into Christ have "put on Christ"—and when he tells the Romans that so many as "were baptized into Jesus Christ were baptized into his death," and, therefore, "buried with him by baptism into death," that they "should walk in newness of life"? Or, again, when in addressing the Corinthians he says, "For by one Spirit we are all baptised into one body"?

CHARLES. By what principle of interpretation can you erase from such passages as you have now quoted the reference to *water* baptism? The rite, as understood by the apostles and practised by them, was administered by the application of *water*, symbolical of inward purification, for which the stain of original sin gave the necessity.

JOSIAH. Certainly, the reference to water baptism is

there: without that, the figure would be unintelligible. It is because the use of "water as a symbol of inward purification" was so well understood, that the apostle describes the change of heart, which the Christian believer experiences, as a baptism "into Christ," and which, he also says, is a putting on of Christ, and being "baptised into His death"; and he goes on to show that this involves the being "dead unto sin, but alive unto God." All this evidently refers to the one spiritual baptism, of which the Jewish rite was an apt figure, and the words, " For by [or rather *in* (εν)] one Spirit we are all baptized into one body," have an evident reference to an immersion in water, and this figure is evidently used to denote that spiritual baptism which unites into one body all the living members of the Church.

CHARLES. The apostles were *commanded* to baptize as well as to preach. It is true that to them was also granted the power of working miracles, and of conferring the extraordinary gifts of the Holy Spirit by the imposition of their hands. But we never find the outward rite of baptism dispensed with, even as respects those of their disciples who were most completely endued with the gifts of the Spirit.

JOSIAH. The command, as I have already explained, was to preach the Gospel, and baptism is referred to as the form usual on the reception of converts. It was no longer to be the outward token of a profession of faith in the Father only, as revealed to the Jews; but of faith in the Father, Son, and Holy Ghost, as now revealed in the new covenant. We are not entitled to assert that water-baptism was administered to *all* the early believers; and many consider that the apostles and others, who became

M

disciples before our Lord's crucifixion, were not baptized, unless they received baptism from John.

CHARLES. The command, as I understand it, was two-fold :—to *preach* to all who would hear, and to *baptize* those who should believe. Baptism is not merely " referred to," as you express it ; it is clearly commanded. When, under the powerful preaching of the apostles, the multi-tude, being " pricked in their heart," asked what they should do, Peter answered them : " Repent and be bap-" tized, every one of you, in the name of Jesus Christ, for " the remission of sins, and ye shall receive the gift of " the Holy Ghost." Here baptism—evidently what you would call " the outward rite"—is made the vehicle of conveying remission of sins, and the forerunner to receiv-ing the gift of the Holy Ghost.

JOSIAH. Peter did tell the multitude to repent and be baptized ; yet, on the next occasion, under nearly similar circumstances, he tells them to " repent and be converted ;" and Paul speaks of his preaching to the Gen-tiles that they should " repent and turn to God, and do works meet for repentance." It was therefore through re-pentance, and not by the outward rite, that they obtained the remission of sins.

CHARLES. Do you mean to infer from this that when St. Peter says, " Repent and be converted," he did not also insist upon the observance of the outward rite, or that he or any other apostle *omitted* to baptize any of their converts?

JOSIAH. The essential object of their preaching, whether to Jews or Gentiles, was that men should repent and turn to God, and the rite which, in accordance with Jewish *custom*, the apostles continued to practise, was a public token of the profession of Christianity, and, in the case of Gentile converts, it was, in Jewish eyes, a legal purification from the defilements of heathenism. The use of this ceremony was no doubt expedient for that time, but the spiritual baptism was gradually to supersede the outward rite which would naturally fall into disuse along with other Jewish customs. The testimony of John the Baptist seems peculiarly applicable to this subject : " He must increase, but I must decrease."

CHARLES. How can you prove from Scripture that " the spiritual baptism was gradually to supersede the outward rite ?" It is nowhere so written, nor do we find the smallest evidence of a neglect of baptism in the New Testament history. Need I add that baptism has never been superseded in the Christian Church. There certainly have been antinomian objectors, of one kind or another, in every age, and some of these, as the Paulicians* of the seventh century, repudiated the sacraments of baptism and the Lord's supper. As to John the Baptist, his mission was fulfilled when he had baptized our Lord and declared Him to the people to be " Him whose shoe's latchet he was not worthy to unloose." But do not the words in St. Mark's gospel, " He that believeth and is baptized shall be saved," imply that all who believed were to be baptized ?

JOSIAH. Many understand these words as implying that to be effectual for salvation, the belief in the good tidings preached should be accompanied by the baptizing,

---

* J. J. Gurney brings forward the "Inspirées" of Germany, and the "Malakans" of South Russia, as holding views on the sacraments similar to those of Friends.

cleansing power of the Holy Spirit—" the renewing of the Holy Ghost." This no doubt is true, but I am inclined to understand this passage as referring to the open profession of Christianity, of which the ceremony of baptism gave proof. There appears to me to be a remarkable parallelism between the expression recorded by the evangelist, " He that believeth and is baptized shall be saved," and that of the Apostle Paul, " With the heart " man believeth unto righteousness, and with the mouth " confession is made unto salvation." In John's gospel we have also a nearly parallel expression, " He that be- " lieveth in Him is not condemned, but he that believeth " not is condemned already, because," &c. Baptism is not here spoken of, it is faith alone.

CHARLES. In other words, " you are inclined to under-. stand" by " baptized," anything rather than baptism. Do you also maintain that outward baptism was not spoken of when Ananias said to St. Paul, " Arise and be baptized, and wash away thy sins ?"

JOSIAH. To reply to all thy insinuations of being prejudiced would involve too many repetitions. I fully admit that the apostles baptized their converts. They had practised this rite during their Lord's lifetime, and before the command was issued to which thou hast referred as giving so solemn a sanction to it; and He placed no restriction on them in respect to this, any more than in respect to other Jewish ceremonies, but directed their attention to the true baptism which the outward rite had symbolized. Thus I understand His words, and not as imparting to the outward form any inherent efficacy, or commanding its perpetual observance by His Church. The *ceremony* of baptism, as practised by the early Christians, was indeed an open confession of their faith, and there may have been an important value, under the particular circumstances of that time, in practising a ceremony which marked distinctly the adoption of Christianity.

CHARLES. Unquestionably it was and is important to mark distinctly the adoption of Christianity, and the reception of the new convert into the Church.

JOSIAH. But to revert to our text, the command was to "make disciples," "baptizing," &c. Now allowing this to have been a command to baptize with water, it only refers to those who were "made disciples," that is, to converts. The Jews baptized those only who adopted Judaism from Heathenism, and there is no proof, either from the command itself, or from the practice of the apostles, that this rite was used or should be used, except in the case of converts,—not to denote, much less to produce a change of heart, but merely to mark the adoption of a new creed, and, in the case of heathen converts, to "purify" those whom the Jews reputed "unclean."

CHARLES. Certainly we have no account in Scripture of the baptism of any but converts, and for the simple reason that the infant Church consisted wholly of converts! It would be more pertinent if you could prove that converts were *not* baptized. You say too that "baptism was not to denote, much less to produce, a change of heart." It was and is a pledge of admission into the Church of Christ, bringing the recipient specially under the covenant of grace. "Change of heart" or conversion comes from God alone, through faith in Christ. Without this faith in the recipient the sacrament is void; but, if faithfully received, we believe that the blessing and grace of God accompany the outward ministration.

We do not believe that the mere immersion or sprinkling is more than the outward shell of the sacrament.

JOSIAH. Thou rests the obligation of the rite, as now practised, not on the authority of Scripture, but on that of the Church.

CHARLES. On the authority of both. St. Paul did not instruct the jailor at Philippi to despise the ordinance; but " baptized him, and all his, straightway." Was this " a spiritual baptism" only ; or, was there not also an outward and visible rite? And St. Peter, at the miraculous conversion of Cornelius and his companions, says of the new converts on whom the gift of the Holy Spirit had just been effused, " Can any man forbid water, that these " should not be baptized, which have received the Holy " Ghost as well as we?" Had George Fox or Robert Barclay been present, they would no doubt have replied, " Yes ; we forbid water, because it is a remnant of the " Jewish ritual, and both out of place and unnecessary in " this instance, where we visibly see the unction of the " Holy One poured out to sanctification and regenera- " tion." Yet not so St. Peter, who commands them to be baptized in the name of the Lord. Not so the new converts, illuminated as they then were with the dayspring from on high. They do not reject the water, nor despise the ministration of the apostle. They do not say, " What " need have we of your typical washings and ordinances, " who have received the Holy Ghost as well as you, and " are therefore as capable of judging as you are?" On the contrary, like their Master, they submit to the ordinance, " for thus it became them to fulfil all righteousness," and we do not find that they were a whit the less spiritual on this account. This case of the water baptism of the Gentile Cornelius and his friends, has always appeared to me to be a complete answer to the casuistry of those who would set aside the outward administration of baptism, as being either a Jewish formality, or an empty ceremony unworthy of the attention of a spiritually instructed Christian.

JOSIAH.   Our early Friends did not presume to forbid water-baptism to others, although they did not consider this Jewish ceremony to be binding on themselves.*   As respects the case thou hast quoted, the apostle Peter appeals to his fellow-believers of Jewish birth who had accompanied him, and asks, could there be any possible objection to receive into the Church men who had already received the graces of the Holy Spirit, although they were Gentiles who had not conformed to the Jewish ritual.   In performing the outward rite, the apostle certainly did not believe that it would convey grace to the recipients, for that had already been conferred on them.   He must have considered it merely as a token of their profession of Christianity, and of their reception into the Church. If I were to cite any case from the New Testament which appears to me to make peculiarly against the sacramental idea, it would be that of the centurion and his friends.

---

* The following extract from a tract entitled *Gospel Truths*, published in Dublin in 1698, and signed by William Penn, Anthony Sharp, Thomas Story, and George Rooke, shews how they regarded the subject under consideration.   " We believe the " necessity of the one baptism of Christ, as well as of His one " supper, which He promiseth to eat with those that open the " door of their hearts to Him—being the baptism and supper " signified by the outward signs ; which, though we disuse, we " judge not those that conscientiously practise them."

CHARLES. Such is the effect of habitually looking through Quaker spectacles. You first settle what St. Peter, had he been a Quaker, "would certainly not have believed," and then you seem incapable of believing that he might have believed differently from what you had settled for him. He certainly *acted* differently from what a Quaker preacher would have done ; " he commanded them to be baptized in the name of the Lord." That act, by your interpretation, was little better than a mockery of baptism.

JOSIAH. That is altogether an unfair twisting of my words. There are others quite as open as we are to the charge of looking at these matters through the spectacles of prejudice. I maintained that the outward ceremony was expedient for the time, as an open confession of faith : but that is no proof of its perpetual obligation. Let us resume our discussion. The apostle Paul was so far from thinking baptism an essential part of the duties of an apostle, which it would certainly have been if the command of their Lord to His apostles was to be understood as thou understands it, that he tells the Corinthians that Christ sent him "not to baptize but to preach the Gospel ;" and he thanks God that he had " baptized none of them, but Crispus and Gaius," and " the household of Stephanas." Could he have spoken thus, if he had considered this rite to have the important value which your Church attaches to it; or if he held the last command of his Lord as intended to imply that baptism was an essential element in his commission as an apostle?

CHARLES. I have often been surprised at the stress laid by Friends on the passage you now quote; for the most cursory examination of the context suffices to show that the expressions used by St. Paul really make nothing for your argument. Parties had risen up among the disciples at Corinth, and had called themselves by the name of favorite preachers.—" I am of Paul, and I of Apollos, and I of Cephas." To whom the apostle sharply replies, " Is Christ divided? was Paul crucified for you? or were ye baptized in the name of Paul?" And, continuing this most natural train of thought, he adds, " I thank God " that I baptized none of you but Crispus and Gaius ; " lest any should say that I had baptized in my own " name." The apostle is thankful that he had not baptized any of these contentious persons, save two or three ; and for a most manifest and sufficient reason ; but he limits this thankfulness to that particular Church, and for that special reason —lest any should accuse him of having betrayed a trust. As to his adding, " For Christ sent me not to baptize, but to preach," it can only have a *special* meaning—that he came to Corinth to preach, not to baptize : others there were whose proper business it was to officiate at baptism. Nevertheless, we find the apostle ready and willing himself to administer baptism whenever the occasion called for it, as at Philippi.

JOSIAH. If baptism was not Paul's business during the year and six months that he spent in Corinth, it cannot have been an essential part of his mission. But we have his own account of the commission given him by the Lord himself when sending him to the Gentiles, viz., " to open " their eyes, and to turn them from darkness to light, " and from the power of Satan unto God, that they may " receive forgiveness of sins, and inheritance among them " which are sanctified by faith that is in Me," (*i.e.* in Christ.) Not a word of the outward rite here, though certainly the baptizing power of the Holy Spirit was necessary to turn his converts "from the power of Satan unto God."

CHARLES. I do not question the primary importance and necessity of the " baptizing power" or grace of the Holy Spirit. But your quotation from St. Paul's speech before King Agrippa proves nothing for or against baptism. If you could prove that authority to baptize was no essential part of St. Paul's mission, it would only show that his commission was less full than that given to the other apostles. Neither of us would accept that inference; and it is sufficiently clear, from St. Paul himself submitting to baptism, from the tone in which he speaks of baptism in his epistles, and from his actions on several occasions, that he did not hold the Quaker interpretation. That he did distinguish John's baptism from Christian baptism is evident from what took place at Ephesus, respecting the twelve disciples of John who "had not so much as heard whether there be any Holy Ghost," and who were, by St. Paul's authority, if not by his own hands, "baptized in the name of the Lord Jesus," as a preliminary to their endowment with the miraculous gifts of the Spirit.

JOSIAH. I draw quite a different deduction from the tone in which the apostle Paul speaks of baptism in his epistles, and I have already quoted some passages which appear to me evidently to refer to the true spiritual baptism. But as respects the apostle Peter, although he did command Cornelius and his friends to be baptized with water, even after they had received the baptism of the Holy Ghost, yet, in his first epistle, he speaks *of the* baptism which " now saves us" as being " not

" the putting away of the filth of the flesh, but the an-
" swer of a good conscience towards God, by the resur-
" rection of Jesus Christ." Surely the baptism to which
the apostle refers is not an outward ceremony, but an
inward spiritual grace.

CHARLES. St. Peter, in the passage you refer to, clearly
combines the symbolical rite with the grace imparted.
He is speaking of the deluge, and of the "eight souls
" saved by water. The like figure whereunto even bap-
" tism doth also now save us ;" but here, as elsewhere in
Scripture, salvation is conditional on inward purity and
faith. This does not dispense with the outward rite, any
more than in the case of Cornelius, or of St. Paul.

JOSIAH. Dean Alford translates this passage literally,
as follows : " which the antitype [of that] is now saving
you also, even baptism, not putting away, &c. ;" and he
maintains that the water of baptism is antitypal to the
water of the flood. Now surely the antitype to water
cannot be water, but must be something different, namely,
the Spirit which purifies the soul, as water purifies the
body. If it were the water of baptism that was spoken of
in the text, it would prove that the outward rite saves,
which thou wilt not maintain. Besides, the apostle says
that "baptism *is now* saving us," which evidently refers
to a *present* operation, not to a rite performed long since.

CHARLES. I do not see the force of your objection to
the waters of baptism being antitypal to the waters of the
flood. There is nothing to prevent a material uniformity
between a type and an antitype. Noah, by faith and
obedience, was saved from the destruction that came by
water ; similarly, " by the answer of a good conscience,"
those who believe and are baptized shall be saved. I do

not contend for more than a union between the saving grace and the *faithful* reception of the baptismal rite. But surely by the word " now" the apostle means the Christian dispensation, as contrasted with the old covenant : not the past or present moment of any convert's life.

JOSIAH. In both the Old and New Testaments water is frequently spoken of as an emblem of purification. The 36th chapter of Ezekiel contains the prophetic announcement, " I will sprinkle clean water upon you, and ye shall " be clean. . . . . A new heart will I give you, and a new " spirit will I put within you. . . . . And I will put my " Spirit within you, and cause you to walk in my statutes," &c. See also our Lord's words, " Except a man be born " of water and of the Spirit, he cannot enter the kingdom " of God." Is not this equivalent to being baptized " with the Holy Ghost and with fire ?" Again, Paul writes to Titus that we are saved " by the washing of regeneration ;" or, as it should perhaps be translated, by the laver of regeneration " and the renewing of the Holy Ghost." Has not this a similar meaning ?

CHARLES. On the contrary, we interpret the words, " to be born of water," as referring to the outward sign in baptism, and to be born " of the Spirit," to the inward grace communicated through the sacrament. None of the ancients, according to Hooker, ever understood this passage as implying anything but outward baptism. The passage from the epistle to Titus seems clearly to be of similar import ; the laver is the baptismal font. God has to the outward ministration of the Church joined an inward grace ; and all attempts to separate what He has joined together, lead through endless disputations to antinomianism, if not to unbelief. The body and the spirit

in man are mysteriously united, but it is only when they
are *united* that the man is MAN ; the body is not "man,"
the spirit is not "man ;" but both together, in the unity
which God hath given, make "the man." And so of the
sacrament ; the water, as water, is nothing ; but, united
to the Holy Spirit by God's ordinance, it is made the seal
of regeneration.

JOSIAH. I regard the words " being born of water and
of the Spirit" as an explanation of what our Lord had
just before said, as to the necessity of being "born again,"
or "from above." Immediately afterwards He drops the
metaphor, and says, "That which is born of the flesh is
flesh, and that which is born of the Spirit is spirit." The
interpretation which explains being "born of water,"
as referring to the outward sign, proves too much ; for it
clearly implies that no one can enter the kingdom of God
unless he have received the outward rite.

CHARLES. Baptism "by water and the Spirit" is the
appointed means of entry into the visible Church of
Christ, or "kingdom of God." Through it the recipient
is brought into a new relation with the Eternal Spirit.
He was by nature a child of wrath ; through baptism he
is adopted a child of God and heir of eternal life. This
is called a being "born again," in other words, being
"regenerate." But, whilst I thus maintain the essential
character and virtue of baptism, where it may be had, I
do not seek to limit the mercy of God in cases where,
from defective views of Christian doctrine, this sacrament
is omitted ; nor do I refer to those special cases (such
as the repentant thief) where the same authority that
had appointed dispensed with it. "Many are called, but
few are chosen." All baptized persons are assuredly

"called" or "elected" to eternal life ; but I fear that thousands do not "make their calling and election sure."

JOSIAH. The term "kingdom of God," as used here, cannot mean the visible Church, because men do enter into the visible Church without being born of the Spirit. Our Lord's words are express, "Except a man be born of water and Spirit," (there is no "of the" in the Greek,) "he cannot enter the kingdom of God ;" so that this "new birth"—this being "born again," or "from above"—this being born of water and Spirit is essential to salvation. I suppose thou wilt also explain the passage in the epistle to the Ephesians, where Paul speaks of "one Lord, one faith, one baptism," as referring to the rite of water baptism, while I think it clearly points out the true spiritual cleansing which the Christian believer receives through the indwelling Spirit.

CHARLES. You are for ever cutting baptism in two, as if there were both "water baptism" and "spiritual baptism" under the Christian dispensation. John's baptism was "water baptism," if you will ; he preached that men should repent and believe in Him who was to come. Christ's baptism is one and one only, a being "born of water and of the Spirit." Quaker baptism seems to be a being born "of the Spirit" alone. I cannot, on your Society's authority, disjoin what neither our Lord nor His apostles disjoined. The passage you refer to is indeed a striking one: "There is one body and one Spirit, "even as ye are called in one hope of your calling : one "Lord, one faith, one baptism ; one God and Father of "all, who is above all, and through all, and in you all." But sectarianism has split the "one body" into splinters; has broken up the "one faith" into "peculiarities ;" has dissolved the "one baptism" into its elements, and cast one away ; and then it asks us complacently to come and taste the spiritual banquet which it has prepared. Ah, Josiah ! you sectarians must come to some agreement among yourselves before we, who hold by the "one body," will eat of your supper.

JOSIAH. Well, we have discussed sectarianism already. The "one body" is certainly not any particular Church, but the whole body of true Christians of every name, and I believe the "one baptism" is that of the Spirit, as already described. But dost thou really believe that the outward sign is always accompanied by the inward grace ?

CHARLES. If the sacrament be received in faith, we believe that "the renewing of the Holy Ghost" does indeed accompany the "washing of regeneration ;" but if faith be wanting in an adult neophyte, I suppose (in accordance with the principle laid down in our Article XXIX) that there can be no true sacrament, but rather a blasphemous mockery of God—an attempt to impose a false oath on the Judge of quick and dead. Hence I infer that the impious person will bring on himself a curse, and not a blessing. "Whatsoever is not of faith is sin." But also, "Whatsoever ye ask in faith, believing, ye shall receive."

JOSIAH. Thou admits then that the inward grace does not invariably accompany the outward ceremony : there must therefore be two baptisms, one outward, and the other inward and spiritual ; otherwise one could not exist without the other. Now, that one may exist without the other is certain, for Simon Magus was baptized, and yet remained "in the gall of bitterness and the bond of iniquity ;" and the penitent thief on the cross did not receive any outward baptism, but was no doubt regenerated by the Holy Spirit.

CHARLES. I apprehend that a body may be present without a soul; as the form of baptism may be without the life-giving faith. Simon Magus is stated at first to have "believed and continued with Philip:" he may have fallen into the gall of bitterness afterwards. As to the thief on the cross, I think his case altogether exceptional and miraculous. Our Church does not limit God's infinite mercy, or presume to question His infinite power. She merely declares "the great necessity of this sacrament, *where it may be had,*" as you may read in the exhortation at the baptismal service.

JOSIAH. It appears most likely that the apostles themselves were never baptized with water, unless they received John's baptism, as we are told that "Jesus himself baptized not," though he permitted his disciples to do so. Dean Alford, in his notes on Acts ii. 38, remarks that "the " apostles and first believers were not thus baptized " (that is, with the outward ceremony) because they had " received the baptism of the Holy Ghost—the thing sig- " nified—which superseded that by water—the outward " and visible sign." Now, if we may receive the inward grace without the outward ceremony, and if the outward rite may be administered without the inward grace accompanying it, can it be necessary to keep it up as an ordinance of the Church? There is much danger that the recipient of the rite may rest in the delusion, that because he has received the outward form, he possesses the inward spiritual grace.

CHARLES. I might ask, how does Dean Alford know that the first believers were not baptized? But, admitting that they were not, I have already allowed that the same authority that appointed baptism can, at will, dispense with it. The apostles, and those early believers of whom Alford speaks, had been miraculously endued with spiritual graces on the day of Pentecost.

JOSIAH. When I refer to facts recorded in Scripture, which thou art obliged to admit make against thy views, thou calls them exceptional cases. To my mind they are the rule, not the exception.

CHARLES. Your last reference was, I think, not to Scripture, but to Dean Alford's Commentary.

JOSIAH. I referred to the case of Simon Magus, and to that of the penitent thief, and I quoted Dean Alford's opinion, that the apostles themselves had not received the rite of water baptism. But how can the "death unto sin and new birth unto righteousness" be communicated through an outward rite like this?

CHARLES. Whence cometh the immortal spirit which shall in time be born into the world, and pass through its stage appointed here? You ask hard questions. I can but answer you that "a new birth unto righteousness" is incommunicable by any act of man, but comes directly from the same Power who giveth to every infant an immortal spirit. If you read the baptismal service carefully, you will find that it proceeds on the assumption that God hears and answers prayer when offered to Him in faith, and when in accordance with His divine will. This surely is plain scripture teaching. He has plainly commanded his apostles and their successors to baptize; and it is quite plain that they understood this command to mean that they should administer the outward rite, as in His name and presence, trusting that He

12

would be with them at the same time, to confer the inward grace and blessing. Now we know from Scripture that the spiritual regeneration of the faithful recipient of Christian baptism is in accordance with the will of God. Hence the collect runs, " Receive him, O Lord, as thou " hast promised by thy well beloved Son, saying, Ask and " ye shall have ; seek and ye shall find ; knock and it shall " be opened unto you; so give now unto us that ask; let us " that seek, find ; open the gate unto us that knock," &c. There is not in this, or in any of the other collects, a single petition put up which has not abundant warranty from Scripture, and that God has not promised to grant to all that ask in faith. " Where two or three are gathered together in His name," He will hear. " Whatsoever two shall agree on earth to ask," He will grant. " God giveth of His Holy Spirit to them that ask Him." " Whatsoever you shall ask in faith, believing, ye shall receive," &c. If there be any truth in Scripture, or any meaning in words, these and other passages assure us that God will raise up into sonship (in other words, regenerate) those that are " buried with Him by baptism into death ; that like as " Christ was raised up from the dead by the glory of the " Father, even so (they) also should walk in newness of " life."

JOSIAH. That text refers manifestly to inward, spiritual baptism, which may be experienced without any ministration of water.

CHARLES. Doubtless it does refer to inward, spiritual baptism, which is the soul and seal of the Christian sacrament. But on your interpretation, which excludes a reference to the outward rite, what is the meaning of the word " buried"? What can it mean, unless that immersion in water, which is compared to the descent into the tomb ?

Josiah. These expressions are figurative, and, as already stated, refer *directly* to the inward operation of the Holy Ghost, the figure being drawn from the practice of immersion. The idea is more fully developed in Col. ii. 12, where the apostle refers both to the death and resurrection of Christ; "buried with Him in baptism, " wherein also ye are risen with Him, through the faith " of the operation of God, who hath raised Him from " the dead." The general idea is purification. It is the " death unto sin and the new birth unto righteousness :" the burial of the old nature in the tomb of Christ, and the birth of " the new man which is renewed in know- " ledge after the image of Him that created him." This spiritual baptism is thus figuratively compared to the burial and resurrection of Christ. Baptism is also spoken of in Scripture, when there cannot be any reference to water ; " I have a baptism to be baptized with ;" " Are ye able to be baptized with the baptism I am baptized with ? " Here it means suffering, not purification by water : that suffering unto death " for the sins of the whole world," of which those experience the benefit who, being truly " baptised into Christ, have put on Christ."

Charles. But was not " immersion " practised in obedience to a positive command ?

Josiah. I have already explained my views as to the meaning of what thou considers " a positive command ;" therefore, I need not repeat them : and for the reasons before stated, I still think that the baptism with the Holy Ghost was quite distinct from the outward ceremony ; and that it was to this true spiritual baptism alone

12*

that the apostle Paul referred when he spoke of "one Lord, one faith, one baptism," and also when he says, " For by one Spirit are we all baptized into one body." I will now repeat, in a somewhat different form, the question which thou left unanswered. Is not the purifying, cleansing power of the Holy Spirit,—effecting " the death unto sin, and the new birth unto righteousness,"—attainable by the Christian believer, whether the outward ceremony be performed or not ?

CHARLES. I can only repeat what I said before, that baptism " by water and the Spirit" is the appointed means of entry into the visible Church, or " kingdom of God;" and that all baptized persons are, by baptism, " elected or called to eternal life ;" that is, they are brought within the covenant of grace, made " children of God," and " grafted into the body of Christ's Church." But, whilst thus honouring the sacrament, because I believe it to be of divine appointment, I do not question God's power and right to dispense with its observance whenever it may please Him to accept a repentant and believing sinner : a matter, however, which no man can *know*.

JOSIAH. The entry into the visible Church is surely not synonymous with being " made children of God," and being " grafted into the body of Christ's Church." Water baptism may be used to mark the entrance into the one, but it is the true spiritual baptism alone which can graft into the other. But if, for the sake of argument, I admit the necessity, or rather the Christian obligation of baptism, I am still at a loss to know how it is to be performed. I see no directions in Scripture either as to the mode of performing it, or the persons by whom it is to be celebrated. All is vague and uncertain, very different in this respect from the ceremonies which were commanded under the old covenant.

CHARLES. Your complaint seems to me unreasonable ; for, admitting the absence in Scripture of rigidly precise directions, the stubborn fact remains against you, that baptism *by water* was invariably administered by the apostles, so far as we read, in apostolic times, as the pledge of discipleship or admission into the visible Church. The proper minister doubtless is whoever is duly appointed by the Church to officiate ; the proper ritual that which any particular branch of the Church may direct. Either may vary at different times, but still the *fact* remains of baptism by water, with the use of the words prescribed by Christ.

JOSIAH. We have no evidence from Holy Scripture that these words were ever used. But supposing you have sufficient warrant for your formal practice, tell me on what scriptural grounds your church administers infant baptism to the children of Christian parents ?

CHARLES. All who are partakers of the fallen nature of the first Adam are fit subjects of the regenerating grace of baptism, by which a new nature is imparted to them. Infants as well as adults belong to this class. In St. Peter's sermon on the day of Pentecost, he says, " Repent " and be baptised, every one of you . . . . for the promise " is to you and to your children." They were to be baptized because of the promise ; but the promise was to their children as well as to them ; consequently baptism would equally belong to their children. Under the old covenant the initiatory rite of circumcision was invariably administered to infants ; the corresponding initiatory rite of the Christian covenant would therefore naturally, by

persons accustomed to Jewish usage, be administered to
infants. If there were to be a difference between the two
covenants on so fundamental a point, we should certainly
have heard of it. Infants are made partakers of the
nature of the old Adam in a state of unconsciousness.
Why then should we doubt their capability of being
grafted, through baptism, in a like state of unconsciousness, into the nature of the second Adam ?—Of Him who
said, " Whosoever shall not receive the kingdom of God as
a little child, shall in no wise enter therein."

JOSIAH. " The promise is unto you and to your
children, and to all that are afar off, even as many as the
Lord our God shall call." · Surely this means, " to you,
and your descendants." However, I do not care to discuss
infant baptism except so far as it bears on the general
question. If baptism be a sacrament, as thou considers it,
the earlier it is administered the better. If it be merely
a formal admission into the visible Church, the same reasoning will apply. There is, however, no record of the
baptism of children in the apostolic age.

CHARLES. Did not St. Paul baptize the whole household of Lydia, and of the jailor of Philippi ? Surely
there must have been children in these households.

JOSIAH. We know that the Jews were accustomed,
when they received a proselyte, to baptize his whole
family, children included ; and therefore, if the households
of Lydia and the jailor included children, they were
probably baptized. All the heathen were reputed " unclean" by the Jews, but when thus purified they became
legally " holy." The apostle Paul, in writing to the
Corinthians, alludes to this Jewish idea ; when speaking
of the unbelieving husband as being " sanctified by the

wife," he says, " else were your children *unclean*, but now they are *holy*," and if " holy," that is, legally pure, they would not, according to Jewish ideas, require to be baptized.

CHARLES. Does not this rather afford a presumption in favor of infant baptism? The apostle may have called the children " holy," because they had been baptized.

JOSIAH. 1 think not, because it was not the Jewish custom to baptize children, except when received into the Jewish Church along with their parents. Besides, if infant baptism had then been in force, the apostle would naturally have appealed to *it* as making them *" holy."* Certainly he did not mean to imply that the unbelieving husband had been baptized, when he spoke of him as " sanctified " by the believing wife. Both were considered " holy" on account of the influence of Christian fellowship. The baptism of children does not appear to have become general before the third century, nor to have been the established practice before the fifth.

CHARLES. There is ample evidence that the baptism of infants was the general practice from the very first, though no doubt baptism was sometimes delayed, during the second and third centuries, on account of the superstitious feelings which began to be connected with the rite. Men misconstrued the doctrine, that their past sins are forgiven to all those who, with hearty repentance and true faith, seek to enter Christ's Church through the appointed door, and deferred being baptized, thinking that " a more convenient season " than the time present would answer their purposes better.

JOSIAH. The existence of these superstitious feelings, at so early a period, affords at least a presumption that the successors of the apostles may have been mistaken, in supposing that a Jewish ceremony, practised by the apostles, was intended to be perpetually observed by the Church. Your baptismal service contains the expression, that "none can enter into the kingdom of God except he "be regenerate and born anew of water and of the Holy Ghost;" and again, speaking of the unconscious infant, we find the words, "Seeing now that this child is regenerate." Now I wish to ask thee if every baptized infant is regenerate, and a member of Christ's kingdom.

CHARLES. I believe that every baptized infant is by baptism "grafted into the body" of the Church or "kingdom of God," as a living bud is grafted into a living tree; also that, as God hears and answers prayer, so He is willing to grant His blessing to earnest parents who present their unconscious infants in His Church, even as His blessed Son was once presented in the Temple. I desire to dogmatize no further.

JOSIAH. And how of unbaptized infants? Are they not regenerate? not subjects of Christ's kingdom? Surely those little children, of whom our Lord said "Of such is the kingdom of Heaven," had not been baptized.

CHARLES. An unbaptized infant is certainly not born anew into the body of the Church or kingdom of Christ. It is born into the world, and we are assured by Scripture that it has been conceived and born in sin, and is liable to all the penalties due to Adam's guilt. As to the little children of whom our Lord spake, we read, "He took "them up in his arms, put his hands upon them, and "blessed them." We cannot doubt that His act did really convey a blessing.

JOSIAH. If the apostle Peter had baptized Simon

Magus according to the forms of your Church, he would have announced to him that he was " regenerate," and yet, very shortly afterwards he would have been obliged to address to him a very different language.

CHARLES. In the English office for the baptism of adults, an express condition (not found in the similar prayer in that for infant baptism,) is introduced, namely, that God will receive them, " truly repenting and coming unto Him by faith." The Church of England (Article XXVII) declares ; " They that receive baptism *rightly* are grafted into the Church." But if " the wicked and such as be void of a lively faith" (Article XXIX), though outwardly receiving the Lord's supper, are declared to be no communicants, as surely, wickedness and want of faith in the adult recipient of baptism are allowed, by our Church, to be obstacles to " regeneration."

JOSIAH. No such ritual as yours can have been in use in apostolic times. Indeed it appears, so far as we can gather from the New Testament, that the form, which some suppose to have been sanctioned by the last command of our Lord, was not generally used by the apostles themselves ; as, in many cases at least, it is stated that the persons baptized were baptized " into the name of the Lord Jesus."

CHARLES. The apostles undoubtedly used that form of words which our Lord commanded, although not expressly stated in every instance. This is evident from St. Paul's reply to the statement, " We have not so much as heard whether there be any Holy Ghost,"—" Unto what then were ye baptized ? " As to the precise ritual used in the administration, it probably varied with every age and in every country : the essential parts of the form have, however, always remained the same. The life of baptism is that it be observed in faith.

JOSIAH. Thou considers the ritual may be varied according to circumstances.

CHARLES. Certainly. But as for the outward body of the sacrament, it is not we who have devised it; but the same who on another occasion said, " Fill the water pots with water ;" " Draw out now and bear unto the governor of the feast." What connection is there between the water and the wine in this miracle ? It were as easy, without water, to create the wine anew in the vessels which had just been emptied, had it pleased our Lord so to do. The filling with water was a work altogether futile, so far as the production of wine was concerned; and had George Fox been present, no doubt he would so have decided. The servants, however, obeyed the command, "Whatsoever HE saith unto you, do it ;"—and the miraculous power of Christ went with them. Precisely thus do I believe respecting Christian baptism ; that we are commanded to do our part in the sacrament in simple faith, trusting that He, on His part, " will most surely keep and perform His promise." But *our* part is not over when we submit to the washing at the hands of the minister. That is only, as the ritual expresses it, " a good beginning." It remains that we follow up this beginning to the end of a Christian education, for " baptism doth signify to us our profession," and is complete only when we carry out by our conduct the professions of self-denial, faith, and obedience which we make, or which are made by proxies acting on our behalf and in our name.

JOSIAH. Thou said " by proxies acting on our behalf." I suppose thou alludes to the godfathers and godmothers.

For this part of your ritual there is certainly no apostolic authority. I believe history is silent as to their origin; but Neander thinks that, in the third century, when infant baptism first became general, sponsors were appointed to make the confession of faith which was expected from an adult convert, but which the unconscious infant of course could not make for itself. How can we reconcile such a mode of proceeding with the general tenor of scripture teaching? Religion is an individual work, and no part of it can be done by proxy. "No man can save his brother." This acceptance of the profession of faith by another as being on the part of the unconscious infant, and considering such a profession to render the sacrament valid, appears to me a subterfuge unworthy of the sacred cause in which it is employed.

CHARLES. Unquestionably the sponsors utter these promises and professions not for themselves, but as mouthpieces or proxies, answering for the infant. But what are these promises and professions, save what every Christian man is bound to observe by the terms of the common faith? namely, to renounce the world, the flesh, and the devil, and to believe in the Gospel message? By their promises on behalf of the infant, the meaning surely is, that so far as lies in their power, they undertake that the child shall receive a Christian education. It is no doubt their duty to assist the parents or natural guardians when called on, or, should these be unfaithful to their trust, to address themselves to the child, if permitted to do so; and I believe that many godparents are careful so to do.

JOSIAH. They promise for the unconscious infant that he " will obediently keep God's holy will and commandments, and walk in the same all the days of his life," and this without any reference to divine assistance, or to the way in which even the best endeavours fall short of our duty. This is a very different thing from endeavouring to give the child a Christian education, and is done by many who use no endeavours to have the promises they have made fulfilled by those for whom they acted. Canst thou pretend that one godfather in ten fulfils, even in the most imperfect manner, what he undertakes in this rite?

CHARLES. I am well aware of the lamentable inefficiency of god-parents in modern times, and the sad prevalence of unsuitable persons chosen for this office—persons who, never having renounced the world themselves, and being willingly led away by its "pomps and vanity," are utterly unfit to guide the child in the Christian path. Such persons frustrate the design of the Church, and turn Christ's sacrament, so far as they are concerned, into a solemn mockery. The original design of the appointment of these witnesses and sureties is, however, wise and good ; and if parents were careful to select for the office none but conscientious persons, and persons likely to come in contact with the child in after life, instead of the name of godfather being a byeword and a hissing, the relationship would be valued as it deserves to be. The design obviously is to ensure for the child not merely the Christian instruction which its parents may give it, but —failing these natural guides—to add the counsel and direction of two other faithful friends and protectors.

JOSIAH. Parents often cannot find such persons willing to undertake the duties' of sponsors ; and I certainly am not surprised that it should be so.

CHARLES. I know that conscientious parents frequently

find it difficult to procure proper sponsors for their children ; partly from the prejudice against the office in the minds of persons who, like you, are shocked at the heedless manner in which its obligations are often undertaken, and who take the opposite extreme, and abjure the office itself. I have heard many of these scrupulous persons say, " I would not be a godfather for any consideration," &c. But I think their scruples unreasonable. The same scruples should prevent them, *a fortiori*, from becoming parents—thereby certainly incurring a still more solemn responsibility. I can conceive a conscientious Christian man objecting to stand sponsor for a child over whose education, in human probability, he would have no opportunity of exercising any control ; but where there is reasonable prospect of his being able to assist, however slightly, in the Christian education of the child, I think his refusal of the office is a spiritual loss to himself, and his acceptance may become a rich spiritual blessing. Many parents, I believe, find that their own hearts are enlarged in the attempt to instruct their children in godliness ; and thus also would it happen with the faithful godparent.

JOSIAH. Thou began our last conversation on these ceremonies by referring to a little book, written by a Friend, which treated on these subjects. I also have lately met with a little book, written by a minister of your Church, entitled, " Baptismal regeneration op-
" posed, both by the word of God and the standards of the
" Church of England." The writer maintains that it was
" the practice of Christ to regenerate souls without the
use of baptism ;" that baptism was " not the instrument of
regeneration, but the sign of profession ;" that "the word
" of God is the appointed instrument for effecting regene-

" ration ;" and that "there is no other instrument in the
use of which we are even warranted at all to expect it ;"
that "regeneration is the pre-requisite for baptism, not
baptism the instrumental cause of regeneration." He
then proceeds to prove that this is the doctrine of the
Church of England, alleging, in the case of adults, that
only regenerate persons are fit for baptism ; and in the
case of infants, that the promise, made by the sponsors on
behalf of the child, is considered as if made by the child
himself, and thus the child is considered by the Church
as regenerate, which appears to me as nice a piece of sup-
posititious logic as I ever saw. This doctrine differs very
much from what thou maintains, and I refer to this little
book to show that doctors in your Church can differ as
much as J. J. Gurney differs from Penn or Barclay.

CHARLES. Our Church certainly tolerates a wide range
for varying opinion. Almost all grades of belief in the
efficacy of the sacraments may be found within her pale.
Much of the wrangling about "baptismal regeneration"
arises out of the different meanings attached by opposite
parties to the word "regeneration." If you wish for a
fuller commentary than the author of the "little book"
you speak of has given, I recommend to your perusal
Hooker's "Ecclesiastical Polity." From that work you
may learn what is the doctrine on the sacraments really
upheld by the Church of England.

CONVERSATION VII.

This do in remembrance of Me.—*St. Luke,* xxii. 19.

The words that I speak unto you, they are spirit, and they are life.—*St. John,* vi. 63.

JOSIAH. Our last conversation turned chiefly on the obligation to observe the rite of water baptism. I suppose thou hast also something to say on the ceremony called the "Lord's supper."

CHARLES. I confess that I am rather puzzled how to address myself to you so as to gain your attention; for I feel as if you did not come to the discussion of this subject with an unprejudiced mind, but rather with a pre-determination to set aside every thing that I might bring forward in favour of the observance. Is it not so, my friend?

JOSIAH. I cannot admit it to be so. Surely it is not unreasonable for me to require a clear proof from Scripture, that our Lord intended to institute any typical rite, under a dispensation in which forms and ceremonies were to be superseded by the great spiritual realities of which they were the figures.

CHARLES. I cannot object to your requiring scriptural

proof; but I so well know how deeply rooted in the mind
of every Quaker is the notion that all outward religious
rites are a departure from the spirituality of the Gospel,
that I feel as if it were useless to speak to them on this
subject.

JOSIAH. We are all liable to be influenced by our
early education, but I am not aware that our body is
more open to the charge just made than others are. I
might fairly retort that it is useless to reason on this subject with a Churchman, because his prejudices are so
deeply rooted that he is not open to conviction. Come, let
us endeavour to discuss this subject fairly, on scripture
grounds, which is the only authority I can acknowledge.

CHARLES. I can bring forward no stronger argument
for the observance of the Lord's supper, than that it
was solemnly instituted by our Lord Himself on the night
in which He was betrayed; that He Himself ordained
the form and the matter of which this rite should consist;
and that He commanded His disciples to observe the
same, saying (as we learn from the statements of St. Luke
and St. Paul), "This do in remembrance of Me." Now
as three of the Evangelists record the first celebration of
the sacramental supper in nearly the same words, you
will hardly deny that, on that occasion at least, our Lord
celebrated it outwardly (as you would say)—that is, by
delivery of the consecrated elements to the apostles. And
His immediately saying, "This do in remembrance of
Me," seems to a plain man to be a sufficient enforcement
of the rite on the apostles and their successors. The
delivery of this rite is almost the last act on earth of
our blessed Lord, and whilst administering it He adds,
"THIS do." Why? "In REMEMBRANCE of Me." Could

He possibly have enjoined the observance by a stronger plea?

JOSIAH. There is nothing in the Scripture narrative to warrant the idea of a "sacramental supper," or of the consecration of the elements. This is a mere assumption, but let it pass for the present. The whole force of thy argument consists in thy interpretation of the word *this.* Thou says our Lord instituted a rite. I say He took part in an ancient Jewish rite, hitherto prophetic, typical and figurative, now on the point of being fulfilled. He did what every master of a family in Jerusalem was accustomed to do at *every* important meal, and especially at all Jewish feasts,—the Paschal supper of course included, —namely ; after having given thanks to God, He broke the bread and distributed it to those at table, and the wine in like manner.* The words "This do," &c., are not an injunction to do anything *new,* but they give a new

---

* *Customs of the Jews at meals.*—In the account of the *Manners and Customs of the Jews,* published by the *Religious Tract Society,* we find this description of their practice at meals, on important occasions :—" The following custom, observed by the modern " Jews after the practice of their forefathers, strongly reminds " us of what passed at the last supper. Before they sit down " they wash their hands very carefully, like the Pharisees of " old, (Mark vii. 3) ; they say that it is necessary to do so. A " blessing is then asked. The master or chief person takes a " loaf, and breaking it, says, ' Blessed art thou, O Lord our God, " the King of the world, who producest bread out of the earth.' " The guests answer, ' Amen,' and the bread is distributed to " them. He then takes the vessel which holds the wine in his " right hand, and says, ' Blessed art thou, O Lord our God, King " of the world, who hast created the fruit of the vine.' The " 23rd Psalm is then repeated. When the meal is finished, the

force and meaning to acts to which His disciples were
well accustomed.   As often hereafter as, at your solemn
feasts, or on any other occasion, you break this bread, and
drink this "cup of blessing,"* do it in remembrance of my
body broken and my blood shed for you.   The Jewish
rites and ceremonies continued to be observed by Jewish
Christians until the destruction of Jerusalem : henceforth
this usage, customary at all their feasts, would be a commemoration showing forth their Lord's death as "the new
covenant" sacrifice for sin.

CHARLES.   The text in St. Luke's Gospel reads,. "And
" He took bread, and gave thanks, and brake it, and gave
" unto them, saying, This is my body which is given for
" you : this do in remembrance of Me."   By the words,
" This do," in this text, the Christian Church, from the
day of Pentecost to the present hour, has understood our
Lord to enjoin His apostles, and through them their
successors in the Christian ministry, to do this : to take

" master takes a piece of bread which has been left on purpose,
" and filling a glass or cup with wine, says, ' Let us bless Him
" of whose benefits we have partaken ;' the company reply, ' Bles-
" ' sed be He who has heaped his favours on us, and has now fed
" ' us on His goodness.'   The master then repeats a prayer, thank-
" ing God for His many benefits granted to Israel, entreating Him
" to have pity upon Jerusalem and the temple, to restore the throne
" of David, to send Elias and the Messiah, and to deliver them
" from their low state.   The guests all answer, ' Amen,' and re-
" peat Psalm xxxiv., 9, 10; then each guest drinks a little of the
" wine that is left, and goes from the table."—*Manners and Customs of the Jews*, (Rel. Tract Soc.) p. 53.

* "The third cup [of wine partaken of at the passover] was
usually called the cup of blessing."—*Rites and Worship of the
Jews*, (Rel. Tract Soc.) p. 99.

bread, to break and distribute it, and to partake of the cup, whenever they met to commemorate their Master's passion. Such appears to me to be the simple, grammatical meaning of the words.

JOSIAH. I need not repeat the arguments advanced in our former conversation, on the general question of typical ordinances, but wish simply to refer to them as being peculiarly applicable to the subject now under discussion. As respects the assumed "consecration of the elements," the word "it," referring to bread, which occurs in our English translation, is not to be found in the Greek, and the literal translation of the text in Matthew would therefore be, " Jesus, taking bread, and having blessed, brake, and gave to the disciples :"—and of that in Luke, " And taking bread, having given thanks, He brake and gave to them." It was God whom our Lord blessed, not the bread.

CHARLES. We build nothing whatever on the words " blessed," or " blessed it," as you may see by referring to the " prayer of consecration" in the communion office, which reads, " took bread, and *when He had given thanks* He brake it," &c. The words of our Lord which do *consecrate*, or set apart for holy uses, the elements of bread and wine, are these, " This is my body,"—" This is my blood," words which no master of a Jewish family could possibly have used, and which clearly distinguish the Christian sacrament from the Jewish feasts.

JOSIAH. These words prove too much or they do not make anything in favour of thy views. Unless I am to take them literally, as the Roman Church does, they only mean, " This signifies or represents my body." This is exactly the sense in which I understand them, but it

13*

contains no idea of consecration. Our Lord pointed out to His disciples that, by the bread which the master of every Jewish family was accustomed to break and distribute at the Paschal supper, and on other occasions of a similar character, was prefigured that body which was sacrificed for them, and that the wine typified His "blood " of the new covenant which was shed for many for the " remission of sins."

CHARLES. But the word "*this,*" which you seem so unwilling to understand, does set apart for a religious use the particular piece of bread of which it is spoken from other pieces of bread, however we may understand the words, "This is my body." That is all I maintain.

JOSIAH. I have just stated the meaning which these words appear to me to convey. But what warrant is there for supposing our Lord to have instituted a rite to be perpetually observed in His Church? The apostle John, who gives a very full account of the transactions which took place on the night of the last supper, makes no allusion whatever to the distribution of the bread and wine to the disciples.

CHARLES. There is nothing positively to be inferred from this omission, for St. John comparatively rarely narrates what had been fully recorded by the other evangelists who wrote before him. His gospel is generally allowed to be a supplementary one. But surely in St. John, chap. vi., the *doctrine* of the Eucharist is unfolded. St. John, similarly, does not record the institution of baptism, but in chap. iii. he relates our Lord's revealing its *doctrine* to Nicodemus.

JOSIAH. We have already discussed the subject of baptism, therefore I need not recur to it. But with respect to thy reference to John, chap. vi., as unfolding the doctrine of the Eucharist, it appears to me that the fact of the apostle John having so fully narrated our Lord's discourse respecting the spiritual reality, only makes it the more striking that he should have avoided all mention of the distribution of the bread and wine, if our Lord had really intended to institute a rite of such paramount obligation as this must be, if it has been ordained as a sacrament. Then, as to the evangelists who do narrate what took place, neither Matthew nor Mark says anything implying the institution of a rite.

CHARLES. It is manifestly unreasonable to infer that a precept is not binding, because it is not repeated by every evangelist and apostle. Where will you find, "Swear not at all," except in St. Matthew and St. James? St. Matthew and St. Mark record enough to distinguish the Christian supper from the Jewish; but because their narrative is less full than that of St. Luke, who is habitually the most circumstantial of all the evangelists, or than that of St. Paul, to whom a special revelation was given, is this any reason why you should discredit the latter witnesses, and abide solely by the former?

JOSIAH. I had no idea of casting any doubt on the testimony of either Luke or Paul. The point under consideration is the meaning of the words recorded by them; and certainly, if these words are so significant that *a binding sacramental rite* is to be based upon them, I do say that it is most strange that Matthew, who was an eye-witness, should have omitted to record them. I cannot see anything, in any of these accounts, which denotes a Christian supper distinct from a Jewish one; and certainly this omission on the part of Matthew and Mark of everything approaching to a command, and the total silence of the apostle John, are very difficult to be accounted for, on the supposition that our Lord was then instituting a rite of perpetual obligation, and a sacrament of such important character as your Church considers it to be.

CHARLES. The record by St. Luke and St. Paul is amply sufficient.

JOSIAH. In continuation of my argument, I wish now to remark that the apostle John's omission of all reference to the distribution of the bread and wine is the more significant, as he so fully describes the occurrences of that last evening which his Lord spent with His disciples, and so circumstantially relates the washing of the disciples' feet which took place during the supper, an act of our Lord which the other evangelists omit.* "If I then, your "Lord and Master, have washed your feet, ye also ought "to wash one another's feet; for I have given you an "example, that ye should do as I have done to you." Is not this an equally strong command for the observance of this ancient Jewish custom? Yet you disregard it, and practice no such washing.

CHARLES. The object of our Lord, in washing the feet

---

* The washing of the disciples' feet took place not after but during the supper; the English version being incorrectly translated. See *Alford's Greek Testament,* John xiii. 2.

It is the custom of the Jews to wash their feet before the Paschal supper, and again after the Paschal lamb has been eaten, but before they have partaken of the bitter herbs. It was on this second occasion that our Lord is recorded to have washed His disciples' feet.—See *Rites and Worship of the Jews,* (*Rel. Tract Soc.*) *p.* 98.

of His disciples, was manifestly to reiterate the lesson of humility which He had enforced on them on many previous occasions.

JOSIAH. I quite agree with thee, and I only quoted the passage to show that we cannot always take that which may appear at first sight the literal meaning of a command, however solemnly given, but must consider the context, and the circumstances under which the command was given.

CHARLES. In this matter we have the practice of the primitive Church to guide us. We hear nothing in the New Testament of the iteration of foot-washing, nor did it ever become an ordinance of the universal Church. But far otherwise with the observance of the Lord's supper. The "breaking of bread" is constantly spoken of, and appears to have been always celebrated in the Church from the very first, on its assembling on the Lord's day, and indeed to have been a principal object in publicly coming together. Immediately after the great day of Pentecost, as we read in Acts, ii., it is said of the new converts, "And they continued steadfastly in the apos-"tles' doctrine and fellowship, and in *breaking of bread*, "and in prayers."

JOSIAH. Many commentators consider that the breaking of bread here spoken of refers merely to a frugal meal partaken of in common, as appears to have been then customary. A verse or two after that thou hast just quoted we read, "And all that believed were together, and had "all things common ; and they continuing daily with one "accord in the temple, and breaking bread from house to "house, did eat their meat with gladness and singleness "of heart." Taking the scope of the whole passage it seems to refer rather to partaking of ordinary food in fellowship, than to a religious rite such as that thou art contending for.

CHARLES. There is a marginal reference in our Bibles to Acts, xx. 7, which affords a clear answer to this objection. There we read, " And upon the first day of the " week, when the disciples came together to break bread, " Paul preached unto them, ready to depart on the mor- " row." Does this look like a coming together to partake of ordinary food at a common table?

JOSIAH. The breaking of bread there spoken of was certainly a meal partaken of in common as a token of brotherly love. It was no doubt one of the agapæ or love-feasts, which were frequently held by the early Christians on the first day of the week. On this particular occasion it was held in the evening, and continued through the night. It was a real meal, and Paul having " broken " bread and eaten, and talked a long while, even till break " of day, so departed."

CHARLES. It was the Lord's supper that was celebrated at one of the agapæ or love-feasts. Such was the custom of the Church at that time.

JOSIAH. I have already referred to the established practice of the Jews, for the master of the house or head of the family, when partaking of food, to ask a blessing while breaking the bread. Thus, when our Lord sat at meat with the two disciples at Emmaus, " he took bread " and blessed (or rather gave thanks), and brake and gave " to them." Thus Paul, on his voyage, " took bread and gave thanks to God in the presence of " his fellow-voyagers. This breaking of bread with thanksgiving, and with the new signification given to it by our Lord at His last supper with His disciples, was certainly an invariable part of the agapæ or love-feasts; and there is no reason to believe, either from the Scriptures or from ecclesiastical history, that it took place, during apostolic times, on any occasion except when the Christians partook of food together. I see in all this no record of anything like a sacramental rite; and yet, if such had been instituted by our Lord, we might expect to find it celebrated with peculiar solemnity, by those who must have had the parting words of their Master so deeply impressed on their memories. The time thou first referred to was just after the great day of Pentecost; the conversion of more than three thousand of their countrymen had filled the apostles with joy and wonder; and the new converts would surely be anxious to partake of a rite, which, if your view be correct, possesses efficacy as a sacrament to nourish the spiritual life in the hearts of the recipients. That no record exists of the celebration of this, which would have been the first " communion" of the Christian Church, is almost a proof that no such thing took place.

CHARLES. I see no reason to doubt that the communion of the Lord's supper was duly celebrated, according to our Lord's model, immediately after the feast of Pentecost, and that, in the text alluded to (Acts ii. 42), there is a brief record of such celebration : and moreover, I think it probable, from the constant allusions to " breaking bread " at the time of prayer, that partaking of the communion formed a part of the ordinary worship of the early Church.

JOSIAH. This is merely supposition: there is nothing that can be fairly called a record of such celebration.

CHARLES. The Lord's supper appears to have been

celebrated in the early Church whenever the disciples met together on the Lord's day, or oftener. It was celebrated equally by Jew and Gentile,—by the circumcised and the uncircumcised. The lamb of the Passover *prefigured* the sacrifice of Christ ; the bread and wine of the Lord's supper *commemorate* that sacrifice.

JOSIAH. It is not quite clear whether it was the distribution of the bread and wine which took place at the love-feast, or the love-feast itself, that was called "the Lord's supper" by the apostle Paul. Neander considers that both taken together were called by this name, and Adam Clarke and others support this opinion.* But to whichever the name was given, it is evident that all Christians, whether of Jewish or Gentile origin, took part in the love-feasts, of which the commemorative distribution of bread and wine formed an important part ; and it is historically certain that the celebration of the ordinance, afterwards called the "Eucharist" or "Lord's

---

* *The feast of love—The Lord's supper.* On this subject Neander says, "After the model of the Jewish passover, and the "first institution, the Lord's supper was originally united with a "*common meal.* Both constituted a whole, representing not only "the communion of the faithful with their Lord, but also their "brotherly communion with one another. Both together were "called the supper of the Lord (δεῖπνον τοῦ κυρίου, δεῖπνον κυριακόν), "the supper of love (ἀγάπη)."—*Neander's Hist. of the Church, vol.* i. *p. 450.*

"So long as the agapæ and the Lord's supper were united to-"gether, the celebration of the latter formed no part of the divine "service. The latter [the divine service] was held early in the "morning, and not till towards evening did the Church re-assem-"ble at the common love-feast and for the celebration of the "supper."—*Neander, vol.* i. *p. 452.*

supper," however its form and idea were subsequently
changed, had its origin in this simple observance. But
what resemblance dost thou find in this to the sacrament,
so-called, as practised by your Church?

CHARLES. St. Paul himself shall supply an answer,
which you will find in the tenth and eleventh chapters of
I Corinthians, where, firstly, it is written, " The cup
" of blessing which we bless, is it not the communion
" of the blood of Christ? The bread which we break,
" is it not the communion of the body of Christ?" Here
the words " which we bless " and " which we break "
clearly show that the apostles *literally* observed their
Lord's command " Do THIS in remembrance of Me." The
whole tenor of the passage in the tenth chapter shows
that he speaks of a religious eucharistic offering, which
he contrasts with the Gentile sacrifices, and then proves
that the faithful cannot partake of both. " Ye cannot
" drink the cup of the Lord and the cup of devils ; ye
" cannot be partakers of the Lord's table, and of the table
" of devils." Language can hardly be stronger to show
that, in those days, under apostolic guidance, the Christian commemorative sacrifice was observed—the blessing
of the cup and the breaking of the bread, even as it is
now, at nineteen centuries' distance, and as it has essentially been throughout the long ages between. But the
eleventh chapter puts this still more forcibly, where St.
Paul declares, " For I have received OF THE LORD that
which also I delivered unto you ;" and then he fully re-
capitulates what took place at the last supper, on the night
of the betrayal ; adding, " For as oft as ye eat this bread
" and drink this cup, ye do shew the Lord's death till He
" come." Now St. Paul was not present at the last

supper, nor converted to Christianity till long afterwards; and yet he declares that he received this narrative "of the Lord." Compare this declaration with what he also says in the first chapter of Galatians, "But I certify you, "brethren, that the Gospel which was preached of me "is not after man; for I neither received it of man, nei- "ther was I taught it, but by the revelation of Jesus "Christ." The question will then rest on the veracity of St. Paul, and the authenticity of his epistles, neither of which you will call in question. For you will observe that St. Paul declares that "the Lord" had specially revealed to him the institution of the holy supper, and that he therefore had delivered the ordinance to the Church. For my own part, I do not desire a higher sanction; nor do I see how historic evidence in favour of the observance can well be stronger. For the observance we have the evidence of three evangelists, and of the great apostle of the Gentiles, supported by the unvarying voice of the Church for nineteen centuries;—against it you put forth the testimony of the Society of Friends.

JOSIAH. Our opinions are based on Scripture, and a taunt of this kind does not prove that we are wrong. We have the testimony of three evangelists that our Lord told His disciples that the bread broken typified or repre- sented His body broken for them—that of Luke and the apostle Paul, that He directed them, as often in future as, following the custom of their forefathers, they distri- buted the broken bread, and partook of "the cup of bless- ing,"* they should do so "in remembrance" of Him,—and

---

* *The cup of blessing.* Neander says, speaking of the cup of wine which was distributed at the Paschal supper :—" The cup " of *wine* over which this giving of thanks was pronounced, was

we know that it has been the almost unvarying belief of succeeding ages, that, by these words, He had instituted a religious rite of perpetual obligation. Now, whether this belief have Scripture warrant or not, is the question we have to discuss. The observance referred to by the apostle Paul is evidently the practice before alluded to, of distributing bread and wine to those assembled at the agapæ or love-feasts; and no doubt this practice was intended by those who partook of it to serve as a memorial of their Lord's death. The apostle Paul speaks of it as if he himself was accustomed to take part in it; but, although this may convince us that, as then practised, it was not inconsistent with Christian doctrine, yet it does not prove that it was intended to be continued perpetually as an ordinance of the Church. Thou finds a " commemorative sacrifice" in the words of the apostle. I cannot see any indication of it. " The cup which we bless"—" the " bread which we break, is it not the communion of the " body of Christ ?" May not this be paraphrased thus : " Does it not represent the communion, or partaking " together in common, of the benefits promised to be- " lievers by the blood of Christ shed, and His body " broken for them ?" Thus I think the bread and wine distributed at the love-feasts were understood, being taken in remembrance of the Lord's death ; and therefore the apostle—when contrasting the agapæ at which they were distributed, with the feasts of the Gentiles on food which had been offered in sacrifice to idols—calls the cup, "the cup of the Lord," and speaks of the table on

---

" called the cup of blessing or thanksgiving, ($\pi o \tau \acute{\eta} \rho \iota o \nu$ $\epsilon \upsilon \lambda o \gamma \iota a s =$ " $\epsilon \upsilon \chi a \rho \iota \sigma \tau \iota a s$.)"—*Neander's History of the Church*, vol. i., p. 449.

which the bread was placed as "the Lord's table." He says, "Ye cannot drink the cup of the Lord and the cup "of devils; ye cannot be partakers of the Lord's table "and of the table of devils." That is:—If you wish to be Christians, and to take part with them in the feasts of love, you must not frequent the idolatrous feasts of the heathen.

CHARLES. I have listened patiently to your explanation. You assert that the κυριακόν δεῖπνον, or Lord's supper, was merely a part of the ἀγάπη or love-feast. Now I maintain that it was an independent and divinely instituted rite; though I am aware that, in early times, it was frequently celebrated in conjunction with the love-feasts. You admit that it was celebrated in commemoration of our Lord's death, and that St. Paul speaks of it as if he were accustomed to take part in it; but you do not see any proof of its perpetual obligation, or of its sacramental character. I have already defended the obligation to observe our Lord's dying injunction, and you have not convinced me that the words, "Do this in remembrance of Me," have ceased to be binding on the Church. As to the sacramental virtue of the Eucharist, I think that it is established by considering the sixth chapter of St. John's Gospel, jointly with the eleventh of I Corinthians. Observe particularly St. Paul's concluding words; "Where-"fore, whosoever shall eat this bread, and drink this "cup of the Lord, unworthily, shall be guilty of the body "and blood of the Lord. But let a man examine him-"self, and so let him eat of that bread and drink of that "cup. For he that eateth and drinketh unworthily, eat-"eth and drinketh judgment to himself, not discerning "*the* Lord's body."

JOSIAH. Here the apostle certainly enjoins the Corinthians to examine themselves whether they are in the faith, before eating the bread or drinking the cup which were intended to commemorate the Lord's death ; and declares that he who partook of this bread or this cup unworthily, that is, without faith in that atoning sacrifice which they purported to commemorate, would be guilty of injurious disrespect to the Lord, by proclaiming His death in an improper spirit, and would thereby incur the Divine condemnation, as trifling with the death of Christ. But this only shows that, while the observance continued, those who took part in it should do so with a pious disposition, and in faith : it offers no proof, either of its sacramental efficacy, or of its perpetual obligation. The injunction of the apostle was not, that the Corinthians should partake of this rite, but that those who did partake should do so in a proper spirit.

CHARLES. You speak as if St. Paul did not *enjoin* his disciples at Corinth to keep the Lord's supper, but merely explained to those who wished to partake of a harmless rite, how they might do so in a proper spirit. His words, you infer, are merely permissive, but imply no injunction or "obligation." I ask you then, who taught the Corinthian *Gentiles* that there was any such rite as the Lord's supper—a rite which, according to you, arose out of a *Jewish* festival ? We know that the Corinthian Church received the Gospel from St. Paul himself ; "For though "ye have ten thousand instructors in Christ, yet have ye "not many fathers ; for in Christ Jesus I have begotten "you through the Gospel." And observe how this eleventh chapter commences, " Be ye followers of me, even as I am "also of Christ. Now I praise you, brethren, that ye re-

"member me in all things, and keep the ordinances, as I
"delivered them to you." Keep what ordinances? Why,
amongst others this very one, of which he goes on to say,
"For I have received of the Lord that which also I delivered unto you." For what purpose did this apostle
of the Gentiles *deliver* to Gentile converts the institution
of the Lord's supper, if it were not that they should *keep*
it? Or why does he praise them for keeping "the ordinances" as he delivered them, if his words imply no injunction to keep those ordinances? Now let me hear your
explanation of St. Paul's account of the original institution
of the Lord's supper, as especially revealed to himself.

JOSIAH. The apostle praises the Corinthians because
they kept the "ordinances," or rather "the traditions,"
(παραδόσεις)--that is, the precepts and doctrines which he
had delivered to them. This proves nothing except their
general attention to his instructions. Thou asks me to
explain Paul's account of this observance. In the tenth
chapter he refers to the custom incidentally, his object
being to warn them against idolatry: in the eleventh he
speaks of it directly, blaming them for the abuses which
had crept in. From the very nature of these abuses it is
evident that it was part of a real meal, as indeed might
be inferred from his comparing that meal to the idolatrous feasts of the heathen. He calls either this meal, or
the distribution of bread and wine which took place at
it, "the Lord's supper,"—whether in memory of the last
supper of our Lord with His disciples, or for the same
reason as a feast in an idol's temple might be called "the
feast of the idol": and he tells the Corinthians that, when
they come together, it "is not to eat the Lord's supper;"
that is, that their object was not to partake of this bread

and wine with thankful hearts, but to satisfy their own irregular appetites. Then he goes on to narrate the circumstances which had given rise to this observance. In all this there is no command except the original, " Do this in remembrance of me." I have already explained that, to my apprehension, this instituted no new rite for perpetual observance, but only meant :—As often as ye take this bread and wine of the solemn feast, take them with thankful hearts, in remembrance of Me, for, in so doing, ye proclaim My death, and the benefits thereby conferred on man.

CHARLES. You grant me that, " as then practised, it was not inconsistent with Christian doctrine ;" but you do not see any reason for its perpetual observance in the Church. St. Paul sanctions its observance till the second coming of Christ, or, as he expresses it, " till the Lord come." Is that event gone by ? or does what George Fox called " the second coming of Christ in the hearts of his people," fulfil the apostolic injunction " till he come," and so abolish the observance ? How do you explain the words, " till He come"? Has our Lord come ?

JOSIAH. The apostle does not say that this ceremony was to be kept up until the second coming of the Lord Jesus, but that every time the Corinthians ate that bread or drank that cup, they showed forth " the Lord's death till he come." Dr. Macknight paraphrases this, as ; " Ye " tell the world that the Lord died to ratify the new " covenant ; and that He will come again to raise the " dead and judge the world." Evidently the words, " ye do shew the Lord's death till He come," as written by the apostle Paul, imply no command, and do not even contain an assertion that this observance would be per-

14

petual in the Church. Dean Alford says that they were "addressed directly to the Corinthians, not to them "and all succeeding Christians ; the apostle regarding "the coming of the Lord as near at hand—in his own "time."

CHARLES. If we were to limit the application of Scripture to the very person or persons to whom each precept was originally addressed, we should quickly reduce all arguments from Scripture to a nullity. Some future "Dean Alford" may say that when St. Paul writes, "All "Scripture is given by inspiration of God, and is profit-"able for doctrine, for reproof, for correction, for instruc-"tion in righteousness," he wrote it *only* to Timothy, and not to the Church for all time to come.

JOSIAH. The Lord's coming is spoken of, in the New Testament, in more senses than one. In several cases it certainly refers to the establishment of His kingdom by the destruction of the Jewish polity, and the consequent termination of the Jewish ritual observances :—" There be "some standing here who shall not taste of death till "they see the Son of Man coming in His kingdom."—"If I will that he tarry till I come, what is that to thee?" The meaning of these passages is clear ; and if we do not receive Dr. Macknight's interpretation, that this observance proclaimed not only our Lord's death, but also His second coming to judgment, then we may take the words, "till He come," as meaning that the observance would be kept up as a memorial until, on the destruction of Jerusalem, and the full establishment of the kingdom of "the Son of Man," it would naturally cease along with other Jewish observances.

CHARLES. Think for a moment of what you say. "Do

this in remembrance of me," says our Lord. "In so
doing," says St. Paul, "ye do shew forth the Lord's
death till He come." Is all regard for our Lord's words
to end with the destruction of Jerusalem? Is no more
"remembrance" of His passion to be observed by His
Church after the few years that the temple survived
Him? If the Psalmist could say, "If I forget thee, O
"Jerusalem, let my right hand forget her cunning; if
"I do not remember thee, let my tongue cleave to the
"roof of my mouth;" how much more ought the Christian to treasure this commemorative rite till his Lord do
indeed come and fulfil all things! If your interpretation
of "till He come" be the true one, how do you account
for the special revelation made to St. Paul? It was
hardly worth revealing a rite so soon to cease.

JOSIAH. Surely it is not necessary to keep up a formal
-rite, in order to enable His faithful servants to bear their
Lord's sufferings and death in thankful remembrance.
As to what thou terms a special revelation made to the
apostle Paul, several commentators think that he did not
mean to claim any such; and they ground this opinion
on the use of the Greek preposition ἀπό, instead of παρά,
which latter word, they say, would have been used if it
had been intended to convey the idea of *direct* revelation.
I do not pretend to offer any critical opinion on such a
subject; but I may remark, that in the passage thou hast
quoted, where the apostle tells the Galatians respecting
the gospel which he preached, that he did not receive
it "of man," the word παρά is used; and it certainly may
be inferred that he would have used the same expression
in another place, if he wished to convey the same meaning. Special revelations are not usually given, unless

there be a special necessity for them, and no such necessity appears to have existed in this case : he might
readily have learned the facts from the other apostles,
who were present, or from his constant companion Luke,
who was probably with him at the time he wrote the
epistle to the Corinthians ; and who says himself that he
had learned the facts he relates from those who "from the
beginning were eye-witnesses and ministers of the word."

CHARLES. I think this gloss is, at best, a very superficial one.   I do not pretend to be sufficient critic to decide on the merits of the prepositions ἀπό and παρά,* both
of which have similar imports in a general sense, and
are often rendered by the same word, though their critical signification may be somewhat different, the one referring to a more immediate action than the other.   Still,
if the apostle had received this account " of the Lord,"
whether by direct or by indirect revelation, the *mode*
in which it was communicated to him is of little consequence to us, so long as we are assured of the *source* from
which the doctrine sprung, and have confidence in the
purity of the *channel* through which it is conveyed to us.
The source appears to be " the Lord ;" the channel, the
" apostle Paul ;" and for my part I am more disposed to
trust to these than to the critical acumen of the commen-

---

* 'Aπό and παρά.   It is well known that the distinction between ἀπό and παρά is not strictly observed in the New Testament.   See, for instance, the use of ἀπό in Gal. i. 1, and especially
its use in verse 3, where "grace and peace" are assuredly communicated *directly* from " God the Father and our Lord Jesus
Christ."   See also Col. iii. 24.   Moreover, in the passage referred
to by Josiah (1 Cor. xi., 23), the verb παρέλαβον includes the
force of παρά.

tators you refer to. The plain words of Scripture, the plain example of the apostles and of apostolic times, and the plain witness ever borne by the Church are all in favour of our view.

JOSIAH. I do not build very much on this criticism respecting the meaning of the words. Still it is not without its value, and certainly, for the reasons already stated, the indirect revelation appears to me the more probable.

CHARLES. You say special revelations are not usually given unless the occasion calls for it. This is true; and therefore I think the special revelation on the present occasion, is one proof of the importance of the sacrament which was the object of it. The miraculous calling of St. Paul, the miraculous sending of Ananias to open his eyes, and many circumstances recorded in the history of this great apostle, are equally departures from the usual course of Divine providence : but we do not reject them on that account.

JOSIAH. No; but the object of these miraculous interventions is evident enough.

CHARLES. Well ! let us pass from this subject. The ἀγάπαι or love feasts are not to be confounded with the Lord's supper; and their connection with the public worship of the Church was dissolved in the fourth century, owing to the drunkenness and other disorderly conduct practised at them.* The disorders at Corinth reproved

---

* "The love-feasts were frequently attended with intemperance "and other serious disorders, which form subjects of grave com- "plaint in the writings of the fathers. This perhaps may be reck- "oned among the causes of the change in the time of celebrating "the Lord's supper, from the evening to the early part of the

by St. Paul consisted in making the pretence of assembling to partake of the Lord's supper an excuse for selfish indulgence in private suppers.* The Lord's supper had become subordinate to the private suppers of the pretended worshippers. Certainly, as you say, there is little similarity between the love-feast and what we celebrate as the Lord's supper. But I apprehend that there is a close affinity between what we celebrate, and what St. Paul tells us he "received of the Lord." Perhaps you are not aware of the almost verbal agreement between 1 Cor. xi., 23, 24, 25, and the main clause of the prayer of consecration in our liturgy; and that the spirit of the whole passage is embodied in the address to communicants. Our service is modelled, as nearly as possible, on the Scripture, and on the practice of the Church in the earliest age.

JOSIAH. I did not contrast the love-feast with your "sacrament," but the simple distribution of bread and wine which took place at the love-feast, with what you now celebrate under the name of the Lord's supper. The apostle reproved the Corinthians for certain unseemly practices, and explained the origin and true purpose of a custom which then prevailed in the Church. Had the abuse been greater than it was; had it, instead of taking the form of drunkenness and gluttony, assumed that of an idolatrous worship of "the elements," dost thou not

---

"morning. And hence it was that afterwards the holding of
"agapæ within the churches was forbidden. And by this regu-
"lation the agapæ became entirely distinct from the Eucharist,
"which continued to be publicly celebrated in the church. It
"cannot be exactly determined at what period the agapæ were en-
"tirely abolished."—*Riddle's Christian Antiquities.*

* See *Dr. Christopher* Wordsworth on 1 Cor. xi., 20, 21.

think that Paul's spirit would have been so "stirred within him," that he would have removed the cause altogether, and wholly abolished the custom, instead of merely showing how it might be practised without offence? In fact the love-feasts were, as thou remarks, abolished after the time of the apostles; but the superstitious corruption of the simple "breaking of bread" with thanksgiving, was enjoined as a rite, and called a sacrament of the Church.

CHARLES. I shall not trouble myself to enquire what St. Paul would have done in a supposed case. I am satisfied with what he actually did under the circumstances before him. He restored the rite to its original purity, and enforced it by the original authority. This is exactly what our reformers did in the case supposed by you, where idolatry had crept into the sanctuary. *Your* reformer, on the other hand, acted as you *suppose* St. Paul would have acted, but as we *know* he did not act! This is, indeed, slight ground for going against the whole weight of historical authority. It is attributing to our Lord's words a meaning different from that which His apostles, to whom they were addressed, and the whole Church has ever attributed to them.

JOSIAH. The case that I put never having occurred, we cannot *know* how the apostle would have acted; the circumstances which he had to deal with were wholly different from those that arose in after ages, so that the contrast thou hast drawn has no force. I am well aware that the meaning which thou attaches to our Lord's words prevailed very early in the Church. Indeed Roman Catholic writers have clearly shown that the germs, at least, of their views are to be found in the writings of the second century, and we both consider the views of the Church of Rome, on this subject, to be superstitious additions to the simple truth of Christianity. But I am not at all inclined to admit that the apostles interpreted these words as your Church does, and we do not think ourselves bound by the meaning which has been assigned to them in after ages, when we find them capable, without any straining, of a different interpretation. The apostles were Jews, accustomed to the breaking of the bread and the pouring out of the wine, with the blessing or giving thanks to God, which was customary when they partook of food together. They continued to frequent the temple and observe Jewish ceremonies for many years after our Lord's ascension, and, probably, until the destruction of the temple rendered it no longer practicable to do so : and I believe they understood the words of their Lord, " This do ye, as oft as ye drink it, in remembrance of Me," as an injunction to them that, in future, at all their solemn feasts, when they should eat of that broken bread, and drink of that cup, they should do so in remembrance of Him who had delivered them from the bondage of their sins.

CHARLES. Your friend J. J. Gurney, in one of his most popular books, argues differently. He says that this command was in itself of a simply *positive* nature, that there is no *internal* evidence of its being binding on any except the twelve persons to whom it was addressed, and others under similar circumstances, and that therefore it cannot be considered as of universal application. Had it indeed been a moral or doctrinal precept, though only spoken to a single individual (as to the woman of Samaria) he considers that its universality would have been questionless; but being merely an observance *in itself* indifferent, he holds that no such universality was intended.*

JOSIAH.   Joseph John Gurney does make use of this argument.

CHARLES.   His is indeed a very special reason, but he forgets to tell us *what* these twelve persons were. What ministry was entrusted to them? These "twelve persons" were chosen to be Christ's witnesses, and the bearers of His gracious message to the people. They were the first ministers of His Church, to whom the commission to evangelize the world was about to be given. Therefore, to them was explained that commemorative sacrifice which was designed, as St. Paul declares, "to shew the Lord's death till he come;" to keep up in the Church, as our liturgy expresses it, "a perpetual memory of that His precious death until His coming again." Who so fit to receive the message as those who were appointed to be the first dispensers of its benefits? That "these twelve persons" understood our Lord to institute a commemorative rite, is manifest from the uniform testimony of every branch of the Christian Church founded by them, and that in all ages, from the apostolic times to the present day.

JOSIAH.   This is merely an assumption; there is no proof that the "twelve understood their Lord to institute a commemorative rite." I think I have fully shown that the words, "This do ye, as oft as ye drink it, in remembrance of Me," were not intended to institute a ceremony of perpetual obligation, and therefore the explana-

---

* See *Distinguishing Views and Practices of the Society of Friends, by J. J. Gurney.*

tion added by the apostle that, "as often as ye eat this
"bread, and drink this cup, ye do shew the Lord's death
"till He come," will certainly not complete the institution
of this ceremony. There is, no doubt, some difficulty in
ascertaining the meaning in which the apostle used the
words "till He come." When our Lord predicted the
destruction of the temple to His disciples, they asked
Him in reply, "When shall these things be? and what
"shall be the sign of Thy coming and of the end of the
"world?"—these three events being evidently connected
in their minds as expected to take place together. Our
Lord's reply does not give any information as to the
time. It is one of those things which are not revealed;
and it appears from several passages in the apostle Paul's
epistles, as if he anticipated it as likely to take place at
an early period. He may therefore, very probably, have
expected that the practice to which he alluded would be
kept up until the actual coming of his Lord. As to the
ceremony itself, the question rests wholly on the *true*
meaning of our Lord's words, and not on the construction
which succeeding ages have put on them, however uniform
may have been the testimony—and I admit that, so far as
we learn from history, there has been a uniform testimony
to the observance of this rite, in some form or other, by
the various branches of the early Christian Church.

CHARLES. I thank you for this admission: the uniform
testimony of the apostolic Churches is of some value—of
more, as I think, than your last argument, which rests
solely on your interpretation of our Lord's words. *If* our
Lord's words do not mean what the church has always
understood them to mean, *then* St. Paul's apparent corro-
boration goes for nothing! Be it so.

JOSIAH. It needs but a slight acquaintance with ecclesiastical history to see how prone the early converts were to make superstitious additions to the doctrines delivered by the apostles, and, as I have before remarked, this was one of the earliest observances corrupted by such superstitions. I cannot therefore admit that the testimony of the various branches of the Christian Church, however uniform it may have been, is sufficient to compel my assent to doctrines which I do not find in Holy Writ. Thou blames us for giving up a practice of the apostolic age. I say you have totally changed its character. The early Christians, when assembled at a social evening meal, partook of bread and wine after thanksgiving and prayer. With you, the rite which has superseded this simple observance forms a most important part of religious worship. With them, the whole assembly gave thanks to God for the material food of which they partook, and for the spiritual blessing which they considered it to typify. You have placed it in the hands of a clergy, who "consecrate" what you call "the elements," and deliver them to the worshipper, kneeling at what is commonly called "the altar." They partook of it as a commemorative observance. You have converted it into a "sacrament" conveying spiritual grace—a "holy mystery"—a "banquet of most heavenly food." Certainly we have given up a practice which appears to us to have had only a temporary meaning and value, and for the perpetual observance of which we cannot find anything in Scripture amounting to a command. You have so changed it, both in form and spirit, that it is no longer the same, and thou hast not brought forward any scripture warrant for such a

change, or any scripture proof of the sacramental character of the rite.

CHARLES. It would be to little purpose to answer your
last words, or to defend the mere *ritual* of the Church, for
your former objections strike at the root of the matter.
To you the maxim, *quod semper, quod ubique, quod ab
omnibus creditum,* is of no value : you deny the authority
on which we found our practice. When you do speak of
the Eucharist, you talk as if it were merely intended for
the time then present, and became of less and less interest
as time went on. But very little consideration ought to
show you the fallacy of this supposition. The supper was
instituted in remembrance of our Lord's passion ; and this
alone ought to teach you the necessity for its perpetual
observance. For, as all our hopes of salvation rest on
the *certainty* of that one sacrifice and atonement, so, whatever recals it to our mind, and vividly brings it before
our view, is assuredly a thing not to be lightly set aside.
Our Lord himself chose and appointed this means of keeping up a perpetual memory of his passion. Why should
you, then, class it among the Jewish customs which were
about to cease, or interpret " till He come" as you have
done this evening ?

JOSIAH. This maxim to which thou hast referred—this
" unvarying voice of the Church"—the " *Consensus Eccle-
siæ,*" as your learned doctors call it, will lead thee farther
than thou art prepared to go. I will again quote from
Dr. Arnold of Rugby : " If I follow this pretended Con-
" sensus in forming my views of the sacraments, I appear
" to myself to be undoing St. Paul's and our Lord's work
" in one great point, and to be introducing that very
" Judaism to which Christianity is so directly opposed,

" and which consists in ascribing spiritual effects to out-
" ward and bodily actions."*

CHARLES. I do not think that the Church of England
can justly be accused of " ascribing spiritual effects to
outward and bodily actions." She requires faith in the
communicant. In her twenty-ninth article she says, " The
" wicked and such as be void of a lively faith, although
" they do carnally and visibly press with their teeth the
" sacrament of the body and blood of Christ, yet in no
" wise are they partakers of Christ : but rather to their
" condemnation do eat and drink the sign or sacrament of
" so great a thing."

JOSIAH. If the ceremony called the Lord's supper had
remained in the simplicity in which it was first celebrated, and had been regularly handed down thus to
the present day, it would indeed have assumed the character of a venerable and pious custom, to which, while
we should not have considered the observance impera-
tive, we should not, I think, have raised any objection,
or borne any protest against it. It would have been
one of those non-essentials in which Christian liberty
should prevail, and with regard to which charity and
mutual forbearance should be exercised. But its whole
force and meaning and form have been so perverted—the
glosses on the words, " This is my body" have been so extravagant—and the delusion thereby spread abroad has led
to such a perversion of Christian truth, that the force of
thy argument is considerably weakened. For how can I
look on the modern mass as a commemorative rite ? I am
told that it is a real sacrifice of the very flesh and blood

---

* *Life of Dr. Arnold,* vol. ii. p. 176.

of Christ; I am commanded to worship the wafer as if it were "very God, of very God, begotten, not made;" and the reception of this consecrated bread into the mouth of a sinner is held to be identical with the precious communion of the body and blood of Christ. Even as this rite is regarded by your Church, how very different is the claim to sacramental efficacy, conveying grace to the recipients, from the simple memorial observance of primitive times! and how many an ignorant man has, on his death-bed, depended for salvation on the reception of this "sacrament," instead of seeking reconciliation with God through Christ!

CHARLES. In discussing this subject we must indeed be careful, lest on the one hand we fail in reverence, or on the other slide off into idolatry. As neither of us believes in the grosser notion of transubstantiation, we may pass it by as a chimera of the times of darkness foretold by the apostle. But, so far as our Church is concerned, your last objection has no force, for the article just quoted declares that "the wicked and such as be void of a lively faith" are not true communicants— a position which is very readily established by such Scriptures as these: "Whoso eateth my flesh and drinketh my blood *hath eternal life*."—"He that eateth my flesh and drinketh my blood *dwelleth in me, and I in him*." But as no wicked or unfaithful person can have eternal life, or dwell in Christ and Christ in him, it follows that such cannot be true partakers of His flesh and blood in a spiritual sense. And this I believe was the doctrine of the early Church.

JOSIAH. Yet this "chimera of the times of darkness" is still the belief of two-thirds of Christendom; and the view thou takes of this doctrine does not seem to be that taken by some of your extreme divines of the present day.

CHARLES. Whoever cannot accept the twenty-ninth article in its natural sense had better pass over to Rome at once ; for a denial of this article is a virtual admission of transubstantiation.

JOSIAH. There is certainly a marked distinction between the Romish dogma of transubstantiation and the doctrine held by the Church of England, as shown in the address to communicants : " For then we *spiritually* eat " the flesh of Christ and drink his blood ; then we dwell " in Christ and Christ in us ; we are one with Christ and Christ with us :" yet, if these words are to be taken in their literal meaning, surely they convey something greater than ought to be attributed to any act of man, such as this ceremonial communion is. They far outrun the notion of a commemorative rite, or a symbolical setting forth of the Lord's death.

CHARLES. Those words are not spoken of all who come to the outward communion, but of those who come " with a true penitent heart and lively faith." To such, on the authority of Holy Scripture, heaven is opened, even on earth. Is it not written : " Behold, I stand at the door " and knock ; if any man hear my voice, and open the " door, I will come in to him, and will sup with him, and " he with me." This is the state spoken of in the Liturgy. Nor do I think the words, so applied, are too strong.

JOSIAH. Thou hast truly said that heaven is opened here on earth to the truly penitent and faithful, and hast cited our Lord's promise, that if any man open the door, He will " dwell in his heart by faith," and will feed him with " the bread of life." But, my friend, this

blessed state is not limited to any particular time, or to
any holy place. It cannot be assumed, at periodic or
stated times, by those who are habitually strangers to it.
It is not confined to those who partake of your outward
sacraments "worthily." The promise is to those who
come to Christ their Saviour in faith. He says, "I am
" the bread of life. He that cometh to me shall never
" hunger; and he that believeth in me shall never thirst."
" Verily, verily, I say unto you, he that believeth in me
" hath everlasting life." " Except ye eat the flesh of the
" Son of Man, and drink His blood, ye have no life in
" you." " Whoso eateth my flesh and drinketh my blood
" hath eternal life." " He that eateth my flesh and
" drinketh my blood dwelleth in me, and I in him."
These words can only refer to the spiritual supper of
the Lord—the " inward and spiritual grace " which your
outward sign is intended to typify. The Christian needs
not only that birth "from above,"—that birth " of water
and the Spirit" which is the commencement of his spiritual life, but also those renewed supplies of spiritual
food by which that life is nourished up for eternity.
This food is obtained through faith in Christ as his Saviour—his risen and glorified Lord—and by the power
of His indwelling spirit. The Christian believer " eats
the flesh and drinks the blood of the Son of Man,"
when, through the quickening power of the Holy Spirit,
he is brought afresh to rejoice in His reconciling love, and
to rely on the efficiency of His atoning sacrifice ; when, to
use the words of your Book of Common Prayer respecting
the sick man who may be prevented from receiving the
outward rite, he " truly repents him of his sins, and stead-
" fastly believes that Jesus Christ has suffered death upon

"the cross for him, and shed His blood for his redemp-
" tion, earnestly remembering the benefits he hath there-
'' by, and giving Him hearty thanks therefor." This
should be his "daily bread ;" and if the occasional or
periodic use of outward symbols have any tendency to
induce the mind to rely on them, as the means of ob-
taining this nourishment of the soul, they must be an
injury rather than a benefit to the Christian believer.

CHARLES. I presume not to limit the grace of God,
through Christ ;—"The Lord knoweth them that are his."
Nor am I so bigoted as to think that the Almighty, having
truly appointed the sacraments as the ordinary means
whereby we are made partakers of special graces, has
therefore (as some would have it) put it out of His power
to receive penitent sinners through any other channel.
Such a doctrine appears to me to be without scriptural
warrant : on the contrary, we know that His mercy is
over all His works. Nor would I venture to deny that a
blessed communion, such as you have spoken of, may not
be mercifully vouchsafed to many who have never participated in the outward communion of the Church. But
this does not lead me to spurn or to undervalue that outward communion which is the appointed means through
which divine grace is ordinarily imparted to the believer.
I look back to its origin. I endeavour to recal that
"upper chamber" which was indicated by "a man bearing a pitcher of water ;" and to repeople it with the
company that there sat down to meat for the last time
together. And I remember the words, "This do in remembrance of Me ;" and, taking them in simple faith,
I seek to be made partaker of the blessing which the
apostle declares is dispensed in the ordinance :—not look-

ing too curiously into the matter—not caring to dispute
about the *how;* but endeavouring to profit by the *what.*
And this I recommend to your consideration.

JOSIAH. We have now, my dear Charles, discussed the
subject of these ceremonies fully. I may not have convinced thee that the views held by our Society are correct,
but I trust I have been able to show that we have not
adopted opinions, so much at variance with those held by
most other Christians, without a deliberate, and I may
add a prayerful consideration of all those passages of Scripture which bear on the subject. "Let every man be fully
persuaded in his own mind." We believe that those who
look on them as religious observances, and partake of
them in faith, are, in so doing, accepted by their Lord,
and we ask from them the same feeling of charity towards
those who cannot conscientiously unite with their fellow-
Christians in this matter.

CHARLES. You certainly have not convinced me that
the views held by your Society are correct; on the contrary, I have not ceased to wonder at your interpretation
of the texts we have discussed. But I willingly assent to
your concluding remarks; and say, "Grace be with all
them that love our Lord Jesus Christ in sincerity. Amen."

CONVERSATION VIII.

"If it be possible, as much as lieth in you, live peaceably with all men."—*Rom.* xii. 18.

JOSIAH. In some of our late conversations, thou charged us with not paying sufficient regard to the literal interpretation of Scripture, in some cases where we deem a different rendering more in accordance with the general scope of Gospel truth. One would suppose, therefore, that you of the Church of England would, on all occasions, stand by the literal interpretation. Nevertheless I think that there are one or two points of grave importance, on which your theory is directly opposed not only to the plainest texts of Scripture, but to the whole spirit of the Gospel.

CHARLES. What may be those cases in which the Church so flatly contradicts the Gospel?

JOSIAH. The cases I allude to are your toleration of WAR, and admission of OATHS, both of which our Lord has most forcibly forbidden in His sermon on the mount; and the whole spirit of the Gospel, the whole New Testament from beginning to end, is in unison with the teaching of this discourse. How, then, can you defend

15*

what is so expressly forbidden? And how, to begin with WAR, can you plead for so great a curse to humankind?

CHARLES. I am quite free to admit that war is a great evil—evil in its origin—the child of the devil, or of that evil principle in man which works in unison with the evil spirit. As St. James says, "From whence come wars and "fightings among you? Come they not hence, even of "your lusts that war in your members?" No one who believes in Christianity can regard "the pomp and circumstance of glorious war" as any other than a great, though a necessary evil.

JOSIAH. Thou calls war a *necessary* evil. It may be so in one sense, while there are so many bad men in the world; but is it necessary for Christians to engage in it? Our Lord said, "It must be that offences come," yet he adds, "But woe to that man by whom the offence cometh."

CHARLES. I fear that an impartial examination will show that it is necessary, and therefore I do not think that Christians are forbidden to engage in warfare. The "offence," no doubt, comes of the evil principle, and woe is pronounced against him who offends, not against those who punish or control offenders.

JOSIAH. If war comes of the "evil principle in man," it must be sinful, and therefore forbidden to the Christian. The world may fight, the true Christian cannot, for has not his Lord said, "Love your enemies"—"Do good to them that hate you"—"Resist not evil;" and did He not Himself show a perfect example of non-resistance, though having "legions of angels" at His command?

CHARLES. Yes. He has said all this, and has superadded a glorious commentary on His own words, in His perfect example of meekness under unmerited suffering. And these words and this example ought to be the guide of each of us *individually.* St. Paul says, "If it be possible, as much as lieth in you, live peaceably with all men." These words suggest cases in which peace may be impossible even for private persons to keep. But war is not in our day waged by individuals, but by national governments; and I maintain that the appeal to the sword, as a last resort, has ever of right belonged to the kingly or ruling power, under every form; and that this right was not abrogated by any ordinance of our Lord, and is not contrary to the spirit of Christianity.

JOSIAH. It cannot be right for any number of Christians in the aggregate to do that which is forbidden to each of them individually. The apostle's words do not imply that there are cases in which Christians may be obliged to fight; but the context clearly shews that he calls upon them to act peaceably towards all men, however others may act towards them; for he goes on to enjoin them not to avenge themselves, but to return good for evil. I know that the appeal to the sword has ever been necessary for the maintenance of human power, but our Lord came to introduce a wholly different principle.

CHARLES. You assert that the commands: "Resist not evil,"—"Love your enemies," and other similar passages in the New Testament peremptorily forbid all warfare, yea, all resistance to evil, or opposing force to force; that our Lord being emphatically styled the Prince of Peace, all his followers should be non-resistant as he was; and, consequently, that the calling of a soldier is unlawful for a Christian man. Now I contend that these passages are *not* to be taken in the bondage of the letter, but according to their evident meaning, as laying down great principles of action. There is a distinction of the most obvious kind between the duties of a society and the duties of its individual members. We are not to harbour revenge, malice, spite, or ill will, even against those who are spiteful or malicious towards us; but, on the contrary, we are clearly commanded "to do good to them that hate us, and to pray for them that despitefully use us;" and briefly, "as we would that men should do to us, so are we to do to them."

JOSIAH. I quite agree with thee, that it is the spirit of these passages, not their literal interpretation, that is binding on Christians. We are not to consider an absolute non-resistance to be thereby enjoined, but rather that we should not repel one outrage by another. We are not to resist wicked men by means inconsistent with Christianity.

CHARLES. Certainly not, but the question is, what means does Christianity permit us to use for this purpose. Human society implies the existence of a ruling power, by which alone it can be held together in peace and good order; and rulers are not only commanded in Scripture to resist evil, but were appointed by God for this very purpose. If you look to the thirteenth chapter of Romans you may read, " For rulers are not a terror to good works, " but to the evil. Will thou then not be afraid of the " power ? Do that which is good, and thou shalt have " praise of the same: for he is the minister of God to thee " for good. But if thou do that which is evil, be afraid; " for he beareth not the sword in vain : for he is the " minister of God, a revenger to execute wrath upon him " that doeth evil." Does not this give to governments the divine sanction in using the sword ?

JOSIAH. The apostle was then enforcing the duty of ready obedience to the rulers of the state. We have never questioned either the necessity or the lawfulness of civil government, or the right of the rulers to suppress and punish crime. Obedience to rulers is clearly the duty of a Christian, when they do not command anything inconsistent with his duty to God. The passage thou hast quoted teaches us that human government is of divine appointment, that the magistrate, even though a heathen, as were the rulers of whom the apostle spoke, is " the minister of God," and, in a certain sense, His representative upon earth, and that the obedience due to him is founded upon this relationship.

CHARLES. If you once admit the right of a government to resist evil, you give it the right to use the sword, for the right to resist evil implies the right to use those means which are necessary to enable it to do so. The power to enforce its authority is essential to its existence.

JOSIAH. The authority of civil government rests on principles independent of Christianity, for it exists equally in all nations, whether heathen or nominally Christian. The Christian is bound to obey the government under which he lives, but he must not take part in any government which is not conducted on Christian principles, or attempt to support it by any means which are inconsistent with Christianity. I fully admit that, in the present state of mankind, no government can maintain its power without armed force, but that does not prove that it is right for a Christian to engage in war.

CHARLES. The notion of a government without the power to enforce its authority is an absurdity. Children should *obey their parents*, no doubt; but if they do not, parents must control their children. The moral law of Christianity was not given for an utopian state of society, but for the world as it is. Ought not a government to repress and punish murder, highway robbery, or house-breaking?

JOSIAH. A government should certainly endeavour to repress crime.

CHARLES. But suppose your murderer or highwayman is armed to the teeth, or that gangs of armed ruffians infest society. Is it not plain that physical force may be lawfully employed by the governor, to overcome such physical resistance to authority; and this in exactly the proportion in which resistance is offered? You cannot limit your policeman to the use of a truncheon if he has to arrest a man armed with a blunderbuss. Such conduct would only lead to further murders. If desperate criminals are to be secured, force must be employed; and in this case the guardians of the peace must be offensively armed.

JOSIAH. I have already admitted that, in the present state of society, governments are dependent upon force for the maintenance of their authority. There is, however, a decided difference in principle between the repression and punishment of crime, and the practice of war—between the calling of the policeman and that of the soldier. The theory of government is, that the magistrate acts for the good of society, with impartial justice and without passion, and punishes the guilty only. War is the reverse of this.

CHARLES. War is only police on a large scale. The distinction is not one of kind, but of degree; and if one be authorized in Scripture, so is the other. It is the duty

of the civil force to maintain civil order ; " to execute
wrath" on every individual that transgresses the laws.
This is to be done with as little violence as possible ; but
violence is to be met by violence. Now armies are the
police of nations. If one government act criminally towards another, that other has the right to resist evil,
and it may become the duty of neighbouring nations to
aid it, so that it may not be overpowered. The aggressor must be regarded as a criminal against the whole con-
fraternity of nations, and as such is in rebellion against
the divine law of " Peace on earth, good will to men ;"
the aggressor therefore becomes the enemy of all nations
that desire the peace and welfare of mankind. Once
the general peace has been violated, the only road to a
renewal of peace is often through war ; and those who
most desire a permanent peace may, under such circumstances, become the advocates of war, without forfeiting
the benediction, " Blessed are the peacemakers."

JOSIAH. An army would bear some analogy to a police
force if it belonged to some power superior to either of the
contending parties, and that its business was to compel
them to keep the peace, and submit their differences to a
duly constituted tribunal : however, I do not defend the
force used by either the police or the soldiers. Thy
view of Christianity is indeed an extraordinary one.
What ! are we to call your troops, armed with the most
deadly weapons, carrying fire and sword, and often plague,
pestilence, and famine amongst whole communities of
men—are we to call these the peacemakers on whom our
Lord bestowed His benediction, " Blessed are the peace-
" makers, for they shall be called the children of God" ?

CHARLES. Observe ; I do not advocate aggressive, un-

provoked war. Such war I consider as rebellion against
the divine law. But I contend for the right of defensive
war; and for the right of a national government, to defend not only its own territory, but also the territory of
others, when it may appear to be for the general good,
more especially when a strong power attacks a weaker
neighbour. The right to avenge the cause of justice exists
in a government under all circumstances; but as the appeal to arms should always be the last resort, so it ought
not to be exercised on occasions where diplomacy will
serve the purpose. When diplomacy fails to bring about
peace on equitable terms, and the criminal government
continues its aggression on the rights or liberties of others,
then I do say that soldiers—though armed with implements of destruction tenfold more deadly than have ever
been invented—may be the truest peacemakers, the best
friends to the welfare of human society; yea, the "mi-
"nisters" (and if ministers, why not children?) "of
"God; revengers to execute wrath upon them that do
"evil."

Josiah. When the apostle speaks of the emperor Nero
as a "minister of God," he certainly does not mean to
imply that Nero was one of His children. A war wholly
unprovoked is very rare indeed. There have been very
few wars in which both parties have not really been to
blame, and yet neither would admit itself to be the aggressor. It is impossible to draw any distinct line of
demarcation between offensive and defensive war.

Charles. Even if you cannot, in all cases, draw an
exact line between defensive and offensive war, yet the
cause of quarrel will always be just or unjust, and I maintain that war in a just cause is not only lawful for the

Christian, but that it may become his religious duty to engage in it.

JOSIAH. I know that government is a divine institution, dependent upon principles inherent in the nature of man ; and I fully admit that, in the present state of society, its ultimate appeal is force—armed physical force. The principle from which the policeman derives his authority may be different from that on which the soldier is appointed, but practically the office of the one slides imperceptibly into that of the other, and both, under present circumstances, are obliged to use physical force for the performance of the duties they undertake. I admit that the object contemplated, or at least presumed to be contemplated by their appointment, is the defence and preservation of society. But all this does not bring me a whit nearer to the proof that war is consistent with Christianity ; that it is right for Christians to engage in warfare ; or that the rulers of a nation, if Christians, have any direction, or authority, or permission, to do that, on behalf of the nation, which it would be wrong for an individual Christian to do in his own particular case.

CHARLES. You allow that government is a divine institution, and that " armed physical force " is necessary for the defence and preservation of society, as now constituted. But " the present state of society " in which good and evil men herd together, is no casual phase of humanity, but what has always been and will continue to be " till the harvest " or end of the world. If human government then be of divine appointment, a Christian may lawfully exercise the offices of governor, of policeman, or of soldier, or any other office necessary for the preservation of society.

JOSIAH. Human government may well be of divine

appointment, and yet it may be so conducted that a conscientious Christian cannot take part in it. This evidently
applies to heathen nations, and, to some extent also, to
those nations in which Christianity is professed. If the
government of a nation were conducted on pure Christian
principles, a Christian man, however conscientious, might
fill any office from the highest to the lowest ; but, under
present circumstances, when so many things are done in
which a truly conscientious man cannot unite, he must
only leave the government of the world to those who do
not see the requirements of Christianity in the same light
as he does. He could not undertake to govern a heathen or
Mahomedan state ; and even in states that are nominally
Christian a similar difficulty exists, because, however high
his own views of the moral duties required by Christianity,
he cannot govern on principles that are much in advance
of those of the majority of the nation. I do not mean to
say that a truly conscientious Christian might not hold
office, even under a pagan or Mahomedan government :
there have been many instances of Christians filling such
offices worthily. Still less am I disposed to assert that
such a man could not conscientiously serve a government
which professes Christianity ; but he will feel himself precluded from those situations in which his Christian principles would be compromised by the duties he would be
expected to perform.

CHARLES. Must then the government of the world be
placed in the hands of infidels ? Is this your idea of " a
divine institution," or would such an arrangement be for
the good of mankind ?

JOSIAH. The government of the world must remain in
the hands of men of the world ; and the distinction be-

tween the world and that Church which is called out of the world, is clearly marked, and must remain so, until men submit to the influence of Christian truth to a much greater extent than they have ever yet done. The Christian's course, if he obey his Lord, must often be in opposition to the maxims of worldly prudence : it is his duty to act according to the dictates of his conscience, without regard to consequences. The world will not be effectually served by Christian men doing what they believe to be wrong.

CHARLES. Nor by Christian men leaving undone what it is their duty to do. If you believe government to be "a divine institution," I cannot see on what plea a conscientious Christian should refuse to take part in it. A conscientious man ought to assist in preserving social order, or in repressing and punishing crime, when called on to do so. The conscience which allows the divine authority and necessity of an office, and yet, on conscientious scruples, refuses to undertake its responsibility, must be weak indeed.

JOSIAH. An office may be both necessary and of divine appointment, the duties of which are performed in such a manner that a Christian cannot conscientiously undertake to fill it ; and if the greater part of the individuals composing a nation be Christians only in name, it is very certain that the nation, in its collective capacity, will do many things in which a true Christian ought not to take part. But let us consider the whole question more closely. We do not base our objection to war so much on any particular passage of Scripture, however clear its meaning may be, as on the general tenor and spirit of the teachings of the Gospel. The New Testament may not expressly forbid war, but it forbids the Christian to indulge those passions which lead to war, and without which it is impossible to carry on war, and it inculcates those virtues which it would be impossible to maintain, while trying to injure our enemy—" Recompense to no man evil for evil ;"—" Overcome evil with good." Among the fruits which ought to be produced in the Christian by the Holy Spirit are peace, long-suffering, gentleness, faith, meekness, humility, forbearance, patience, forgiveness of injuries, and charity. Can any man maintain these virtues whilst engaged in strife and war? The whole scope and tenor of the Gospel preaches the same language. The Christian is the subject of a " kingdom which is not of this world." " He is not his own, but is bought with a price." His life here is but the preparation for an endless life hereafter. " He is dead" —dead to this world ; and " his life is hid with Christ in God." His business here is to " work out his own salvation with fear and trembling," knowing that " it is God " who worketh in him, both to will and to do of his good " pleasure." It should be the object of his life to endeavour to extend the kingdom of his Redeemer in the hearts of his fellow-men. If afflictions befall him, from whatever source they appear to come, he knows that they cannot come except by the permission of his Lord, and he has His word "that all things work together for good to them that love God." How then is he to fight or inflict injury upon his fellow-men for the sake of any earthly possession, or even for life itself ?

CHARLES. The precepts you quote are obviously of individual application in our relation one to another, and to that spiritual kingdom which is not of this world. But a Christian, dwelling in the world, owes allegiance also to the human government which God has appointed, and he ought not to refuse to bear part in it. Christianity cannot have enjoined what is impracticable. There must be government, and you have admitted that its objects cannot, in the present state of the world, be attained without force; therefore those precepts cannot have been intended to prevent Christians using force under every circumstance.

JOSIAH. The precepts I have quoted are of universal application, and can no more be set aside by communities of Christians than they can by individuals. The Christian unquestionably owes allegiance to the human government under which his lot has been cast by Providence, and is bound to render it a cheerful obedience in all things which do not interfere with his duty to God. Christianity has not enjoined anything that is impracticable; but, unless it can be shown that the affairs of this world are of paramount importance, it cannot be necessary for Christian men to put themselves forward as the governors of nations.

CHARLES. My argument is that we not only owe a personal duty to God, but also a duty to our fellow-members of society; that both these duties are equally binding on the truly conscientious man; and that they do not clash together. We may indeed sometimes act from mistaken views of duty. But, if God has established the office of governor, he has not put it out of the reach of a Christian to fulfil all the duties of this office, amongst which you allow that the repression and punishment of crime are included.

JOSIAH. The repression and punishment of crime are no part of the duty of a Christian, such as I have already

described. " He is not his own, but is bought with a
price," and his duty is to endeavour to extend his Redeemer's kingdom by the example of a pious life, if not by the
public preaching of the word. No principle of human
expediency can render that lawful for him which Christianity does not sanction.

CHARLES. It is well for you that, living under the protection of a settled government, you can enjoy your utopian ideas in peace, without being made to feel their
impracticability by the sharp experience of anarchy.

JOSIAH. I have already said that, when a government
is conducted on pure Christian principles, the most enlightened and conscientious Christian may lawfully take
part in it. I believe this to be impossible at the present
time, because the majority of men do not truly seek to act
in accordance with Christianity, and the government of a
nation cannot be much in advance of the nation itself.
A good government is indeed a great blessing, and the
Christian who believes that his Lord's commands forbid
him to fight, assists in maintaining it, by the influence of
his example in a willing submission to those who rule.
When Celsus called on the early Christians to take up
arms, like other subjects, in defence of the emperor, and
fight in his armies, Origen replied, " We do render the
" emperor a divine assistance, when we put on a divine
" armour, wherein we follow the commands of the apostle.
" The Christian renders greater service to his country
" than other men, by forming the hearts of the citizens,
" and teaching them piety towards God, on whom the
" well-being of the state depends."*

---

* Quoted from *Neander's Hist. of the Church*, vol. 1, page 377.

CHARLES. I do not see how, on your showing, a good government is possible, except perhaps in heathen countries. For if force be necessary to government, as you allow that, in the present state of the world, it is; and if force be forbidden by our Lord's commands; it is clear that no Christian ought to take part in government; although government is, as you admit, a divine institution. Surely you are arguing in a vicious circle.

JOSIAH. I do not think of refusing the name of Christian to those who do not see this subject as I do. I only contend that their view is not the true and highest idea of Christianity. Difference of opinion existed among the early Christians on this subject, and this difference must, I think, continue to exist, until Christianity really obtain a much greater prevalence than it now possesses, even among those who profess to be bound by its teachings. It was a long time before men became convinced that it was inconsistent with Christianity to hold their fellow men in slavery. I do not refuse the name of Christian to those who, even now, think it lawful to do so; but I consider that their views are not those which the New Testament teaches, when examined fairly and without prejudice. Many sincere-hearted Christians have searched the Scriptures, and have not drawn from them the same conclusions as respects war that we have done. " Let every one be fully persuaded in his own mind." Until the time come when the government of nations is conducted on true Christian principles, I cannot see any course for those who entertain what I believe to be the true and highest idea of Christianity but to submit to be subjects, and leave the rule and authority amongst men to those who, as I think, take a lower and less enlightened view of the morality enjoined by the Gospel.

CHARLES. The ideal that Christianity holds out is, no doubt, higher than we see actually realized in the world; but still I cannot admit that my view of the teachings of Christianity is lower than yours. I think it much to be desired that the government of Christian nations should be in the hands of good Christian men, who are ready to stand up for truth and justice, and to oppose evil and wrong in every shape, whether within or without the bounds of the nation over which they rule. If a Christian man be chosen as chief magistrate of a state, or if he succeed to such office by hereditary right, would it not be weakly shrinking from the path of duty, if he gave up the post which Providence had assigned to him?

JOSIAH. I think he ought not to give it up, provided the people were satisfied that he should govern according to his own views of duty; but as, under present circumstances, this is not to be expected, I see no course left for him but to resign his power. He may safely leave to others the government of the world, satisfied that an enlightened sense of self-interest will be sufficient to secure the maintenance of order and the administration of justice. The true way for Christians to serve their country is, not by the exercise of power, but by "labour-"ing continually to infuse a holier temper in the whole "body of the citizens."

CHARLES. They may do all that while they fill offices of trust or authority, or while they serve the state in a lower capacity. Have you never read the life of Sir Matthew Hale?

JOSIAH. There are certainly many offices in the state,

in which the man who believes the use of armed force to be inconsistent with Christianity, may yet serve his country with a clear conscience ; but he will feel himself precluded from any, in which force would be required for the performance of its duties. Christianity is not an ab_stract declaration of doctrines to be accepted by the intellect, but a living reality which is intended to mould and govern the whole life, and which must separate the faithful Christian from the world in which he lives, but to which he does not belong. Your Church, by upholding the lawfulness of war, has, as it seems to me, lowered the standard of Christian truth. There are other considerations which we cannot properly pass over ; one is the dreadful evils which are inseparable from war. I do not merely allude to the carnage, the pain and suffering of wounds and hardships, and the cruel deaths indiscriminately inflicted. These are the necessary results of repelling force by force. But glance for a moment at the moral evils of the system ; or consider the callousness of heart which the habitual sight of the horrors of the field engenders in the breast. All these evil fruits clearly bespeak their parentage.

. CHARLES. I am far from excusing or palliating the dreadful crimes which have often accompanied the state of warfare. But to argue fairly on this matter, we must distinguish between those evils which are *essential* to warfare and those which (however common) are *accidental* to it. I am arguing for the right of a Christian to be a soldier ; and you must allow that such an one may fight, without indulging vices which no more belong to the calling of a soldier than to that of a hatter, or any other tradesman. You must also allow that a soldier

16*

may be merciful in the hour of victory, and may treat the conquered as brethren. How many cases have there not been, in naval engagements, of heroic efforts made to save the lives of conquered enemies from sinking or from burning ships, and often at great personal risk. Look at the care taken of wounded prisoners, and the forbearance of commanders to inflict unnecessary misery on the countries through which they pass. All these acts show a.Christian spirit; and were armies wholly Christianized, such acts would be universal, and would greatly mitigate, if not drive out, the evils of which you complain.

JOSIAH. Armies wholly Christianized! Impossible. Our Lord says, "Love your enemies," and the soldier's business is to destroy them. To prove thy position, thou must show that the slaughter of enemies is an act of love. Mercy in the hour of victory is no proof that hatred and malice did not previously reign in the hearts of the combatants. The grosser sins, which too commonly infect the soldier's life, may be avoided, but he cannot avoid the evil passions which must burn in the breast of one whose *business* it is to destroy his fellow-creatures.

CHARLES. Never having been myself engaged in battle, I cannot tell you what a soldier's feelings are. But I can well believe that a generous and brave man can go to battle wholly free from the evil passions of "envy, hatred, malice, and all uncharitableness;" and can conduct himself therein with a single eye to the performance of his *duty*, whatever that may be. His "business" is not, as you assert, "to destroy his fellow-creatures," but, to finish the strife—"to abate the pride, assuage the malice, and confound the devices" of the enemy; and these ends are to be accomplished as effectively and quickly as possible. The soldier's aim is not carnage, but victory.

Josiah. But the only road to victory is carnage, and this too often in a bad cause. The soldier has no choice but to fight, whether the cause be just or unjust. He has sworn to obey, and he must do so, however criminal he may feel the command to be. He lays the blame on his commander, and the military commander lays it on the civil ruler under whom he acts. But how can a Christian think that by such a subterfuge he gets rid of his own individual responsibility? Or how can he attempt to place his conscience in another man's keeping? And this in respect to acts of destruction, and blood, and rapine, which, if the cause in which they are done be unjust, must be acknowledged by all to be among the blackest crimes that man can commit. I think it was the Duke of Wellington who said, that " a man of nice conscience had no business to be a soldier." This saying has always appeared to me to be strikingly illustrative of the incompatibility of the profession of a soldier with Christianity.

Charles. I suppose my conscience is not a nice one, for I own I do not see the force of this objection. Unquestionably a soldier's first duty is to obey the orders of his officer. He is an instrument in the hands of others, and cannot be allowed to debate about the cause he has enlisted to defend. Would you have the policeman debate whether or not he should obey the orders of the civil magistrate? You have already allowed that " the office " of the policeman slides imperceptibly into that of the " soldier."

Josiah. Can the Christian safely place himself in a position, in which he is wholly precluded from following the dictates of his own conscience, because he has bound himself implicitly to obey another, whether right or wrong? Will this plea avail him at the last day, before the Judge of all? Holding such views as thou dost, I suppose thou wilt also defend the religious dedication of the regimental colours—a "service" of your Church which I have ever looked upon as semi-heathen, to say the least of it, and quite inconsistent with the spirit of the Gospel of peace.

CHARLES. No such "service" is authorized by the Church; but the religious dedication cannot surely be objected to on Christian grounds.

JOSIAH. Certainly, if it be right to engage in war, it is right to invoke the blessing of Heaven on the undertaking; and then there is the extraordinary spectacle of two Christian nations engaged in a destructive contest, and both, in good faith, praying the God of peace, to strengthen and give success to their arms, and confound their enemies.

CHARLES. The character of the Almighty is unchangeable. Throughout the Bible history, His most abiding title is "the Lord of Hosts"—the God of armies. When Moses sang before Him, he said, "The Lord is a man of war; the Lord is his name." And if this be so, surely the solemn dedication of the colours of our army to "the God of Armies" is not inappropriate. Believing as I do that a Christian man can lawfully follow the profession of arms, I see an obvious necessity why our regiments should have their chaplains. Why should not the chaplains teach those under their superintendence to look in all things to God, as "the only Giver of all victory?" As we are taught that all our works should "begin, continue,

and end in Him," so this work also—the soldier's duty—
may be and ought to be brought within this limit. But
what say you to the wars of the Jews, which were often
divinely commanded?

JOSIAH. There are difficulties in both the Bible and
the book of nature which I am unable to fathom. I see
clearly that war is inconsistent with Christianity, and
that is enough. Why the Israelites were commanded to
wage war—to be the executioners of the Divine justice
on the idolatrous Canaanites—is a question which I do
not venture to answer. They were not permitted to go
to war unless specially commanded, and victory was
certain so long as they obeyed. But Christians receive
no such command from Heaven, and victory is doubtful
even in the most righteous cause. Even under the Jewish
dispensation, it is evident that the character of the war-
rior, however pious, was not that of the perfect man ; for
David was forbidden to build the temple of the Lord,
because he had " shed blood abundantly and had made
great wars."

CHARLES. If all warfare were inconsistent with Christianity, we might expect that the calling of a soldier
would be stigmatized in the New Testament. On the
contrary, John, the forerunner of Christ, "who came to
restore all things," when asked by conscience stricken
soldiers, "What shall we do?" did not say "Quit the
army," but he justified their calling, saying, "Be content
with your wages." Nor did our Lord reprove the centurion who besought Him to heal his servant ; but said of
him to His disciples, "Verily, I say unto you, I have not
found so great faith, no, not in Israel." Neither did the
profession of Cornelius hinder his being chosen of God to

be the subject of miraculous intervention, and the means of teaching the apostles that a door was open to the gentiles. On his head the Holy Ghost descended, as on the disciples at the miracle of Pentecost. And why ? Because, " he was a devout man and one that feared God with all his house." Nor did St. Peter, after receiving him, through baptism, into the Church, admonish him to give up the profession of arms. If a soldier's duty call on him, during war, to take life in battle, man against man, it is equally his duty, in peace, to protect the weak and defenceless, " to do violence to no man [or put no man in fear], neither accuse any falsely." Indeed a good soldier's life is a life of self-devotion for the preservation of the lives and properties of others.

JOSIAH. In all these cases the presumed approval of the soldier's profession is founded on nothing having been said against it. It is at the best but a negative proof, and really amounts to nothing, when we consider that both our Lord and His apostles evidently acted on the principle of not interfering *directly* with the established institutions of society. The centurion's servant was a slave (δοῦλος), and yet our Lord did not denounce slavery : therefore, if thy argument be valid, slavery is in accordance with Christianity. I pass by the case of John the Baptist as wholly irrelevant in a question of Christian teaching, and proceed to that of Cornelius. Certainly we have no record that the apostle Peter admonished him to give up the profession of arms, but neither have we any record that he did not. The scripture account leaves us wholly in doubt; but as we know that very many of the early Christians did give up that profession, I think we may infer it, as being probable, that Cornelius also ceased to be a soldier. The apostle Peter's silence on this occasion is no more evidence that he approved of war, than the apostle Paul's sending Onesimus back to his master is evidence that he approved of the system of slavery. They both preached Christ crucified, and called on men to repent and turn to God; and thus they sought to purify the heart, knowing that, if the spring of action were made pure, the conduct would accord with it. They did not *directly* interfere with the established institutions of society, trusting that the doctrines they preached would destroy those that were irremediably bad, and reform those that were capable of improvement. Thus Paul, in his epistles to the Romans and Corinthians, never denounces the licentious spectacles of the theatre, or the cruel sports of the circus, and he nowhere explicitly condemns slavery. Yet we know that all these were soon felt to be inconsistent with Christianity; and respecting the gladiatorial shows in particular, the early Christian writers speak with horror, and consider the attendance at them as implying the total renunciation of the Christian character. If we are to take the silence of the writers of the New Testament as implying approbation, then we must consider that the early Christians were wrong in condemning the combats of gladiators, and that modern Christians are wrong in denouncing slavery.

CHARLES. What we read of the good centurion and of Cornelius may at least assure us that a faith which called forth our Lord's admiration, and a devotional spirit which caused the visit of an angel and the miraculous descent of the Holy Ghost, can flourish in the breast of a soldier. This is some proof that the profession of arms is not inconsistent with a devout life. It is true that our Lord did not interfere with Cæsar's prerogative; the kingdom he came to establish was not of this world.   It is true, also, that a day is foretold in which men " shall not learn war any more," and that the more fully the " gospel of the kingdom" is received into the heart, and the more widely it is disseminated, the nearer will that prophecy be to its fulfilment.   But it is manifest that the day of universal peace has not yet dawned ; the earth is not yet " full of the knowledge of the Lord ;" and nothing has yet disproved—on the contrary, everything confirms—this saying of Christ, " Think not that I am come to send peace " on earth ; I came not to send peace, but a sword."   The sword is often judicially sent.   The Roman army which destroyed Jerusalem was a divine instrument to punish the Jews, " because they knew not the day of their visitation."   And, to the present day, I believe that armies are one great means, in God's hand, for carrying civilization to the ends of the earth, as they are also for punishing the disobedient and unthankful.

JOSIAH.   The passage of Scripture which thou hast quoted has no reference to war, but to the division among families which would result from the preaching of the Gospel.   I fully admit that the sword has often been judicially sent, and that armies may be instruments in the Divine hand to work God's purposes in the earth ; but that only proves, what we learn from many parts of Scripture, that evil is overruled for good, and that bad men often unconsciously work out His will.   The example of the early Christians may possess no authority, still it is noteworthy that, as in the case of the amusements of the theatre and the cruelties of the circus, so in respect to war also, they drew the legitimate inference from the teaching of Christianity, and therefore refused to enter the military service, or abandoned it if they had been bred to arms before they had become Christians. " It is not lawful for a Christian to bear arms for any earthly consideration "—" I am a Christian, and therefore I cannot fight." Such were among the sayings recorded of those who were called to suffer martyrdom for their refusal. Towards the end of the second century the heathen Celsus charges the Christians with refusing to bear arms, even in case of necessity. Origen admits the refusal, and justifies it *because war was unlawful.*

CHARLES. You are sharp enough in appealing to the example of the early Christians when it makes in your favour. Many of those who refused to fight under the Roman eagles refused because of the idolatrous rites required from the soldiers. When the emperors became Christian, we hear no more of the refusal to bear arms.

JOSIAH. When Christianity became the religion of the court, many were ready to adopt the name of Christian who had no intention of practising the Christian morality, and the objection to war was soon forgotten.

CHARLES. Do you then refuse the name of Christian to those who do not see with you in this matter?

JOSIAH. Certainly not. We know that many sincere-hearted Christians have not drawn the same conclusions from the Scripture teaching on this subject as we have done. We believe that many soldiers have been good Christian men. Still we think they have erred in their views on this point, being warped by the prejudices of education, or the circumstances by which they have been surrounded, and their example does not shake our conviction that war is inconsistent with Christianity.

CHARLES. This is a modest confession from one of the smallest of Christian sects; and particularly so after your admission, in the earlier part of our conversation, respecting the *necessity* for an armed police, and the virtual similarity between the calling of policemen and soldiers. Your deduction from Scripture is applicable only to a state of society which has never yet existed on the face of the earth.

JOSIAH. There is a wide difference in principle between the calling of the policeman and the soldier, though I admit that the office of the one slides imperceptibly into that of the other. There may not be any part of the world sufficiently under the influence of Christianity to admit of its being governed without the appeal to the sword; but that affords no warrant for the Christian to set aside or explain away the precepts of his Lord, though I think it does afford a good reason for his not undertaking a position, the duties of which he cannot fulfil without compromising his principles. The difficulty, as it appears to me, does not lie in the interpretation of Scripture, but in our own want of faith; and whatever hesitation I have, in advocating what appears to me to be the teaching of Christianity on this subject, arises from my feeling that the gentle, long-suffering spirit which alone would enable a man to bear injuries unresistingly, and still to feel love for those who injure him, is among the highest of Christian attainments. To support the pacific principles of the Gospel, if really put to the test, would require the faith and patience of a martyr. The promptings of instinct and the teachings of natural reason incite us to stand up for our rights, and contend with those who would injure us while there is any hope of success. Christianity, on the contrary, teaches us to be willing to suffer wrong, rather than infringe the commandments of our Lord, by doing injury to any of our brethren, "for whom Christ died."

CHARLES. To support your views consistently under every circumstance would call for the abnegation of every civil right. We must not shut our door against a thief, or, if one break in, we must permit him to do as he pleases. We must give to every one, bad or good, who asks of us; and lend to every one who would borrow of us, looking for nothing again, neither for repayment nor interest.

JOSIAH. I have already repudiated the idea that the words of our Lord in the Sermon on the Mount are to be taken in the bondage of the letter. Their spirit is evident enough, and by that spirit the Christian ought to endeavour to regulate his conduct. His resistance to injury should be only by Christian means. He must not repel outrage by outrage. Thy arguments *ad hominem* scarcely require an answer. To give to every one whatever he asks for would often be no kindness; but how few are there who fulfil what they admit to be the meaning intended by this precept!

CHARLES. Well, even though you are not inclined to bind yourselves by the literal meaning of these precepts, you must, if consistent to your own views, decline any appeal to the magistrate for protection or redress: you cannot resort to a court of law for the recovery of a debt, or for the redress of any injury, because force is requisite to give effect to its decision: these are the necessary results of carrying out your theory consistently into the common affairs of life. Is the practice of your Society in accordance with its theory? On the contrary, are you not glad, not only of the protection to property afforded by the civil power, and in times of civil tumult by the military, but also of the security to commerce guaranteed by the naval forces?

JOSIAH. I think no such inconsistency exists. Those who think war unlawful, and whose view of Christianity forbids them to defend themselves by force of arms, must not seek themselves to be rulers; but they yield a willing submission to " the powers that be," and thus faithfully fulfilling the duties of subjects, they are entitled to claim from their rulers the reciprocal duties of justice and protection. It is not for them to dictate the mode in which the government shall be carried on; but because they cannot, under present circumstances, make any claim to power themselves, they do not thereby give up the right to call on those in authority to perform the duties of their office: they maintain that all war is totally repugnant to the spirit of Christianity; but they do not, therefore, deprive themselves of liberty to claim the protection of the civil government under which they live, and to which they are subject, "for conscience' sake." Thus the apostle Paul acted when his life was in danger from civil commotion, and thus he appealed, as a Roman citizen, to the highest tribunal of the state.

CHARLES. You have anticipated me in referring to St. Paul. I would say that by availing himself of a military force for his protection, he sanctions my side of our argument.

JOSIAH. If a man will not fight in defence of his rights he must take the alternative, namely, submission to whatever, in the ordering of Providence, may befal him at the hands of violent men. He is bound to obey what he believes to be the precepts of his Lord without reference to the results. He may become a martyr for his obedience to the moral law. Many have been preserved unharmed in the midst of danger, but many also, who would not defend themselves, have suffered. We have no right to presume that Providence will always protect those who, for conscience' sake, decline to use force for their own defence. Their sufferings may be useful to others as a testimony to the truth. They are as truly martyrs as if they suffered at the stake for their faith.

CHARLES. Far be it from me to withhold the meed of approbation from those who, with a firm reliance on the overruling providence of God, so conduct themselves as to live void of offence in the sight of all men ; and who fulfil, to the best of their ability, the apostolic precept,—"If "thine enemy hunger, feed him; and if he thirst, give him "drink." I do not say that Christians should " avenge themselves," but rather that they should " give place unto wrath," and " overcome evil with good." What I have contended for is, that it is the *right* and the *duty* of a government to protect or " avenge" society ; and *that* because the same apostle who commands individuals " to live peaceably with all men " since " vengeance" belongs to the Almighty, in the next breath speaks of a human ruler as being " the minister of God, a revenger, to execute wrath upon him that doeth evil." Hence I infer that the power of the sword has been, under the gospel dispensation, entrusted to the " powers that be."

JOSIAH. Recollect that the ruler whom the apostle directed the Roman converts to obey, and whom he described as " the minister of God," was a heathen emperor : and, therefore, the authority with which he was entrusted was altogether independent of Christianity, and is possessed as fully by a heathen as by a Christian. The apostle enforced the duty of being subject, " for conscience sake," but said nothing about fighting the emperor's battles. If such had been the duty of the early Christians in Rome, no doubt it would continue to be the duty of those who live under governments professedly Christian ; but both appear to me equally inconsistent with Christianity.

CONVERSATION IX.

Ye have heard that it hath been said by them of old time,
Thou shalt not forswear thyself, but shalt perform unto the Lord
thine oaths: but I say unto you, Swear not at all.—*Math.* v.
33, 34.

JOSIAH. Well, thou seems to have satisfied thyself
that Christianity does not forbid war. What canst thou
say for the practice of judicial swearing? How do you
get over the express command, "Swear not at all," confirmed by the words of the apostle James, "Above all
things, my brethren, swear not"?

CHARLES. My reply to this question is very similar to
what I have already said on the subject of war: for as we
admit that civil strife and personal revenge are forbidden
to Christian men, and at the same time hold that it belongs to the state to repress evil by force and to avenge
the injured, so we also believe that the command you have
quoted refers to "vain and rash swearing," that is, to the
use of oaths in common conversation, or in dealings between one person and another, and does not refer to
solemn oaths imposed by the authority of the state, in
the administration of justice.

JOSIAH. Let us consider the whole passage. "Ye have

" heard that it hath been said by them of old time, Thou
" shalt not forswear thyself, but shalt perform unto the
" Lord thine oaths : but I say unto you, Swear not at all.
" · · But let your communication be yea, yea ; nay, nay;
" for whatsoever is more than these cometh of evil."
This forbids something that was before permitted : now
profane swearing—that is, " vain and rash swearing,"—
was always forbidden :—" Thou shalt not take the name
of the Lord thy God in vain." Solemn oaths were permitted, but were to be performed "unto the Lord :"—"Ye
shall not swear by my name *falsely.*"—"If a man vow
" a vow unto the Lord, or swear an oath to bind his soul
" with a bond, he shall not break his word." Therefore,
what our Lord condemned in the words referred to was
not "vain and rash swearing," nor false swearing, but
those solemn oaths which had been previously permitted,
but which were required to be "performed unto the
Lord." Surely this prohibition must include "solemn
oaths imposed by the authority of the state." Such were
the views of the early Christians. " The old law," says
Basil, "is satisfied with the honest keeping of the oath ;
but Christ cuts off the opportunity of perjury."

CHARLES. As the appointed minister of God, the judge
stands in a very different relation from that in which
common persons stand. His duty is to elicit the truth ;
and if this cannot be assured to society without the confirmation of an oath, or solemn appeal and declaration
addressed to the Omniscient, the judge may demand such
an appeal.

JOSIAH. Thou says that " the judge may demand an
oath to elicit truth." On what dost thou ground this
opinion ? Our Lord makes no exception when he forbids

swearing, nor does the apostle James when he reiterates the prohibition.

CHARLES. Our Lord's command against swearing was addressed to individuals only, and not to the governing power; therefore that power, not being affected by the command, still retains all the rights with which the old law invested it; and the right to administer oaths for the welfare of society was one of its prerogatives, as you may learn from the whole Old Testament history, throughout which a solemn "oath of the Lord" is held to be final— "the end of all strife," as St. Paul says.

JOSIAH. Thou might as well tell me that the command, "Thou shalt not steal," was addressed to individuals only, and not to governments, and therefore that governments might rob and plunder as much as they liked; and I presume they might afterwards divide the spoil. This mode of procedure is common enough; but I never thought it very Christian.

CHARLES. I think, if you attentively read over the whole of the Sermon on the Mount, you will agree with me that all the other precepts enjoined throughout that discourse are addressed to men *as individuals,* for their guidance in a private capacity, and are not applicable to governments. For to apply some of them to governments would be to dissolve all human society, which could never be our Lord's desire. Thus, "Resist not evil" cannot refer to governors, for governors, as we have already settled, are appointed by God expressly to resist evil. "Judge not, that ye be not judged" cannot be spoken to a judge who sits to administer justice. Most of the other precepts are so purely personal that they can have only an individual application.

JOSIAH. These precepts are addressed to Christians, whatever station in life they may occupy. If we are to set aside our Lord's commands because we consider them impracticable, we shall not readily find a resting place. Some men consider *they* cannot live without stealing : some, that *they* cannot help getting drunk. There is not a sin forbidden in the decalogue, but you may find men to say that it is impossible for *them* to avoid it. Our Lord, in His introduction to His Sermon on the Mount, says, " I am not come to destroy the law, but to fulfil," which Dean Alford explains as meaning, "to fill out or expand, that is, to give a deeper and holier sense to it." I cannot explain my meaning better than in the words of Gregory of Nyssa : " He who has precluded murder by " taking away anger, and who has driven away the pollu- " tion of adultery by subduing desire, has expelled from " our life the curse of perjury by forbidding us to swear ; " for where there is no oath, there can be no infringe- " ment of it."

CHARLES. The moral law is, no doubt, equally binding on all Christians, whatever be their station in life. But still actions are commanded to rulers and judges which are forbidden to private persons, living under a government. The command, "Thou shalt not kill," for instance, does not apply to a governor whose duty it may be to take life, in order to protect society. Our Lord's command is, " Swear not at all," (or, use no oaths), "but let " your communication (one with another) be yea, yea, nay, " nay." Now the words, " let your communication," fix the command pointedly to the intercourse between man and man, and do forbid us to use colloquial asseverations to enforce belief in our words. Such asseverations, in our private discourse, are manifest breaches of the third commandment, and as such are forbidden by our Lord, because they "come of evil."

JOSIAH. The Greek word is λόγος, that is, "word spoken"—"discourse." It surely will not bear the restricted meaning which thou puts on "communication," but must include *all* cases in which swearing may occur, and not merely those conversational oaths which the good of all ages agree in condemning, and which do not require a new commandment to prove their evil origin. An oath is defined by Milton as "that whereby we call God to witness " the truth of what we say, with a curse upon ourselves, " either implied or expressed, should it prove false." Is this awful appeal to Heaven, this conditional imprecation of a fearful penalty, consistent either with the reverence due to God, or with a proper feeling of the fallibility of man?

CHARLES. The moral distinction between lying and perjury is more apparent than real. He who wilfully breaks the command, "Thou shalt not bear false witness," exposes himself to the same curse as if he had taken and broken a formal oath. Why then is an oath added? Simply, I suppose, to bring forcibly before the mind and conscience of the person sworn the guilt which he incurs by violating his word. St. Paul's expression, " I say the " truth in Christ, I lie not, my conscience also bearing me " witness in the Holy Ghost," seems to me to express that solemn and reverent appeal to the Almighty that constitutes the "virtue" of an oath. I cannot suppose that an oath is in its nature immoral, as has been maintained by an esteemed writer on morals, a member of your Society. The morality or immorality of an oath does not depend on the *act itself*, but on the occasion that calls it forth. The *act* itself may be shown by Scripture to have been performed by the Almighty, by His angels, by His prophets, by the patriarchs and the holy men of old who are ensamples in righteousness. But these all swore " in truth, in judgment and in righteousness." To such swearing there is no condemnation recorded in Scripture. That which is condemned by our Lord and by His apostle is, as I have said before, the habitual use of oaths and asseverations in our communications one with another.

JOSIAH. I have already shown that our Lord's condemnation went much beyond this. As respects the morality of oaths, it must be admitted that, in a certain sense, they are in their nature immoral, because their origin is evil. They were adopted as a means of guarding against deceit and falsehood, and have been used among all heathen nations : and, although the evil consequences of swearing were seen by some of the heathen moralists, yet the use of oaths is not condemned by the intuitive perception of morals common to all mankind. They were recognised as lawful under the Jewish dispensation, and even commanded in some cases. Solemn oaths were among those things which were permitted under the old dispensation, " for the hardness of their hearts," but which are forbidden under the new. The old law said, Thou shalt swear only on solemn occasions, and " shalt perform unto the Lord thine oaths ; " but He who came to fulfil that law, and to reveal to man a higher law, upholding a purer morality, said, " Swear not at all," but let the simple assertion or denial only be used, " for whatsoever is more than these cometh of evil," or of the Evil One.

CHARLES. Oaths will certainly become less frequent and more sacred as the moral sense of society becomes purer. My object is not to defend the abuse of legal oaths, but to show that *all* oaths are not unlawful; and this I maintain on the authority of the Old Testament Scriptures, confirmed and illustrated by a very remarkable passage in the New. In the Old Testament God Himself is repeatedly represented as making use of an oath, as in Gen. xxii. 16, " By myself have I sworn, saith the Lord." And St. Paul, commenting on such passages, says in Heb. vii. 20, 22, referring to our blessed Lord,—
" And, inasmuch as not without an oath He was made
" priest (for those priests were made without an oath ;
" but this, with an oath, by Him that said unto Him,
" The Lord sware and will not repent : Thou art a priest
" for ever after the order of Melchisedec) : by so much
" was Jesus made the surety of a better testament." " *By*
" *so much*"—that is, by the virtue of the Divine oath. Did that oath come of evil ? Was it not rather a gracious act of Him who, " willing more abundantly to shew unto
" the heirs of promise the immutability of His council,
" confirmed it by an oath : that by two immutable things
" in which it was impossible for God to lie, we might have
" a strong consolation," &c.

JOSIAH. The essential part of an oath is the imprecation of a curse on the person of the swearer, if his word be false. Now in the case to which thou refers this is impossible, therefore it is not an oath in the sense in which we understand the term ; we can only regard it as the strongest form of promise. I consider that when in the Bible God is spoken of as swearing, the word is used, in condescension to human ideas, as implying absolute security of performance, and as a mode of adaptation to the limited comprehension of man ; just as, in other cases, He is spoken of as being angry—being jealous—being sorry—repenting—changing His mind, &c. Even if it were an oath, it cannot be an example for us.

CHARLES. I had supposed that the essential part of an oath between man and man is the appeal to the Almighty to vouch for our truthfulness ; the curse is but the consequence of our untruthfulness in that appeal. But let us take a lower example. In the Apocalypse, the angel which stood upon the sea and upon the earth "sware by "Him that liveth for ever and ever that there should be "time no longer." This is an example of an oath being uttered by a created and finite, but unfallen and pure Intelligence, acting (as we must suppose) under the express command of the Judge Eternal.

JOSIAH. There are many difficulties in the Book of Revelation, which far exceed our limited comprehension. It is stated that the angel swore—no doubt under express command. This cannot be any example for us who have received no such command ; but who, on the contrary, have been commanded not to swear.

CHARLES. The example given at least proves that an oath is not necessarily immoral. But did not the high priest examine our Lord Himself upon oath ?—"I adjure thee by the living God ;" and our Lord, although He had previously kept silence, immediately answered, "Thou hast said," thus admitting the authority of the high priest to use this mode of examination.

JOSIAH. If our Lord did take an oath it would not be an example for us, because the Jewish law was still in force, and He always conformed to it. But I see no oath here at all. The word used, ἐξορκίζω, means only, as explained by Schleusner in his Lexicon, " I solemnly, and in the name of God, exhort and enjoin." A nearly similar word ὁρκίζω, occurs in other places, where it evidently is not an oath : viz.—a man with an unclean spirit addresses our Lord with the words, " I adjure thee, by God, that thou torment me not." The sons of Sceva address evil spirits with, " We adjure you by Jesus whom Paul preacheth ;" and lastly, Paul writes to the Thessalonians, " I charge [or adjure] you, by the Lord Jesus, that this epistle be read to all the holy brethren."

CHARLES. Even allowing what you say to be satisfactory, did not St. Paul make use of oaths ?—" Behold, before God, I lie not ;"—" I call God for a record upon my soul ;"—" God is my witness;"—" God is my record ;" —" I protest by your rejoicing, which I have in Christ Jesus, I die daily."

JOSIAH. In these expressions the apostle appeals to Him who was a witness of the thoughts of his heart. The Greek particle which usually implies an oath is used in the last expression ; but the idea of swearing by the " rejoicing" or " boasting" of the Corinthians is absurd. The only one which has any appearance of that self-imprecation which is essential to an oath, is the second, " I call God for a record upon my soul." This has been supposed by many commentators to imply an imprecation against either his soul or natural life ; but others consider it to be an appeal to the Deity as a witness of his condition of mind. "The holy apostle," says Theodoret, " wishing to persuade them of the truth of his assertion, " calls in the testimony of Him who was the inspector of " his thoughts." Thou hast before stated that a Christian

is not at liberty to swear, except when required to do so
by a magistrate ; but, if these be oaths, the apostle swore
without any such authority, and his example would therefore warrant the Christian in taking an oath whenever he
thought right, which would, I think, set aside our Lord's
words altogether.

CHARLES. The morality or immorality of an oath does
not depend on the act itself, but on the occasion that calls
it forth. My previous statement referred to the general
principle ; but is it not easy to see that, though swearing
add nothing to the word of an upright man, an occasion
may occur when it will be proper for him to make a solemn asseveration, for the satisfaction of some individual
man no less than of society ?

JOSIAH. No idea of expediency will warrant us in setting aside a Divine command, if it be really such. Good
men would give true evidence without an oath, and the
bad are induced to do so more by the fear of punishment
or the force of public opinion, than by any reverence for
the oath itself.* Where public opinion is weak or uncertain, and the law does not interfere, we see, in many

---

* The following extract from a speech of M. Desmarest, of the
French bar, before the *Jurisprudence Section of the Association for
the Promotion of Social Science*, at its meeting in Dublin, is interesting as showing the progress of public opinion in France on
this subject. M. Desmarest said : " In France there was a gene-
" ral movement going on against oaths, and it was very generally
" thought that the man who would tell a lie would swear to it.
" Children were not sworn in the French courts, and still the
" verdict of a jury might be founded on their evidence." See
*Transactions of the National Association for the Promotion of
Social Science*, 1861, page 254.

cases, that there is no bond in the oath which prevents men from taking it unthinkingly, and, no doubt, in many cases falsely.

CHARLES.   There are, no doubt, some men who would give true evidence in any case, and others to whom the oath is no bond whatever ; but still there is a large class between both, whose religious convictions are weak, but who do feel the sanctity of an oath, and will not knowingly break it. For such men judicial oaths are necessary.

JOSIAH.   I do not believe in the necessity ; and if any such appear to exist it is caused by the practice of judicial swearing. This teaches men to make a distinction between evidence given on the simple word and that under the bond of an oath, and to think lightly of the former. It lessens the value and the dignity of truth, by attaching to perjury the disgrace which would otherwise attach to falsehood. Thou says oaths are needed because bad men exist in the community, but that furnishes no reason for a good man to swear. "The rule of the Christian com-
" munity," says Dean Alford, " is, *not to swear at all ;* for
" every such means of strengthening a man's simple affir-
" mation arises out of the evil in human nature, is ren-
" dered requisite by the distrust that sin has induced, and
" is therefore out of the question among the just and
" pure of heart."

CHARLES.   Read farther, and you will see that he supports my view of this subject.

JOSIAH.   I am aware of it, but I cannot agree with him there. If it be " out of the question for the just and pure of heart," the Christian ought to refuse to do it, and let those who do not so understand the commands of their Lord do as they think right. But as respects the expediency of oaths commanded by the authority of the state, did not fearful prevarication, if not perjury, daily take place in our custom-houses and other public departments, before the act of parliament was passed which allows of declarations in lieu of oaths?[*]

CHARLES. I agree with you that the custom-house oaths you allude to, although imposed by lawful authority, were little removed from ordinary profane swearing, and as such are justly to be condemned. Here the state manifestly exceeded its authority, and profaned and degraded a sacred ordinance. Nor do I justify the too frequently irreverent mode in which oaths are administered in our courts of justice. And further, I admit that oaths are still, by law, required in many cases where they had better be omitted. I look upon an oath as the gravest civil act which a Christian can be called on to perform—almost equalling in solemnity his reception of the blessed sacrament,—and therefore I would not put him to his oath on every trivial or merely formal occasion. It is lowering to the dignity, and consequently weakens the force of the oath.

JOSIAH. Thou objects to custom-house oaths, and yet defends oaths taken in a court of law. On what is this distinction founded? Both were imposed by the governing power. Is it the importance of the occasion on which they are taken? Many of the cases which occupy

---

Oaths were formerly taken on almost every occasion in which the revenue was concerned : their frequency and the carelessness with which they were taken were notorious. They are now superseded by "The act for allowing declarations in lieu of oaths," and, in many cases, no declaration even is now required.

our law courts are surely of less importance than a fraud on the revenue. It is not possible to define what oaths are lawful and what unlawful. The only safe conclusion is, that all are forbidden.

CHARLES. It is one thing to argue for authority in the abstract; and another to palliate the abuses of authority. All human government is subject to error. I would not defend its misdeeds or excesses, though I uphold it in its place, and obey its mandates so long as it enforces nothing contrary to God's word. I am merely contending that to the civil governor, as the minister of divine justice, has been committed the power to put such oaths as shall be, between man and man, " the end of all strife :"—just as I have maintained that to the same governor is given the power to take life in order that the law may be avenged. Both these powers, the highest civil preroga- tives exercised by man, may be and are abused; and therefore I may freely condemn the wanton abuse of law- ful power.

JOSIAH. I need not again assert that all Christians, whatever station they may occupy, are bound by the same law; but I think that there are other oaths also, which are as questionable as those formerly taken in the custom- houses, and which are taken as thoughtlessly. What is the precise meaning of the oath of allegiance? Did it ever yet prevent treason? Paley says that " it excludes " all design *at the time* of attempting to depose the reigning " prince." What then can be the use of imposing such an oath, if it do not bind the future conduct? The soldier swears " to obey the orders of the officers set over him." If his officer command him to do what his conscience for- bids, he has sworn to obey his officer—to obey man rather than God. So all military men read it, and so the court-martial decides when such cases occur. How many men who take bribes at an election will hesitate at the oath against bribery? Is not the oath against simony a snare for the integrity of the clergy, who sometimes sail so near the wind, that they are in doubt whether they swear truly or not? No, Charles, the only safe way is to give up oaths altogether.

CHARLES. I am not disposed to defend all these oaths, some of which are relics of a barbarous age, when morals had been so corrupted that an oath was required on almost every occasion, as the only means of ending strife. And now I suppose we may conclude. You know my sentiments on the use of oaths in general. Whilst I cannot agree with you in your unqualified interpretation of our Lord's command, I freely admit that the frequent and irreverent use of civil oaths does tend to lessen the force of simple truth, and therefore to promote immorality. But, on the other hand, I am clearly of the opinion that the state has rightful authority, when it sees fit, to demand the test of an oath from Christian men. This power, nevertheless, like every other civil power, may be, has been, is, and will be abused. With the abuse of authority I have nothing, in argument, to do.

JOSIAH. The state has no authority over the conscience of Christian men, neither can it set aside those commands of their Lord which Christians are bound to take as the rule of their lives.

CONVERSATION X.

When the Son of Man cometh, shall he find faith on the earth ?—*St Luke*, xviii. 8.

JOSIAH. In reading over the order for morning prayers in your liturgy, I observe that the people are desired to repeat the articles of belief, called "the creeds," after the minister. I have already objected to some of the terms or forms of expression used in these creeds. Dost thou suppose that all who repeat the words understand their meaning? Do not many say them as something which they have got by rote, but about which it never enters into their thoughts to enquire, what does this mean? And if so, is there not too much of formalism, not to say irreverence, in your practice?

CHARLES. It is doubtless probable that in large congregations there may be some who repeat the creed in a formal way, and this not from lack of capacity to understand the words, but from indifference to their import. There may also be other cases of sheer ignorance. Where the catechetical instruction of children has been neglected, the simplest creed will probably be, for many years, an incomprehensible jargon; and among the uneducated portion of the community this ignorance may remain for life undispelled. Hence the dark state of semi-heathenism into which parts of this Christian land have sunk. Hence the reason why so many fall a prey to the teachings of infidels. But these evils are not to be laid to the fault of the Prayer Book, but to want of sufficient extension of the Church, and in great measure to unfaithful pastors, who have neglected their charge, and who allow their people " to be destroyed for lack of knowledge."

JOSIAH. And is there no one to blame but the unfaithful pastors? What are the higher officers of the Church about? Why do not your bishops interfere, and expel these unfaithful pastors from the ministry?

CHARLES. Why do they not? Why, but because their hands are tied. Our discipline is shackled by the laws of the land; and unless a clergyman be a murderer or incestuous, it is next to impossible for a bishop to get rid of him. He may silence him, it is true; but if he be possessed of the " vested right " of a parish, he cannot dislodge him. Such is one of the grievous evils which the English Church suffers from her connection with the state. Every denomination of dissenters has its code of bye-laws, and its rulers can expel unruly members. But our Church is bound hand and foot; and those who ought to be her guardians and rulers are forced to endure what they have not authority to prevent. By example and precept a bishop can do much good, but when it comes to dealing with refractory priests, his efforts will, in most cases, be defeated by " law," or by " appeals to the Privy Council."

JOSIAH. You might take example by us, and arrange monthly meetings for discipline in every parish, quarterly meetings for each diocese, and a yearly meeting for the whole realm. Thou wilt recollect that, in a former conversation, I maintained that all the members of the Church ought to participate in the management of its affairs; and certainly you must allow the laity to take some share in the discipline and government of the Church, if you mean to have its affairs managed with prudence and discretion. Arrangements such as these, but better suited to the circumstances of your case, would control all cases of clerical irregularity. The example of the conscientious clergy being brought at stated times under the general notice, would stimulate the lukewarm and careless; and the exercise of a godly discipline, enforced in tenderness, would lessen the number of the " unfaithful pastors."

CHARLES. I should be very glad to see a well ordered synod, consisting of clergy and laity in due proportions, restored to the Church; and a reformed system of vestry meetings instituted. But let us keep to the subject you started with. You objected, I think, to the formal repetition of the creed in our services.

JOSIAH. Yes. It looks to me like a sort of lip-service, which might better be omitted.

CHARLES. Your objection can, of course, only apply to the merely formal repetition. You cannot suppose that there are whole congregations so destitute of faith that the recital of the fundamental articles of Christian belief is to them an empty form and mockery; and unless you suppose this, I do not see the force of your objection.

JOSIAH. Our Christian faith is best manifested by a consistent walk amongst men; a very different matter from the daily repetition of a creed. The faithful do not require this constant lip-repetition of truths which are to them so bound up in their being, that they may be said to constitute their life ; while, in such repetition, the unfaithful or the ignorant assert a belief in what they do not understand, and thus stand up, in the very presence of the Judge of quick and dead, with a lie in their mouths.

CHARLES. As to the faithful not *requiring* to repeat their creed day by day, I do not quite agree with you. We are taught by our Lord to ask, day by day, for our daily bread ; not merely for the daily nourishment of our perishing bodies, but much more for the daily sustenance of the inner life—for that " bread which " cometh down from heaven, and giveth life unto the " world." And if it be expedient and delightful for the faithful Christian daily to show forth the praises of God, so ought it also to be good for him daily to recal to memory what the Lord has done for him. A heartfelt repetition of the articles of belief brings before the mind, as in a picture, the whole scheme of redemption ; and if this be not absolutely *required* (perhaps it is not) by the faithful, it ought to be one of his delights. The apostles' creed, which is but an enlargement of our Lord's words when he instituted the sacrament of baptism, is the confession required, as an essential condition, previously to admission to the baptismal covenant. The renewal of this covenant every morning can be no unseasonable service, even to the most devout servant of God.

JOSIAH. We have already discussed the question of baptism, so I will not enter into it again. It is certainly no unprofitable occupation, day by day, to meditate upon all the Lord has done and suffered for us. Such thoughts are sweet to every one who has been redeemed from the hand of the enemy : but they are best enjoyed in silence, and may be dissipated by the rapid vocal utterance of a dry string of articles, repeated after a minister when called on to do so. The objection I made was to the superstitious repetition of the creed by those who do not understand it, or to the careless repetition by those whose thoughts are wandering. In fact, the same objection applies, in my mind, to the formal repetition of a creed, as to the formal repetition of a prayer.* It is the worship of the lips and not of the heart.

CHARLES. Let us not lose sight of the distinction between the devotions of the closet, and the public congregational service of God. In the former, I grant you, quiet meditation, unrestricted by forms, will probably be best for the individual worshipper; but where many join together to worship God in fellowship, a common utterance must be employed, and for this there must be a form known to all and approved by all. We have only, therefore, to consider whether the united repetition of the creed be profitable, and whether the symbol itself be a form of sound words.

JOSIAH. Well, why dost thou think it expedient to introduce this profession of faith into the public worship of God? Unless the feelings of the heart accompany the words of the lips, it is not worship but a solemn mockery.

CHARLES. I have already said that the daily renewal

---

* Archbishop Whately says, "I know the caution given in "Dr. Hawkins' excellent ' *Manual for Christians after Confirma-* "*tion*,' that ' to repeat the Creed is not to pray,' startled some "persons as being needless. But the fact bears him out. The "practice is by no means uncommon of reciting the apostles' "creed as a portion of prayer."—*Whately's Errors of Romanism.* *Essay* i. § 6.

of the covenant we have made in baptism is no unseasonable service. Had it pleased the Almighty to enunciate from heaven a *formula* of faith, no human symbol would have been needed; but as we are left to gather Christian doctrines from the volume of inspiration, where they are indicated under a thousand varieties of form, it is the duty of the Church to put together briefly "the first principles of the oracles of God," in order that the young disciples may keep in mind the faith which they have solemnly professed.

JOSIAH. I do not see the force of this reasoning. For although no *formula*, enunciated like the decalogue from heaven, has been given in the new dispensation, yet we have, even in the oral teaching of our blessed Lord, ample material to establish all the doctrines of the Gospel, were the rest of the sacred volume completely blotted out. How much may be gathered from even a single text, as where it is said, "This is life eternal, that they might " know thee, the only true God, and Jesus Christ whom " thou hast sent!"

CHARLES. And what is the Creed, (whichever of the three *formulæ* you take,) but a setting forth, with clearness and precision, of that very text, and of others which hang as corollaries upon it?

JOSIAH. Thou speaks of "the Creed." Which creed dost thou mean? For I find that three are set forth in your Prayer Book.

CHARLES. Though the Creed appears under three forms of words, yet there is but one faith, one Creed. The variations do not involve any essential difference, but are merely amplifications, intended to render more explicit what is briefly asserted in the earlier form. Of the three, that which is called the apostles' is the most ancient, and was the symbol used in very early times. Afterwards, when perverse men began to question the divinity of our Lord, the Nicene, or, strictly speaking, the Constantino-politan creed, was composed to meet the emergency, by defining, with greater precision and emphasis, the Sonship of Christ and the divinity of the Holy Ghost. And finally, the creed known as the Athanasian was introduced, to set at rest for ever mischievous questionings respecting the nature of the Godhead and the plan of man's redemption. These three are called the Catholic creeds, because they have ever been received as true symbols of the Catholic faith by every branch of Christ's Church.

JOSIAH. In so saying thou must exclude many who consider themselves Christians, and who trust that they are members of Christ's Church, but who do not receive these creeds as having any authority.

CHARLES. I would not willingly exclude from fellowship in Christ any sincere believer in the Son of God, merely because he differed from me in some of the words of a formula. No such stringency exists in the reformed Church.

JOSIAH. Thou hast just said that all branches of the Church accept the three creeds. But I think I have heard that the Episcopal Church in the United States has rejected the Athanasian.

CHARLES. It is true that, on the revisal of the American Prayer Book, at the time of the political separation of the American from the English Church, the American divines removed the Athanasian creed from their Prayer Book ; not because they objected to it as untrue, but because they did not think it expedient to be retained in the Church service. Many conscientious persons object to the wording and to the congregational repetition of that venerable composition, even while they fully receive the doctrine which it is designed to declare.

JOSIAH. This is true, and I think it was remarked by an archbishop of your Church, that he wished you were " well rid of it." We strongly object not only to the damnatory clauses, but to what appears to us to be a somewhat presumptuous attempt to define, in logical terms, a mystery of the Christian faith which is beyond human comprehension ; and perhaps the attempted definition rather obscures than clears up that most important doctrine which it is intended to explain.

CHARLES. I wonder when we shall hear the end of this archiepiscopal dictum.

JOSIAH. You will hear no more about it, when the Anglican Church has followed the example of the Episcopal Church in America.

CHARLES. Whilst I do not go so far as the archbishop, I am conscious that the stated repetition of the Athanasian creed by a mixed congregation of worshippers, is objected to by many who cordially assent to the doctrine it declares, but who do not feel called upon to seem to pass sentence on those who dissent from it.

JOSIAH. In the apostles' creed, and also in the Athanasian, it is said of our Lord, " He descended into hell ;" but this phrase is omitted in the Nicene formula. How is this discrepancy accounted for ? Or what is meant by the descent into hell ?

CHARLES. In certain ancient forms of the apostles' creed, where this article occurs, that of our Lord's burial is omitted (as it also is in the Athanasian creed), and *vice versd.* Hence one interpretation is, that it simply implies our Lord's burial.

JOSIAH. Then thou supposes that all that is meant by, "descended into hell," might be more intelligibly expressed by the words "into the grave."

CHARLES. Such is the opinion of many. I own, however, that a deeper meaning appears to me to be required, and yet so little is revealed to us on this subject that I am fearful of advancing further than what is written. Dean Comber, a learned divine of the seventeenth century, in a meditation for the Easter communion, speaks of our Lord passing through "the scorn and cruelty of "men, the malice and rage of devils, the just but severe "anger of God, yea, the shadow of death and the regions "of eternal horror." But our Lord's alienation from the bosom of the Father could only be momentary; therefore the promise of immediate paradise made to the repentant thief might still be fulfilled.

JOSIAH. I fear there are many in your Church who never think of taking the word "hell" in any but the ordinary meaning, and to such the word conveys an idea which has certainly no foundation in holy Scripture, unless thou think the passage in the first epistle of Peter, where he speaks of our Lord's ministrations "to the spirits in prison," has reference to it.

CHARLES. Some ignorant persons may mistake the meaning of the word "hell" in the creed; but it is not likely that any Sunday-school teacher would omit an explanation of it. Besides, in the prayer-book version of the Psalms, the word "hell" occurs more than once in the older sense; as in Ps. xlix. 14,—"They lie in the hell like sheep." The text you have quoted from St.

Peter's epistle is one of those difficult passages of Scripture respecting which we can afford to await God's good pleasure. It cannot concern us individually; nor can our speculations upon it lead to any good result, and they may possibly divert us from the way of truth.

JOSIAH. I am of the same opinion. But some men seem strangely possessed with "itching ears," which are always open to receive such speculations as these. A favorite employment with many, for instance, is to attempt to describe in detail the glories that await the redeemed in heaven; as if it were possible that it "could "enter into the heart of man" to conceive what "God "hath prepared for them that love Him."

CHARLES. I have no sympathy with such fanciful dreamers. There is a verse in Psalm xvi. which to my mind is far more sublime in its simplicity, and more satisfying in its depth, than all their gorgeous descriptions: "In *Thy presence* is fulness of joy, at Thy right hand there are pleasures for evermore."

JOSIAH. In the apostles' days those who denied the resurrection of the body mockingly enquired, "How are the dead raised up, and with what body do they come?" and the apostle Paul has most fitly prefaced his answer with the words, "Thou fool!"

CHARLES. Yes. And his sublime answer completely meets the cavil of the materialist who scoffs at the Christian belief in corporeal resurrection because, during life, our bodies are in perpetual change—not a particle of the substance of early youth remaining in the man of mature age. Such cavils are sufficiently met by the apostle, when he says, "There is a natural body, and there is a spiritual body," and "Flesh and blood cannot inherit the king-

" dom of God, neither doth corruption inherit incorrup-
" tion."

JOSIAH. Gross ideas respecting the resurrection of the body are held, I apprehend, by many well meaning but imperfectly instructed persons, and hence much of the superstitious anxiety which prevails respecting sepulture in what is called hallowed ground.

CHARLES. True. And an equally gross opinion appears to me to be entertained by many, respecting those passages of Scripture which declare that death entered into the world because of man's sin : as if they required us to believe, that immortality on this earth would have been the lot of all its inhabitants, had man not brought in death by his fall.

JOSIAH. Thou dost not then agree with Milton, that " man's first disobedience

" Brought death into the world, and all our wo,
" With loss of Eden."

CHARLES. Death is indeed denounced in Scripture as the punishment of sin, and this death passed upon all men through Adam's disobedience. But it has always appeared to me to be a shallow misconception of a great truth, to regard the mere separation of soul and body as the death to which Adam's sin exposed his posterity. Nor do I think that Scripture requires us to believe that, had Adam preserved his purity, natural death would never have been introduced into the world. From the moment that the charge was given to our first parents, " Be fruitful and multiply, and replenish the earth," one of two things must eventually have taken place. Either the earth could not, after a comparatively few generations, have supported its inhabitants; or God must have appointed a means by which they should be successively removed. That means, in existing circumstances, is the natural decay of the body, and the closing scene is a seasonable gathering to rest, and in no respect necessarily a punishment. Scripture fitly calls it "a falling asleep."

JOSIAH. I have no doubt that the penalty which Adam incurred was, as thou says, alienation from God, or spiritual death. Still it is not necessary, for those who believe in the original immortality of man, to point out the precise mode in which provision might have been made for human existence, if man had never sinned.

CHARLES. It is difficult for a physiologist to conceive of a natural *growth* without a corresponding *decay*. Natural life is indissolubly bound up with natural death; and St. Paul's expression, "I die daily," which he meant in a spiritual sense, may be as correctly said of our bodies, which during growth, maturity, and decline are continually "passing away," and replenished day by day. As for all animals having been, but for man's sin, intended to have been restricted to a vegetable diet, I should think that no one who had compared the teeth and stomachs of cows and sheep with those of lions and wolves, could entertain such an opinion for a moment. Depend upon it, the lion was never intended, except in a figurative sense, to "eat straw like an ox."

JOSIAH. I fully agree with thee. Still there are those, I believe, who insist on the literal acceptance of that part of the account of the creation which says, "And to every "beast of the earth, and to every fowl of the air, and to "every thing that creepeth upon the earth, wherein there "is life, I have given every green herb for meat: and it

" was so." They say there is here no mention made of beasts devouring each other, but "every green herb" is given to them for food. For my part I entertain no doubt that, from the beginning of creation, there have been carnivorous as well as herbivorous animals. The investigations of geologists fully prove that many of the monsters of former ages were carnivorous, and the bones of animals eaten by them have actually been found in the cavity of the stomach.

CHARLES. We cannot reason on a subject like this from such evidence as one or two verses in the first chapter of Genesis supply. God has given us a revelation, not to instruct us in natural history, but to lead us from the passing shadows of earth to the enduring substances of heaven. Facts of natural history must be gathered by observation. Observation teaches us that certain organizations in the animal world indicate certain propensities ; and this with such exactness that an expert comparative anatomist will give you a tolerably correct description of the habits of a previously unknown animal, by merely inspecting his jaws, his claws, and his maw. The whole material world is an adaptation of means to ends, and each contrivance is as aptly fitted to its office as are the cogs of neighbouring wheels in a chronometer.

JOSIAH. I think we may dismiss this question as one which very little concerns us.

CHARLES. Let us dismiss it with the reflection that all things here below are ordered for us in a far more profitable way by the Omniscient and Omnipotent, than they could be dressed up by all the dreamers and schemers in the world. But have you anything further to say of the clauses of the creed?

JOSIAH. In the Nicene creed it seems to me that there are some redundant expressions used in describing our Lord's person. I allude to the words, "God of God, Light of Light, very God of very God."

CHARLES. . You must bear in mind that this creed was composed to stop the mouths of the Arians, who denied our Lord's divinity, and hence the very emphatic manner in which that fundamental doctrine of Christianity is here expressed.

JOSIAH. I presume then that these words are designed to show forth the divinity of our Lord. I cannot say that they reconcile me to the attempt at defining that which seems to me above our comprehension.

CHARLES. Is there anything else in the services of our Church to which you object?

JOSIAH. Not in this *formula*. But why do you bow at the mention of the name of Jesus? The text in Philippians, sometimes referred to, will not bear you out, being a mistranslation of " at " for " in."

CHARLES. As the practice of bowing at the mention of the name of Jesus existed long before the mistranslation of the text in Philippians, it cannot be defended by that text. From very early times it has been the custom to stand whilst the weekly gospel is read at the Communion service, as a mark of respect to Him from whose words the gospels are (with one or two exceptions) invariably taken; to utter the exclamation, " Glory be to Thee, O God," or some similar words; and at the name of Jesus to bow. " Which harmless ceremonies," says Hooker, " as " there is no man constrained to use, so we know no rea- " son wherefore any man should yet imagine it an insuffer- " able evil." The bowing is an act of worship intended apparently as an acknowledgment of the divinity of our Lord, and as such it seems an appropriate action during the recital of the creed. The early Puritans objected to it that it seemed to advance the Son "above the Father "and the Holy Ghost ;" but, says Hooker, "Seeing that "the truth of His equality with them is a mystery so hard "for the wits of mortal men to rise unto, of all heresies "that which may give Him superiority above them is "least to be feared."[*]

JOSIAH.   Again, I wish to call thy attention to the power claimed by the ministers of your Church to grant absolution.   In the " Order for the visitation of the sick" we find the words, " By His authority committed to me, " I absolve thee from all thy sins, in the name of the " Father, and of the Son, and of the Holy Ghost."   This phrase certainly claims a miraculous power, which we have no record of the apostles themselves claiming, and which throws quite into shade the highest claims made by any Friend from George Fox to the present time.

CHARLES.   It is hardly fair to take these words apart from their context, and from the uniform teaching and explanation of the reformed Church.   The Church of Rome claims the power of exercising priestly absolution, in the miraculous sense you attribute to the words you quote ; but our ministers only " declare and pronounce to the penitent the absolution and remission of sins." Even in the *formula* from which you quote, and which is the *strongest* to be found in our ritual, the right to absolve is restricted in its exercise to the truly repentant, and is expressed in the form of a prayer, " Our Lord Jesus

---

[*] *Hook. Eccl. Pol., Book* v., *chap.* xxx.

" Christ, who hath left power to His Church- to absolve
" all sinners who truly repent and believe in Him, of His
" great mercy forgive thee thine offences : " and then follow the words that offend you.

JOSIAH. But the words I quoted clearly convey the
very idea of priestly absolution, which thou says your
ministers do not claim.

CHARLES. Taken by themselves they may have that
signification, but they are immediately preceded by an
assertion which implies that it is Christ who forgives sin;
and the ministerial absolution is grounded solely on the
authority derived from Christ,— " Whosesoever sins ye
remit, they are remitted unto them ; " and they are followed by a prayer for forgiveness. But this does not
claim a power over men's souls. Hooker is very clear on
this point. " The act of sin," he says, " God alone remit-
" teth, in that His purpose is never to call it to account,
" or to lay it unto men's charge; the stain He washeth out
" by the sanctifying grace of His Spirit ; and concerning
" the punishment of sin, as none else hath power to cast
" body and soul into hell-fire, so none [hath] power to
" deliver either, besides Him. As for the ministerial sen-
" tence of private absolution, it can be no more than a
" declaration what God hath done ; it hath but the force
" of the prophet Nathan's absolution, ' God hath taken
" away thy sin.' " Such is the explanation given by the
great defender of the Church against the Puritans in the
reign of Elizabeth, by one who ought to have known the
mind of our reformers on this subject. After quoting
" the Master of the Sentences "* and St. Jerome in corro-

---

* Peter Lombard was called *the Master of the Sentences.*

boration, he concludes thus : " For there is nothing more
" apparent, than that the discipline of repentance, both
" public and private, was ordained as an outward mean
" to bring men to the virtue of inward conversion ; so
" that when this by manifest tokens did seem effected,
" absolution ensuing (which could not make) served only
" to declare men innocent."*

JOSIAH. The complete formula is as follows :—" Our
" Lord Jesus Christ, who has left power to His Church
" to absolve all sinners who truly repent and believe in
" Him, of His great mercy forgive thee thine offences; and
" by His authority committed to me I absolve thee from
" all sins, in the name of the Father, and of the Son, and
" of the Holy Ghost." This surely is not " an assertion
that it is Christ who forgives sin," but rather an assertion
that He has given to His Church the power of absolution,
which the minister is about to exercise, and which thou defends by quoting the words, " Whosesoever sins ye remit,
they are remitted unto them." Whatever may be the
precise meaning of these words, I feel sure that they do
not confer on the ministers of any Church the power
to forgive sins. Archbishop Whately explains them as
giving the Church power to inflict penalties, and, in extreme cases, to excommunicate ; and to remit those penalties, or " to re-admit an expelled member, on his testifying
contrition." He denies that " fallible men could presume
" to claim the Divine privilege of forgiving sins as against
" God."† If the words referred to have the meaning that
I understand thee to put on them, they must confer on the

---

* *Hook. Eccl. Pol.*, Book vi., chap. vi., sec. 8.
† *Whately's Errors of Romanism. Essay* iv. § 1,

Church the power which is claimed by the Church of Rome. When Hooker speaks of "the discipline of repentance," I presume he means "penance," which is another adaptation from Rome; and I see also that the minister is directed "to move the sick man to a special confession of his sins," and it is only *after* that confession that he is to absolve him. All this is very little removed from Rome.

CHARLES. I think you misunderstand not only the passage from the "Order for the visitation of the sick," but also the explanation given by Hooker. The words you quote do not assert that Christ has left [unlimited] power to His Church to forgive sins, but only "to absolve" [or release] "all sinners who truly repent and believe in Him;" namely, those, and those only, whom He has Himself already forgiven. He alone forgives sin; His commissioned minister assures the repentant sinner of His forgiveness. The minister cannot act of his own mere motion; he must be well convinced that the penitent's repentance is sincere and his faith alive, otherwise he has no authority whatever "to loose him and let him go." This is what I understand by Hooker's explanation. As to confession previous to absolution, it is manifestly intended to relieve the troubled conscience of the penitent, and further to certify the minister that the repentance is sincere. I see no objection to what is ordered in the rubric.

JOSIAH. The minister cannot know whether the repentance be sincere or not; and this form of absolution, which thou calls conditional, seems to me well calculated to delude the ignorant into a false security.

CHARLES. Such objection strikes at the root of every

ministerial action. Our ministers do not pretend to omniscience; neither do their people give them credit for possessing such power over the soul as you suppose.

JOSIAH. There is a ceremony in your Church called " Confirmation," which seems to be designed as a sequel to the rite of baptism, as by it young persons take upon themselves the vows made for them by their sponsors. I am far from objecting to the principle of this ratification, or to the instruction which is understood to precede it. But are not a very large number of persons baptized who are never confirmed, and who yet look upon themselves as members of your Church?

CHARLES. The rite of confirmation is excellent in its intention; and if parents and sponsors were heedful of their duty, it would not be neglected as it too generally has been. A great improvement, however, has taken place of late years, and I hope, therefore, the reproach of neglecting this ordinance will soon cease to be deserved. By the order of the Church no person ought to be admitted to the communion—which is the true test of full membership—until he has been confirmed. In practice, however, this rule is often disregarded.

JOSIAH. We know that, during the first three centuries, baptism was frequently deferred until children had attained to such an age as to be able to act for themselves; and I take it that when infant baptism became general in the Church, the laying on of the hands of the bishop, which was supposed to convey the graces of the Holy Spirit, and thus to complete the sacrament, was separated from baptism, and converted into a separate rite.

CHARLES. Baptism may sometimes have been deferred,

19

but there is incontrovertible evidence that the baptism of infants was the general practice from the days of the apostles. When adult converts were admitted to the communion of the Church by baptism, the rite of confirmation was usually administered at the same time ; but as the baptism of adults became more rare, owing to the growth of the Church, this usage died away.

JOSIAH. The superstitious idea prevailed in early times that the mere *opus operatum* of baptism washed away all previous sins, and the words now used by the bishop seem to countenance a similar idea as respects confirmation, when he says in his prayer, that " forgiveness of all their sins " has been given to the persons confirmed. Are not these words objectionable ? Do they not in fact imply that the rite of confirmation purifies from all sins previously committed ?

CHARLES. It is to the scriptural connection between baptism and the remission of sins, and not to the rite of confirmation, that the bishop's prayer refers. The prayer is offered up *before* the laying on of the bishop's hands, and speaks of regeneration " by water and the Holy Ghost," and of " the forgiveness of sins," in the past tense, obviously referring to regeneration in baptism.

JOSIAH. Possibly that may be the reference intended ; but, certainly, when the bishop, praying on behalf of the young persons on whom he is about to lay his hands, says, that God " has given unto them forgiveness of all their sins," it is difficult to believe that he means no more than that the rite of baptism, which was celebrated some sixteen or eighteen years before, had washed away the original stain inherited from Adam.

CHARLES. It is assuredly the reference intended. But

you seem to forget that these young persons who were baptized sixteen or eighteen years before, have not meanwhile been neglected, but have been carefully instructed by their parents and guardians, and specially prepared and examined by the pastor to whose charge they have been committed, previously to being brought to the bishop. This is of great importance ; and I think your Society suffers much loss from admitting to the full privileges of membership every one who has a "birthright" among you, however ignorant or void of vital religion he may be.

JOSIAH. We certainly suffer much loss from the number of merely nominal members; but it is the same in every religious community. Among the minutes of advice adopted by the Yearly Meeting of London in 1861, there is one addressed to young persons, reminding them that although they are recognized as entitled to "the outward privileges of Christian fellowship, such "recognition cannot constitute them members of the true "Church, and that nothing can effect this but the power "of the Holy Spirit working repentance towards God and "faith towards our Lord Jesus Christ." In truth, you suffer from a similar cause : with you all children are baptized, and all persons baptized by your ministers are considered members of your Church, though certainly many of them are not properly taught, and do not receive confirmation; and even of those who are confirmed are there not many who are "ignorant and void of vital religion" ?

CHARLES. Nominal members have abounded in every communion since excommunication fell into disuse.

JOSIAH. I know well that nominal members are to be found everywhere : I only wished to show that your

Church and ours are in the same position, in reckoning
as members all the children of their members until they
unite themselves to some other body; except that we
preserve the power of excommunication, and you do not.
There are some other matters in your liturgy which appear to me objectionable, or which need explanation.

CHARLES. Which be they?

JOSIAH. Firstly, as regards the marriage service; do
you consider that the minister or priest marries the parties, or does he only attend to receive their mutual vows
as a witness, and to read the prayers and advices which
are appointed for the occasion?

CHARLES. Marriage is partly a civil contract and partly a religious engagement. The mere civil marriage sti-
pulates that the parties shall live together as man and
wife, and that their children shall be deemed legitimate in
the eye of the law. The religious engagement before the
priest adds a far more important element to this formal
stipulation required by the civil law. By it the parties are joined together by God, and "what God hath
joined together let no man put asunder." The priest
attends as God's appointed minister, to receive the vows
of the parties, and to bless them in the name of the
Church. These two acts, taken together, combine the
civil and the religious ceremony : they are necessarily
performed by the priest, who ratifies the marriage thus :
" Forasmuch as M. and N. have consented together in
" holy wedlock, and have witnessed the same before God
" and this company," &c., " I pronounce that they be
" man and wife together, in the name of the Father, and
" of the Son, and of the Holy Ghost. Amen."

JOSIAH. I must object to the part assigned by your

Church to the priest in the celebration of marriage ; and to the idea that this solemn contract must be deprived of the sanction of religion, unless an "ordained" minister be present to receive the vows of the parties, and to bless them in the name of the Church.

CHARLES. You mistake my meaning. I am very far from thinking that the *idea* of the Quaker marriage is not religious. Persons who take each other in marriage in one of your meetings for worship profess to do so as in the immediate presence of the Great High Priest, the Judge of quick and dead. Such a marriage is wholly distinct in idea from the civil contract before the magistrate. I have nothing to object to it.

JOSIAH. But besides this, there is the form of giving a ring, which seems a strange thing in a religious ceremony ; and this ring is first laid by the man on the Book of Common Prayer, along with the fee to the clergyman and the clerk, and then given back by the minister to the man to put it on the woman's finger. What is the meaning of this? Is it in order to consecrate the ring that it is laid on the book, and then given back to the man by the officiating priest?

CHARLES. Marriages in church take place in front of the rails of the communion-table, within which the minister stands. The ring, a well-known type of eternity, symbolizes, I suppose, the indissoluble nature of the vow which is about to be made before God and His Church. It is therefore properly given by the man to the priest, as to God's minister ; and the giving back to the man is in token of the acceptance of the vow by the Church. It is laid on the Book of Common Prayer, I suppose, much for the same reason that a person taking a legal oath is re-

quired to "kiss the book." No doubt the idea of consecration, in the same sense I have formerly allowed this
word, is involved in this ceremony.

JOSIAH. Then follow the words, "With this ring I thee
" wed, with my body I thee worship, and with all my
" worldly goods I thee endow." This seems to me, to say
the least of it, very much out of place in such a ceremony,
and especially after the solemn pledge of their troth which
they have just given. I know that "worship" means
" honour," "respect," but the idea of marrying a woman
by means of a ring is difficult to account for, if it be not a
very questionable relic of a former superstition. I should
not like to term any portion of a religious rite ridiculous,
but certainly this matter of the ring has an appearance of
absurdity which tempts one to laugh at it.

CHARLES. A clerical friend of mine once told me an
anecdote which your last words tempt me to repeat to
you. He was called on to marry a couple of stage actors,
who came accompanied by a rather disorderly company of
friends, who were disposed to make merriment of the
ceremony, and to titter at some of the prayers. Seeing
this, he determined to read the whole service, from beginning to end, including some parts which are often omitted,
and to throw into his reading such solemnity as would
bring out fully the intent and meaning of every portion
of the ritual. The effect was that the tittering ceased,
several of the company were melted to tears, and the
bridegroom afterwards thanked him for the lesson he had
received.

JOSIAH. I can well believe that the solemn character
of the service, taken as a whole, may have had this effect,
but this only makes it more desirable to get rid of a form

which appears so incongruous. Why is a ring made use of at all ?

CHARLES. The use of the ring in marriages is of very old date, earlier than the Christian era. " The ring," says Hooker,* " hath been always used as an especial pledge " of faith and fidelity. Nothing more fit to serve as a " token of our purposed endless continuance in that which " we never ought to revoke. This is the cause wherefore " the heathens themselves did in such cases use the ring, " whereunto Tertullian alluding, saith, that in ancient " times ' no woman was permitted to wear gold, saving " ' only upon one finger, which her husband had fastened " ' unto himself with that ring which was usually given " ' for assurance of future marriage.' The cause why the " Christians use it, as some of the fathers think, is either to " testify mutual love, or rather to serve for a pledge of con- " junction in heart and mind agreed upon between them."

JOSIAH. So then the custom of giving and receiving a ring is of heathen origin. You do not even pretend to defend it by any scriptural authority. Ought you not therefore to omit it ?

CHARLES. I see no reason for discontinuing so harmless a ceremony, and one which, properly interpreted, is significant. I do not attach any superstitious value to the ring, as if it were an essential item of the marriage contract. But, at least, it serves a married woman as a sort of portable certificate of marriage, and may, on occasion, protect her from annoyance or impertinence. I believe that some of your members, when travelling abroad, make use of a pseudo-wedding ring for this very purpose.

---

* *Eccl. Pol.* Book v. ch. lxxiii. §. 6.

JOSIAH. I can have no objection to the ring as a sign of marriage. To wear it for this purpose is very different from using it as part of a religious ceremony.

CHARLES. Is there anything else in our ritual to which you object ?

JOSIAH. In the burial service, appropriate as are the portions of Scripture chosen for it, I must say that it peculiarly exemplifies the evils of all stated forms. The minister is obliged, in *every* case, to declare that " it has " pleased God of his great mercy to take unto himself " the soul of our dear brother here departed :" and that " we therefore commit his body to the ground, in sure and " certain hope of the resurrection to eternal life ;" and again, in the prayer, the words, " We give thee hearty " thanks that it hath pleased thee to deliver this our " brother out of the miseries of this sinful world." This is very strong language, even over the body of one whose life has been such as to give the survivors the firm trust that he has died the death of the righteous ; but to be said over all indiscriminately, if they have received the rite of baptism, whatever have been their manner of life, does seem to me to go much further in the way of charitable hope than we are warranted in doing. I recollect well the injunction—" Judge not"—" Condemn not," but I think, where the outward conduct has not been evidently that of a Christian, that silence best becomes both the recollection of the dead and the deep feeling which we ought to have of our own frailty.

CHARLES. Cases do occur in which silence, or at best the expression of a trembling hope, would be preferable to the " hearty thanks" of the ritual, but I do not think them so numerous as you suppose. The chief design of both the declaration and the prayer is to profess our belief in the doctrine of the resurrection of the body;* and also to declare our trust in the promise of eternal life to all who have lived and died in the faith of the Gospel. The burial service is not to be used over the excommunicate. All others are charitably taken to die in the faith which they have outwardly professed. No man can judge of the belief of another, or whether God have not accepted the veriest sinner at the last moment. Assuredly to all who die repentant and in the faith, death is a deliverance for which all should render " hearty thanks."

JOSIAH. Your ministers sometimes read it over those who may have been baptized into the communion of your Church, but who have openly avowed their disbelief of the Gospel.

CHARLES. To read the burial service at the graves of such persons is certainly an abuse which was not contemplated by the framers of the Prayer Book. No clergyman ought to be required to officiate at the burial of an openly avowed infidel, who is virtually " excommunicate ;" and were the ancient discipline revived, we should have no cases of such profanation.

JOSIAH. Your liturgy needs revival and reformation, which I hope it may receive when you get a proper dis-

---

* *Resurrection of the body.*—This appears by comparing the form used in the case of a burial at sea, which reads :—" We " therefore commit his body to the deep, to be turned into cor- " ruption, looking for the resurrection of the body (when the " Sea shall give up her dead), and the life of the world to come, " through our Lord Jesus Christ ; who at his coming shall change " our vile body, that it may be like his glorious body, according " to the mighty working, whereby he is able to subdue all things " to himself."

cipline for the management of your Church affairs. If thy interpretation of the several passages referred to be the correct one, it would be much better to put it into plain language, so that there might be no doubt as to the meaning.

CHARLES. The revisal of the liturgy, in the present state of opinion within the Church, is simply an impossibility. I trust a day may come in which, under the Divine guidance, a complete revision may be made ; but not after the manner of Lord Ebury and those who join with him. Meanwhile we have unceasing cause for thankfulness that, throughout the many fluctuations of popular theology these two hundred years, hasty fingers have been held back from meddling with the Prayer Book on the pretence of improving it. As it stands, it has fewer faults than any similar ritual in existence ; no human composition is absolutely perfect ; but one which combines so many excellencies and in which even you can point out so few blemishes, ought, by those who possess it, to be carefully guarded ; yea, as the very "apple of the eye." But it is time to separate for this evening. Goodnight.

CONVERSATION XI.

All things are lawful for me, but I will not be brought under the power of any.—1 *Cor.* vi. 12.

JOSIAH. Well, Charles, is there anything else in our practice or profession to which thou objects ?

CHARLES. I have yet a few words to say on some matters which may perhaps be classed among things indifferent.

JOSIAH. What may these be ?

CHARLES. I more immediately allude to the unqualified manner in which Friends have condemned music ; and also the little countenance that they give to polite literature and to the fine arts in general. It is true that latterly the custom of the Society respecting pictures and poetry has materially altered. You have learned to discriminate between the poets, and to cast out from your bookcases only the profane and immoral. The taste for pictures, too, is gradually spreading among your more wealthy members. Time was, within my memory, when the only prints allowed to hang up in a Friend's parlour were engravings of "Penn's Treaty with the American Indians," and, as a companion, the print of "the West Family." But now, engravings of a great variety of subjects are displayed on the walls of many of your members, and even oil-pictures in gilt frames are gradually creeping into fashion among you. In a generation or two, therefore, we shall perhaps have little reason to complain of the non-patronage of art by your Society.

JOSIAH. Friends have no objection to the fine arts, considered in their general relations. We have always loved good poetry. Recollect how Thomas Ellwood acted as secretary to Milton while writing "Paradise Lost," and suggested to him the idea of "Paradise Regained." Our members visit the galleries of art in museums or exhibitions; the children at our public schools are taught drawing, and many who have a taste for it practise painting also. Some of our members, however, look upon paintings or engravings hung against the walls of their houses as an unnecessary decoration, and therefore object to them, as they do also to showy furniture of all kinds.

CHARLES. There is a broad distinction between the decoration of walls by pictures (supposing them to be good ones), and the gaudy ornamentation which is inconsistent with Christian simplicity. A picture is not an ornament which addresses itself merely to the eye, or which awakens pride and vain glory. It pleases the eye, it is true, but it is also calculated to call up the better emotions of the mind. Is it a landscape? We enjoy again through it, if it be truly painted, those inexhaustible pleasures which the beautiful in external nature is calculated to afford us; and thus transfer to the fireside the gatherings of our country rambles. Is it a historical picture, or a home-group like that of Wilkie's "Blind Fiddler"? Human actions and passions are immortalized on the canvas, and emotions of the deepest character are fixed in our minds.

What are Hogarth's moral series but powerful eye-sermons? And so also of many of the works of the great masters. They call up feelings either of patriotism, of philanthropy, or of reverence, according to the subject treated.

JOSIAH. We have nothing to object to the legitimate use of painting : in its proper place it ministers largely to the innocent gratification of the mind. It is to be regretted however that amongst the many hundred pictures of, so called, sacred subjects which have come down to us from the great era of this art, so many should be tinged with debasing superstition, or rendered almost loathsome by semi-blasphemous attempts to put on canvas that which mortal man " neither hath seen nor can see."

CHARLES. It is indeed lamentable that the noble efforts of great artists should often have no other interest in our eyes than that derivable from the artistic manner in which the work has been performed. Harmony and balance of colour, contrast of light and shade, foreshortening of limbs, natural representation of flesh, and all the other etceteras that conspire to make up " a good picture"—these are but the shell of the artist's conception. The soul and substance of a painting lie in the treatment and the subject. It is quite clear to me that Raphael painted with his soul as much as with his brushes, and that unless we can place ourselves in the valley of vision in which his magnificent conceptions were embodied, we realize but a small part of such a heavenly dream as he has perpetuated in his great picture, the Transfiguration.

JOSIAH. We must enter into an artist's feeling if we wish to realize the poetry of his work. Therefore it is that I so much regret that the middle-age painters have, by the subjects they have ~~too generally~~ chosen, put themselves out of the pale of our sympathies. ~~Scripture~~ subjects, except when absurdly treated, have an innate vitality; but not so the endless pictures of the Saint Catherines, Francises, Dominics, Sebastians, and Jeromes with which most of the continental galleries and churches overflow.

CHARLES. There is a class of "religious pictures" which I at once allow to be of a positively mischievous tendency, and of which the existence is much more to be deplored than the representations of saints and martyrs, whose endless repetition is simply a bore. I mean that very favourite class to be seen in every Roman Catholic church, and often in every room of a Roman Catholic house, where the Virgin Mother and her Son are represented—she, as the Queen of Heaven, crowned and enthroned—He as still a helpless infant in his guardian mother's arms. Perhaps, however, we have said enough on the subject of pictures; let us now discuss the question of music—a science which is, I believe, altogether repudiated by your Society.

JOSIAH. The practice of music, whether vocal or instrumental, sacred or profane, has generally been discouraged among our members; not as being in itself sinful, but as consuming time that might be much better employed, and often leading those who acquire a passion for it into much temptation. Music calls itself the language of heaven and of angelic natures; but how little of this world's music leads its votaries heavenward! Need I attack the opera, or point to the degradation of the female sex which may be said to cling to this musical display as

closely as his shadow clings to one who walks in sunshine? A man without a shadow is not more singular
than a theatre without vice. But our objections to music
do not stop at the opera. See the thousands of hours
which, in modern female education, are squandered in
teaching the fingers to thrum a piano—hours which, devoted to the cultivation of the understanding, might result
in raising the whole tone of the female character. Or
even take music in its highest form—that which is called
sacred music—wilt thou tell me that the oratorio leads
the thoughts from earth to heaven? On the contrary,
is not the mind of the listener spell-bound by the skill
of the " performers ;" and that to such a degree as
to lose all feeling for the sublime words that are " performed"? And just in proportion to the appreciation of
the music is the non-appreciation of the subject set to
music. The musical ear is drunk with pleasure for the
moment, but the soul is not lifted thereby a step nearer
heaven ; and heavenly thoughts may be far, far away. If
a false note be accidentally struck by an unfortunate " per-
former," all the listener's " divine rapture" vanishes ; his
devotion is no deeper than the tympanum of his ear, and
flies off when that is unpleasantly tickled.

CHARLES. You have certainly, in a few sentences, con-
trived to rake up against music in general many accusa-
tions that only apply to the abuse of music ; and thence
you argue, rather unfairly as I think, against the proper
use of powers and talents which have undoubtedly been
implanted deep in the human mind by the Author and
Giver of all good things. Why should your Society set its
face against all music? Would it not suffice to condemn
that which is manifestly licentious? In your other pecu-

liarities you are satisfied with clipping and pruning, but
in this matter the cry is, "Raze it, raze it even to the
foundations thereof."

JOSIAH. As thou hast not made any reply to my remarks on what is called sacred music, I presume thou
agrees with me in condemning it as commonly practised.
Music is a luxury which is peculiarly liable to abuse, and
Friends have therefore thought it safest to avoid it altogether; still I must admit that much may be advanced in
favour of the moderate enjoyment of a gratification the
capacity for which has been implanted in us by our
Creator. There have, at all times, been many of our
members who gratified themselves by listening to music,
and some who studied its practice ; and of late years the
number has considerably increased. I do not think it is
within the proper limits of the discipline of any religious
body to do more than offer advice against the excessive indulgence of it; but what is the exact limit of lawful indulgence, must be left to the conscience of each individual.

CHARLES. I knew that the practice of music had increased among the members of your Society, but I was not
prepared to hear you say that it was a matter that must
be left to each individual to decide for himself. In this
case, we may expect before long to find that the piano is
considered to be a necessary piece of furniture in a Friend's
drawing-room, just as it is in the drawing-rooms of other
people.

JOSIAH. We live in days of change, and therefore such
things may take place.

CHARLES. As respects sacred music, though I allow
that it is often listened to without its exciting devotional
feelings, I would not dispense with it ; nor do I think the

oratorio, except when theatrically performed, is to be condemned. Throughout the Bible history music is invariably spoken of as a part of the worship of the sanctuary. Will you erase the songs and hymns from the Bible? or blot out the Psalms as a profane book, for they were all set to music and constantly sung? Or will you condemn David because he took his harp to sooth the passion of Saul? Or, passing on to the New Testament, what say you to the text, "And when they had sung an hymn, they went out into the mount of Olives"? Just reflect for a moment *who* were the singers, and *what* was the occasion when that hymn was sung; and then tell me candidly whether your objection to sacred music be scriptural or not.

JOSIAH. It does not appear to me that that hymn was sung as an act of worship; but even if it were, it forms no precedent for the pealing organ and the full choir of hired singers, by whom the music in churches is "performed." Music may attract some persons to attend, but will that sanction it? They go to church for the same reason that on other days they go to the opera, that is, to hear the singing. Some say that it assists devotion, by softening and solemnizing the feelings. It may act on the passions, and produce a state of temporary excitement which passes away with the last sounds of the instrument; but is this devotion? Is this the worship in spirit and in truth which the Christian ought to offer to his Maker? It cannot reach the heart; and so far as the music is concerned, the sinner leaves the church as dead in trespasses and sins as when he entered it. There is nothing in the New Testament which indicates the use of music in worship during apostolic times, nor does it appear to have been introduced until the fifth century of the Church.

20

CHARLES. If hymns or songs of praise to God be not acts of solemn worship, what are they? You are the only religionists I ever heard of who religiously repudiate them. No doubt sacred music, whether vocal or instrumental, may, as may also preaching, be converted into a mere theatrical performance, but you are hardly justified in saying that " it cannot reach the heart." Perhaps you have no ear for music. Language reaches the heart, and why not music, which is but a subtler form of language? In some states of the mind, under the influence of joy or grief, or of deep religious emotion, I believe music becomes the most natural expression of our spiritual wants. It is told of George Herbert that, the Sunday before his death, he rose suddenly from his bed, called for one of his instruments, took it into his hand, and said—

> "My God, my God,
> "My music shall find Thee ;
> "And every string
> "Shall have his attribute to sing ;"

and having tuned it he played and sung his own hymn, commencing :

> "The Sundays of man's life."

" Thus," says Isaac Walton, who tells the story, "he sung "on earth such hymns and anthems as the angels, and as "he and Mr. Ferrar now sing in heaven."

JOSIAH. Thou art right in supposing that I have no ear for music, or at least my taste has not been cultivated.

CHARLES. Then you cannot possibly judge of the feelings of one who has an ear. But unless all your members, young and old, are equally deaf to the melody of sweet sounds, you will not find them to agree with you in thinking that music cannot reach the heart. Have you never observed the delight which children take in tune ? The nurse knows it well. Even the dullest and most prosaic mother will, by instinct, throw musical tones into the nonsense-words with which she fondles her infant ; or invent extemporary tunes either to excite its mirth or to hush it to sleep. Suppose then, if you reject sacred music from the worship of the congregation, you try the effect of introducing hymns into your nurseries and schools.

JOSIAH. The hymns, without the music, are much used in Friends' families and in our schools.

CHARLES. I think you would find that hymns *with* the music, particularly with such music as could be sung by a whole school of children in full chorus, would be far more effective, for all the purposes for which hymns are designed, than the bald repetition of metrical words can possibly be. Such sacred lyrics as the Old Hundredth Psalm :—

> " With one consent let all the earth,
> To God their cheerful voices raise ;"

or as the well-known missionary hymn—

> " From Greenland's icy mountains ;
> From India's coral strand ;"

lose half their power when stripped of the music.

JOSIAH. There are some hymns which are at least as instructive, and take as deep a hold on the mind, if simply repeated. I think it is William Allen who, in advanced life, records with grateful feelings the benefits which he derived from his mother's having taught him to repeat, nightly as he lay down in bed, the noble Evening Hymn,

> " Glory to thee, my God, this night,
> For all the blessings of the light."

CHARLES. Such an anecdote as that from William Allen's life very forcibly shows the value of the *poetic form* (the same will apply to the *musical*) in inculcating sacred truths. I do not merely mean that poetry and music serve to fix the memory and impress the heart of a child, though this is an important fact; but I allude chiefly to the mother, in William Allen's case. It was the *poetry* that fixed her attention, and induced her to teach the hymn to her child. As a consistent Quaker she dare not teach her child to repeat, at lying down in bed, a form of prayer; and to teach him to get by heart a Collect would have seemed to her to be causing her child to use " vain repetitions :" but she has no scruple to teach him to use this *metrical Collect*, for so it most truly is—every line, except the two first, being an earnest petition to God. Your scruples are of a very peculiar kind ; they allow you to teach your children to repeat sacred poetry, but prevent you from teaching them the same words and thoughts when expressed in " sacred prose," as I may call the Collects.

JOSIAH. The children are taught to repeat hymns, as they are also taught to repeat portions of the Holy Scriptures, including the Lord's prayer ; but they are never taught to consider such repetitions either of hymns or portions of Scripture as prayers, and this makes a great difference. But let us not wander from our subject.

CHARLES. I am glad to hear that your members are more disposed than they were some years since to cultivate the musical faculty in their children. It is, I think, their duty to do so, and thus to direct this natural gift so that it may redound to the glory of the Giver. If the taste for music be strong in your children's minds, they will seek to gratify it by stealth if you do not permit them to enjoy it openly. Herein lies the great peril of an absolute prohibition. It makes that a sin which the Almighty designed to be a blessing; and your children fall into temptation and a snare through your means.

JOSIAH. I agree with thee as to the injurious effect of an absolute prohibition of that which, even if its tendency be dangerous, is not in itself sinful. Many advocate the practice of music as tending to increase the attractions of home, but I fear there are cases in which it has had a different effect. The home music has not been sufficiently exciting, and the young people go out to musical parties or to the opera, in order to gratify the musical taste which their home instruction has created.

CHARLES. Well, we need not discuss the opera, and perhaps we have said enough about music. But I think you also object to your members practising field sports?

JOSIAH. We do.

CHARLES. Field sports when pursued in moderation, are healthful and exhilarating pastimes, and often prove a most salutary change to persons whose ordinary occupations are sedentary, or who are much engaged with harassing business, either public or private. I should be sorry, therefore, to put a ban on these amusements, as if it were a sin to follow hawk or hound.

JOSIAH. But look at the lax tone that the indulgence in such pastimes gives to the mind. When we hear a man spoken of as " a foxhunter," do we expect to meet a sober religious man? And what opinion do we form of a foxhunting clergyman?

CHARLES. The inordinate love of foxhunting, when the chase becomes the chief thought and business of life, like any other inordinate affection, has a tendency to disorder the mind : but the chase itself may be followed in moderation without injury to the mind, and with much benefit to the bodily powers. I do not know any exercise more likely to knit the frame in youth and early manhood, and produce that vigour of body on which, in many cases, strength of mind and character very closely depends.

JOSIAH. Horse exercise is a manly and healthful recreation, and should be encouraged in young people of both sexes. But all the benefits that accrue from it may be attained without the aid of fox-hunting, or the pursuit of any other animal, wild or tame. The inferior animals have a natural right to live and to enjoy life; and man has no right to deprive them of life, unless there be a real object to be served. Now our mere amusement surely cannot be a sufficient object, and therefore it cannot be lawful for the Christian to seek his pleasure in their death or sufferings. If the real object were to take the hare for food, or to rid the country of foxes, it would be a different question; but we know that this is not the case. In truth, the foxes are bred for the sake of being hunted, and are carefully " preserved" in covers planted for the purpose.

CHARLES. The habit of breeding foxes, hunting them down, and then sending them back in a sack to their cover, you may well call a cruel and useless sport.

JOSIAH. We are then, after all, pretty well agreed.

CHARLES. If I saw the taste for field sports very strong in a young person, I should hesitate to oppose it very strongly, lest in attempting to enforce a rigid principle, I might drive him to follow some less harmless pursuit—as racing, for instance. There can be no comparison, I presume, between the evils resulting from a love of the chase and the vices which the turf almost always fosters.

JOSIAH. If a choice between evils be a necessity, let us by all means have the chase in preference to " the turf," as a moral school. Certainly I should much prefer seeing a young man on his horse following the hounds, to finding him with thoughtful face, on the race ground, calculating the odds, or betting on the horses. Mere animal spirits may be the impulse in the former case, but a vitiated taste must be at the bottom in the latter. However, I do not admit that either is necessary.

CHARLES. Even if you consider the practice an evil one, there are yet many cases wherein large allowance should be made for young men who occasionally follow the hounds. Those who live all their lives in a large city, are very differently placed from youths bred up in country habits, accustomed to horse exercise from the time they can sit a pony, and who happen to live in a sporting neighbourhood. England has, for a thousand years, been famous for her noble field sports, which are to the present day such as they have always been; and much of the manly vigour which distinguishes the gentlemen of England, taken as a class, from the enervated aristocracy of other countries, is justly attributable to the healthful character of their ordinary pastimes. It would be a sad day should her gentry exchange, for the vitiated tastes of the continent, those native pastimes which have been handed down, with the oaks on their hills, from father to son, for so many generations. I believe you do not condemn the minor field sports in the same degree that you do the major?

JOSIAH. If the game be wanted for food, as is often

the case in those countries where the flesh of wild animals constitutes a large part of the supply, we certainly should not object to its being procured by the rifle. But in this country, where no such necessity exists, we think, for the reasons I have already stated, that these amusements are not such as Christians should take pleasure in ; and therefore we advise our members not to engage in such sports.

CHARLES. The minor field sports offer excellent opportunities for studying the habits of animals. Look at the extraordinary feats performed by sporting dogs, when of pure breed and well trained. The amount of instinct developed in the dog under man's teaching seems so far above that which properly belongs to the species, that we begin to question how much of this is instinct and how much is reason. But the habits of the dog form only a small part of the naturalist's enquiries. The science of ornithology is greatly indebted to sportsmen. I know several instances in which the aim of the individual at first was no higher than that of the ordinary sportsman—to bag the greatest quantity of game : but the constant habit of traversing the country at all seasons seemed to rouse up dormant powers of observation. Strange birds were met with ; they attracted attention; their doings were watched, and their haunts discovered ; their times of coming and going, their nesting, all the peculiarities of their dispositions were carefully observed and noted down ; specimens were obtained and preserved ; and thus, by little and little, and almost unconsciously, the mere sportsman was changed into the naturalist. And how greatly his enjoyment was increased I need hardly say. Now I am convinced that it requires but a little skilful guiding in early youth to give similar tastes to many, if not to most of the young men who show a partiality for shooting or fishing. Nothing is commoner than to hear old sportsmen regret that they were not thrown into the company of naturalists when young. They feel conscious of having possessed and neglected opportunities innumerable of making observations, which they now perceive, when too late, are both interesting to those that make them, and of real benefit to the world at large.

JOSIAH. So that, instead of discouraging shooting or fishing, thou would endeavour to render these amusements subservient to the advancement of science? Our Society is friendly to every scientific enquiry, and we particularly encourage a taste for natural history, which we hold to possess for young people that true zest which so many spurious pleasures claim to have, but have not. When the study of natural history is the object, I think the capture and killing of animals as legitimate as the taking of game when wanted for food. I fear, however, that the scientific sportsmen form a very small minority of the corps.

CHARLES. Such is no doubt the case at present, but looking back for the last thirty years, to which my memory stretches, I see a wonderful change in this respect. I should say that the number of observers in this country has increased tenfold, and is yet rapidly increasing. Natural History has not yet attained its legitimate status, either in our schools or colleges, but it is making way surely and steadily; and, in another generation, it will be properly appreciated as an essential element of education. The stars that shine above us, and the flowers that spring up under our feet, may be alike the agents of our advancement in knowledge, if we but listen to their teaching. Each created thing, whether great or small, is, in its vocation and ministry, a preacher to mankind. "In season, out of season," this voice is never weary, but "wakeneth us morning by morning," and is ready to give "the tongue of the learned" to all that follow it steadfastly.

JOSIAH. I wish it could be said with truth, that advancement in knowledge was a sure criterion of advancement in the scale of moral being. I fear that it is not always the most cultivated heads that possess the best disciplined hearts. The head may be ever busy, observing, and noting, and adding to the store of knowledge, while the heart is a prey to every evil passion, or at best indifferent to its highest interests, idle, unthankful, unholy.

CHARLES. This is, no doubt, true; but it affords no good reason for ceasing in our efforts to increase a taste for useful or entertaining knowledge. In all cases, whether of the well informed or of the ignorant, the direction of the heart is a separate consideration from that of the head, and belongs to a higher agency. All things considered, the observant mind is in a healthier state than the slothful. A few cases may happen in which "ignorance is bliss," or at least better than the superficial knowledge which is put in its place; but when can the rest of the paradoxical line be true? It never can be "folly to be wise."

JOSIAH. Such phrases, however witty, are extremely liable to abuse, as they may be made to excuse wilful ignorance. It is a feather in the cap of the sluggard, if he can boast good company in prating about the folly of wisdom and the bliss of ignorance. There is an amusement very generally practised in every rank of society, but which has been objected to by many serious persons of all religious persuasions, concerning which I should like to know thy sentiments. I mean dancing, an "accomplishment" which ordinarily forms part of the education of young persons, and to which the Society of Friends has always strongly objected, as being not merely a waste of time, but also as leading to improper familiarity between the sexes, and to dissipation of mind.

CHARLES. I remember, when a little boy, being greatly horrified by an expression which I found in one of William Penn's writings. I think it occurs in his "Advice to his Children," a short tract which contains many wise and just thoughts forcibly expressed. Amongst other things he says, "Dancing is the devil's procession," and then draws a strong picture of the evils that accompany it. This description, and particularly the opening words, for a long time influenced my judgment, for it never occurred to me to question a maxim proceeding from such an authority as William Penn. Consequently I could not look without horror on dancing assemblies, or without pity on the scores of unfortunates who were continually carried off by the heels to the bottomless pit, through such meetings.

JOSIAH. And what may have changed thy opinion in this matter?

CHARLES. My early opinions having been formed from unreasoning submission to authority, were not likely to stand after I ceased to put faith in that authority. When I began to question William Penn's inspiration, my mind was free to examine his words on their own merits. I had seen something of general society, and had mingled in social gatherings, not only among Friends but amongst persons of various denominations, and I failed to discover, in the re-union of young people among Friends, any superiority (as far as the discipline of the mind is concerned) over those of other denominations. The same silliness, the same petty scandal and jealousy, the same waste of time, all that make such assemblies immoral, may and do sometimes flourish in the Quaker evening party as well as in the ball-room. Dancing is not the evil thing in such parties; nor, in the abstract, do I see any evil in it at all.

Josiah. The silliness and scandal of Quaker parties, where such silliness and scandal exist, do not, in any degree, prove dancing to be a suitable amusement for a Christian, or meet my objection to its tendency to lead to undue familiarity between young persons, and to dissipation of mind. We must look at things as we find them actually existing, and so viewed I think it cannot be denied that dancing leads to dissipation, and to the degradation of the moral feelings. Young girls follow it for the vain desire of displaying their persons so as to allure the gaze of the other sex, and excite the envy of their own. Hence the thousand evil passions that spring up in a ball-room, as in a hot-bed. I do not frequent such places, but have read descriptions of them in works written to illustrate fashionable life; and almost every writer, in describing balls and dancing parties, has a bye-play of jealousy, spite, scandal, or some other evil passion, as if it were impossible that this amusement should be indulged in without its leading to immorality.

Charles. I am no advocate for that unnatural state of

society which fashionable novels depict. The fashionable ball-room is too often a place where the young of both sexes, but especially the weaker one, are exposed, night after night, to influences that must destroy the freshness of character which it ought to be the aim of parents to perpetuate. Those who habitually turn day into night, in their habits of life, are likely enough, in morality, to put darkness for light and light for darkness. You much mistake me if you suppose I am defending such dissipation as this.

JOSIAH. But thou art defending that which gives zest to such dissipation. Take away the dancing from the fashionable assembly, and what remains? People will not congregate merely to look at each other, and talk scandal.

CHARLES. You know but little of the world, Josiah, or you would not say so. You may make dancing a capital offence; but even if your law could put it down, you would not thereby diminish the vices of fashionable life. You must cut much deeper than the trimmings of fashion to effect a cure.

JOSIAH. I look upon the practice of dancing with very different feelings from that of music. The latter may be to some persons a temptation from which they may feel themselves bound to abstain; but, in itself, it is the cultivation of a natural taste, implanted in us by the Great Author of nature. Dancing, on the contrary, appears to me to be evil both in its root and its effects, and is an amusement utterly unsuited to those who are seeking to "adorn the doctrine of God our Saviour in all things." Public opinion is so far correct on this point that it will not sanction dancing as an amusement for a minister of

religion. Why have a different rule of morality for ministers and other Christians? There is nothing in the New
Testament to warrant such a distinction. We do not
pretend to put down dancing; all we do say is that it is
very unsuitable amusement for a Christian to indulge in,
and in this opinion we have a large amount of support
from other religious societies, from the Church of Rome
down to the Methodist. I only wonder how thou canst
defend it.

CHARLES. There is a clear distinction between recreation and dissipation. Dancing, within proper limits, is
a healthful, as it is a graceful, exercise; and serves to
rub off the disagreeable stiffness and shyness that school
discipline often leaves behind. I own that I like to see
young people thus enjoying themselves, while the old sit
round the room and chat of their own young days, in a
spirit of healthful gaiety. Nor do I think such reunions
a whit less innocent than your Quaker gatherings, where
small games and forfeits (thoroughly childish, for the most
part) take the place of music and dancing.

JOSIAH. Small games and forfeits! This is an anti-
quated idea—the recollection of some twenty or thirty
years ago. Dancing is not practised, nor ever will be
practised merely for those quiet family parties, though
even there I would object to it; but it will always be
connected with balls and large mixed parties, and all
the evils which thou hast denounced. Dancing rubs off
something more than "disagreeable stiffness," and something which it were better for the young woman to retain. A peach gains nothing by the bloom being rubbed
off. Certainly nothing except habit could reconcile a
modest pure-minded girl to waltzing, and you cannot

readily, in practice, draw a line between one kind of dance and another.

CHARLES. Remove but the glasses of Quakerism, and I think you will see that it is only the *abuse* of this amusement that is reprehensible. They tell a pleasant story of two Quaker ladies who formerly conducted a girls' school, and who were, in all but knowledge of the external world, lady-like women, and accomplished, as far as Quakerism allows. Dancing they had read of as being " the devil's procession ;" but dancing they had never seen, and had formed no idea of it, except, perhaps, that it was something very wicked. And so their school flourished in virgin purity for many years, until at last a clever girl, who in her previous studies had picked up a knowledge of steps and figures, came to the school. She found the girls in want of some new game, and conceived the thought of teaching them to dance ! But she took good care to conceal the true nature of the abominable thing, and called it " *Weaving the Diaper;*" and under this name she taught all the steps and figures of the quadrille to the other girls, to their no small gratification, and to the delight of the two innocent lady governesses, who used to come and watch the girls going through " this new and very pretty game." Nay, frequently they would encourage lazy girls to enter into what seemed so healthful an exercise : " Thou looks " cold ; do, my dear, go join the girls in ' weaving the dia- " per.'" Thus things went on pleasantly till a luckless day, when some Friends, who knew a little more of the world than the governesses, came to visit the school. As a matter of course, they were invited to see the girls " weaving the diaper ;" weaving it, alas, for the last time, for the truth could no longer be concealed. You may imagine the horror of the two innocent ladies when they discovered that they had been unwittingly enjoying and encouraging " the devil's procession."

JOSIAH. The story is amusing, and I have heard it before : yet I doubt the governesses having been so ignorant of the world. They probably saw no harm, considering it merely as a game for children ; but their visitor looked on it differently, and they yielded to her objections.

CHARLES. The story is not merely amusing; it has much point in reference to our present discussion, for it shows that dancing, prejudice apart, is not that diabolical device you would have us believe. Call it "weaving the diaper," and the most innocent minds will see its beauty, and take pleasure in it.

JOSIAH. That which may be very suitable as a play for children, may be very unsuitable as an amusement for grown up men and women. But I wish to remark, with respect to the popular amusements thou hast referred to in this conversation, that although they may not be worse than many other modes of spending time, yet all may be utterly unsuited to the character of a Christian.

CHARLES. " Happy is he that condemneth not himself in the thing that he alloweth." Nevertheless, we must not be too hard on " muscular Christians," who may not see things in the light in which they appear to you or to me.

CONVERSATION XII.

Let brotherly love continue.—Heb. xiii. 1.

JOSIAH. We are soon to part company, perhaps for ever in this life. We have had many conversations, in which, I trust, much as we have differed on matters of opinion, we have kept our friendly feeling for each other uninterruptedly. Let us then devote the present evening to the consideration, not of those points which separate us one from another, but rather to some of those subjects on which our opinions agree.

CHARLES. I willingly consent to your proposal. It is very much pleasanter to agree with those we love, than to be obliged to differ from them, especially in matters of faith ; and though, so far as I am concerned, I remain a much attached to Church principles as ever, yet I do not feel disposed to think hardly of those who do not see everything in the same light in which it appears to me.

JOSIAH. And, for my part, though still firmly attached to the principles I have advocated, I hope that I can tolerate the "peculiarities" of other bodies of Christians, even as I desire them to tolerate those of the Society to which I belong. We may walk with consistency in our several

ways, each keeping to the path marked out for him ; and
yet, for all this, we may enjoy each other's company as we
move heavenward.

CHARLES. Assuredly so. Within that great enclosure,
circumscribed by love to God and man, all the pathways
tend in the same direction, and unite at the end of the
way. As all must enter into the fold by the same gate, so
all must pass over the same river, and find their rest
in the same " green pastures, beside the still waters."
Minor differences are more apparent than real ; or, at
least, they obstruct our view more than their importance
warrants.

JOSIAH. Yes. A midge, if brought close to the eye,
occupies a great space in the field of vision ; and objects
in the foreground of a landscape, although only a few feet
in height, appear to tower over distant mountains.

CHARLES. Have you ever looked down from the top of
some high and isolated mountain over a wide extent of di-
versified country ? Your last remark reminds me of one
of the first excursions I made in early youth to the sum-
mit of Mangerton, Killarney, from which you know there
is a magnificent prospect, comprising a great variety of
scenery, viewed at different distances, and consequently
with greater or less clearness. The lakes and their wood-
ed mountains lie immediately at your feet ; the Reeks are
seen beyond these ; then the various ranges of the Kerry
mountains and their lakes, successively less and less perfectly defined ; and, last of all, the sea, which shuts in the
whole. I remember that this panorama struck my young
fancy as an apt picture of our individual memory. Everything has its real place and just proportion in the landscape if you explore it in detail, but the bird's-eye view

shows every object, except those immediately around you, under a false light. The objects near at hand represent time present ; those at a little distance, time just past ; and so, from distance to distance, till at the horizon we have nothing to dwell on but the faintly outlined monotony of childish days—days which have left few incidents to mark their place, whilst a dreaminess, like the haze of heaven, gives to their remembrance a glory which they had not in reality.

JOSIAH. The simile is a just one, and might be transferred to the stream of history, especially to that of oral history or tradition. The distance that "lends enchantment to the view" also encircles long past events with a halo which the actors in them could not perceive. And so of the ancient worthies. All the commonplaces which surrounded the object of our reverence return with him to the dust ; while the heroism that makes him live in history gathers strength from age to age.

CHARLES. No doubt this was the origin of hero-worship in old times, as it has been of saint-worship in the Church of Rome. Now it occurs to me, that almost all the so-called " developments of Christian doctrine" which have, grown up through the course of ages, have in the beginning, originated among the people themselves. Some solitary enthusiast has started " a pious opinion ;" he dreams of it by night, and dwells on it by day ; he has visions and revelations. He communicates his thoughts to others, and is believed ; and, as time goes on, the opinion gathers strength, till, after long delay perhaps, but certainly at last, the matter is taken up by the monks and friars, and receives the *imprimatur* of Rome.

JOSIAH. This is the old story, *vox populi, vox Dei.*

CHARLES. Rather say, the voice of the god of this world, whose name is *Legion.* These "pious opinions" are the tares sown by the enemy among the wheat. Expressing, at first, but the superstitious thoughts of weak and ignorant minds, they seem of no importance; but like the snow-wreath, that gathers size and weight as well as impurity as it rolls along, till it grows up into an avalanche, they gradually "develop" into dogmas of which their "pious" originators little dreamed. A somewhat similar development takes place in Protestant communities, though it leads to a different result.

JOSIAH. Thou compares the tendency to sectarianism which is characteristic of the reformed Churches, with the tendency to invent new doctrines and to corrupt the old which is equally characteristic of Romanism.

CHARLES. I think the resemblance is striking. At Rome, in order to preserve intact her boasted unity, the Church every now and then adopts some fantasy that commands a sufficient amount of popular support. In Protestant communities new opinions and new varieties of discipline of necessity drive their originators to form new sects.

JOSIAH. The Church of England has always pointed reproachfully to the conflicting opinions which exist among Dissenters, whilst the Church of Rome brings the same reproach against Protestantism in general. Such differences must show themselves wherever thought is free: and, in fact, your Church contains within itself as great a diversity of opinions, as is to be found amongst those who have seceded from you.

CHARLES. I have always considered it the peculiar merit of the Church of England that she has not attempted to chain down the intellect. Thought is free within her borders. Surely you do not allege this liberty as a reproach, or as an excuse for dissent and schism.

JOSIAH. There is a wide range of freedom in matters of doctrine joined with strict uniformity in the externals of religion.

CHARLES. Uniformity in externals is a very wholesome bond of society, and seems a necessary result of having a liturgy. What but the rubric protects the laity from the impertinences of silly curates, or from the heresies of unfaithful ones ?

JOSIAH. Nevertheless, the rigid enforcement of uniformity has cost you dear. It has been the great cause of dissent in England. I would refer particularly to the secession of the Wesleyans, the most active and influential of the modern dissenters. If ever there were men imbued with " Church feeling," the two brothers Wesley were those men; yet the elder, and more daring, was at length driven by the force of circumstances to break through your Church-order, with respect to the ordination of ministers ; and thus to sever, at one blow, from the communion of your Church, the many thousands in England and America that followed his leading. The separation of the North American colonies from England, which occurred about the same time, is an event in the political world of similar importance to what the revolt of the Wesleyans was in the ecclesiastical; and both were brought on by the tyranny and intolerance of the governing power.

CHARLES. There is much truth in what you say. I fully agree with you in thinking that there is nothing in the essential doctrines and discipline of Wesleyanism incompatible with the good order of our Church, were she loosened from her state fetters. Wesleyans use our liturgy and love it, and the *spirit* of our Church would not necessarily forbid the extra machinery of class-meetings, extempore prayer, and lay-preaching, which was adopted by Wesley, and which forms almost the only difference between his society and the Church. Had Wesley, instead of being frowned upon by punctilious churchmen, been heartily sympathized with as he deserved to be, how much more solid and lasting good would he not have effected! His mission was peculiarly to the waste places—the desolations of many generations, where the poor and illiterate ("lost sheep") had been neglected by their proper pastors, and suffered to fall into a state of semi-heathenism. He effected much good among such populations, but the good was greatly marred by the subsequent withdrawal of the societies he formed from the body of the Church, and the setting up of a new ecclesiastical power, like that of the Wesleyan Conference.

JOSIAH. It is much to be regretted that the spirit of your Church is so bound up by outward regulations, that she cannot develop herself so as to embrace Methodists and all such, as the Church of Rome would certainly have done. It is recorded of our Lord, that though scorned by the rich and great, yet "the common people heard him gladly;" but the reverse of this seems to be the case with the Established Church : her consecrated buildings are filled with the rich and great and learned, but the "common people" seek elsewhere for the consolation of religion and the teaching of the Gospel. The lay assistance, which you have certainly discouraged, would be a great advantage. Were not the rulers of the Church chiefly to blame for Wesley and his followers having been driven from amongst you ?

CHARLES. Assuredly so. If Wesley could have obtained for his assistant ministers the episcopal ordination which he possessed himself, and highly valued, and had he been assured that such a ministry would be continued after his decease, there would have been no excuse for his overstepping the limits of church order, by assuming the episcopal function to himself and his successors. If you read his life, you will find that it was not until the supposed necessity of such a measure was forced upon him, in extreme old age, that he adopted it.

JOSIAH. But according to thy own church principles, as advocated in previous conversations, he was not authorized to revolt. He should have meekly submitted to the orders of his "superiors," and remained himself, and retained his followers, at whatever spiritual loss, within the church hedge.

CHARLES. I neither excuse his conduct nor sanction it ; nor did his brother Charles Wesley. But I think the temptation was a very strong one, hardly to be resisted by a man of Wesley's ardent character ; and the sin appears to me to lie more justly at the door of the bishops of those days, who exerted all their power to crush him, and, failing in that, so rigidly refused ordination to the Wesleyan ministers. Had a man of Wesley's fervent piety, and zeal, and church loyalty appeared among the Roman Catholics, and effected such a reformation of life and such a revival of doctrine for them as he effected in our communion, how differently would he have been treated ! The Pope would probably have appointed him head of a new " order," with full authority to " develop"

its idea ; church power and patronage would have flowed
through his hands ; and his honours would have been
consummated by canonization at last.

Josiah. Has the resemblance between Ignatius Loyola
and Wesley never struck thee ? Different as were the
men and their doings, there is still a certain likeness in
their characters, and in the world-wide influence, for good
or evil, to which they have attained.

Charles. The resemblance is very striking, and has
been often noticed. Both were men of extraordinary
strength of purpose, of inflexible will, unwearying energy,
and fervent zeal for the spread of those doctrines which
they believed to be the truth. Both have left on the
world greater and more enduring influences, perhaps, than
the greatest of military heroes. There is no reason to
doubt the sincerity of either. In fact, men less thoroughly in earnest could not have acted their part in history. Both have gone to their long account ; the fruit
only of their labours remains as a legacy to the world.
Shall we not judge, then, the wholesomeness of the tree
by the fruit it has borne ? Loyola was the devoted son of
the Roman Church, whose teaching had entered so deeply
into his soul that it became part of his being ; and, acting
on the illumination of that teaching, he founded the
society of the Jesuits. Wesley, equally devoted to the
Church of England, and equally embued with her teaching and spirit, founded the Methodists.

Josiah. The difference in the result is indeed great,
and plainly shows the different nature of the fountains
from which each drew its inspiration. Many uncharita-
ble persons amongst Protestant dissenters look on the
English Church as but little removed in spirit from the

Roman; but, so long as the English Church refers to Holy Scripture as the only standard of doctrine, the contrast must be great; and the results respectively obtained by the teaching of Loyola and of Wesley offer an excellent illustration. The *idea* derived from Rome has developed into a system which puts darkness for light and light for darkness. The idea derived from England, on the other hand, like the spirit of English institutions, has changed the wilderness into a fruitful field, and called forth springs in the desert. Loyola's guiding principle was unlimited obedience to infallible Rome; Wesley's, unlimited obedience to God's teaching in Holy Scripture. If any one thing more than another can exhibit the unsoundness of Rome's claims to infallibility, the history of the Jesuits is that thing; for their whole system proceeds on the assumption that Rome is " the light of the world," the centre of orthodoxy, that city "whose builder and maker is God." If this were indeed so the Jesuits would be angels of light, for their doctrine is "the sincere milk" of Rome; and their mission should bring peace to him that is afar off and to him that is nigh. That it does not, proves the fallacy of their leading principle.

CHARLES. Looking back to the origin of the Jesuits, there is something very singular in their career. We do not see in them anything like the course of an ordinary river, which gradually increases from a streamlet to a flood that bears all before it to the sea. Their course is one of interrupted prosperity regularly alternating with adversity, like the ebbing and flowing of the tide; as if some power, mightier than that of their leader, had said, " Thus far shalt thou go, and no further, and here shall thy proud waves be stayed." So long as they exhibit

only the fair side of their system, there is something so
plausible in it that it wins its way among men, and appears to bask in the sunshine of God's favour. Their zeal
for learning, their seeming morality and sweetness, recommend them above all the other orders of the Roman
Church to the notice of parents, who fearlessly intrust
them with their children. Frequently, in Roman Catholic countries, almost all education has flowed through
their hands. They have had possession of the lower and
of the higher schools, the private tuition of nobles and of
princes, the direction of families, and the very helm of
the state. And what has been the issue? Have they
ever maintained for long their hard-earned power?
Have they not been continually driven out and pro-
scribed? Not in one place, but in every place, this has
happened over and over again. Even Rome herself, at
one time, suppressed the order.

JOSIAH. Perhaps the fair side of Jesuitry was never
more remarkably displayed than in the history of the early
Jesuit missions to the East Indies, and to Central and
South America. I think we cannot question the sincerity
and single-heartedness of Francis Xavier and many of his
companions; and among the missionaries of Paraguay
there appear to have been similarly devoted men. No
pains were spared on these missions. Whatever zeal
could accomplish, whatever money could effect, whatever
the aid of governments could compass, all these agencies
were in the hands of the missionaries. In Paraguay, for
a long time, they reigned supreme. In India, through the
influence of the Portuguese, they enjoyed the favour of
princes. The field of work was before them, ripe, and
ready for the sickle. We accordingly hear of the tens of

thousands that in India flocked to their churches, " as
doves to the windows ;" and in Paraguay the wild tribes
came and sat at their feet, as at the feet of Gamaliel. If
the teaching of the Jesuits to these dark heathen had
been what it ought to have been ; if they had set before
them the Gospel in its simplicity, and held up to their devotion Christ alone as the Way, the Truth, and the Life ;
if they had not checked their advancement in knowledge
by keeping them in leading strings, and being to them as
gods—directors of the body as well as of the soul—keepers
of the conscience in things temporal as well as spiritual ;
if, in fine, they had acted not as Jesuits but as Christians,
how different might not the present state of India and of
Spanish America have been ! Were ever opportunities of
spreading the Redeemer's kingdom greater ? Were ever
opportunities more completely misapplied ?

> Their promises were, as they then were, mighty,
> And their performance, as they now are, nothing.

Where are the fruits of their labours ? If we look for
them in the Christianization of those countries in which
they laboured, we shall look in vain. It is true that the
populations over which they ruled still call themselves
"Catholics," but their Catholicism is a mere pretence.
They are heathen in everything but the name ; ignorant as
the heathen around them, depraved and debased in mind
as they. Read the accounts which modern travellers give
of the state of Roman Catholicism in the fields of the
great Indian mission, and in those of their various missions in America. There is not, at the present day, a
single bright spot over the whole area to which we can
turn and say, " Here hath God wrought." The picture

is one dreary waste, strewn with the dry bones of men, and "the light is darkened in the heaven thereof."

CHARLES. This is indeed a melancholy but too true picture of the present state of these boasted missions. The Jesuits have been tried in the balance and found wanting. A similar fate arrested their progress in Japan, where at one time there was every prospect of successfully introducing Christianity, but where the good work was marred by their trying to force the papal supremacy on that people. You have alluded to great opportunities of spreading Christianity having been neglected or misapplied by the Jesuits. What do you think of the opportunities which our own government has enjoyed, and the use that it has made of them? How can we, as a nation, stand before the Master when he comes to reckon with his servants? England has received her ten talents in the vast population subjected to her sway. She boasts that the sun never sets upon her empire; would that she could, "in this confidence of boasting," appeal like St. Paul to what she had done and suffered for her Lord. Look at the millions of India. Instead of using its power for the furtherance of our Lord's kingdom, the late Indian government systematically sought to uphold heathenism as "the established religion" of that country. And this it defended on maxims of state policy, as if there were no more difference between truth and falsehood than what might be ascertained by a vote or a census. I do not say that a government ought to persecute heathenism, nor do I think that it should. Let the temples stand and the gods be worshipped as long as the heathen choose. But let us, as a government, have no part in the profanity.

JOSIAH. Certainly the government of India did very

wrong in allying itself with heathenism. There is a wide difference between persecuting a false religion and upholding it.

CHARLES. Opinions may be divided respecting the duty of governments in regard to religious education, where the population, as in England and Ireland, consists of various denominations of Christians. For though one sect may be more worthy of support than another, yet if all be Christian, all have a claim on the government, which, in such a country, ought not be of any one sect exclusively. Compromises, within Christian bounds, must, in such cases, be sometimes made. But there can be no compromise between Christianity and heathenism. Heathenism is not a *religion*. Thus to parley with heathenism is to make the existence of the God of Truth a mere matter of opinion, which we may either hold or not hold as we feel inclined, like an "open question" in Parliament.

JOSIAH. But as respects education ?

CHARLES. I think that every government is bound to provide for the education of its people. In the case of a Christian government ruling over a heathen population, a question may arise as to the nature of the education to be provided. Were I the ruling power, I should endow schools in which, besides the usual school courses, Christian literature didactic, historical, and scientific, should be read, and Christian ethics taught. I should not compel scholars to attend the government schools, nor forbid the heathen starting opposition schools : but I would not give money to support the heathen schools. As for the rest, let truth and error fight their own battle. My sympathy should ever be given to truth, as a duty I owe to the Source of Truth ; my toleration to error, as a tribute to the frailty of man.

JOSIAH. In the case of India thou would not permit the Shasters or other heathen books, or the Koran to be read in the endowed schools?

CHARLES. Certainly not; no more than I should permit the "Book of Mormon" to be read in the national schools at home. If the heathen and Mahommedan priests chose to instruct the pupils, out of school hours, in their sacred books, they should have full liberty to do so, if the parents wished it: I should neither obstruct them at all, nor favour them at all; nor should I place the Bible in such schools, as a common class book. It is very right that Christian children, in a Christian school, should have the privilege of reading lessons in Holy Scripture; but the Scriptures should not be thrust, like a primer, into the ruthless hands of young Buddhists or Mahommedans. That would be casting pearls before swine. Let the Bible be reserved for missionary schools, where doctrinal teaching may accompany its introduction.

JOSIAH. Well, if England, as a government, has shown herself unworthy of her high calling, it is at least some consolation to know that the Gospel of peace has been published by Englishmen in every clime, and perhaps in three-fourths of the languages spoken by mankind. I cannot boast of much that has been done by the Society to which I belong in the way of missions to the heathen. Many amongst us, I believe, contribute to the mission funds of other bodies of Christians, and our sympathies attend all those who love the Lord in sincerity. But I could wish to see our Society, as a Christian body, taking a more active and direct part in the evangelization of the world. The subject has engaged much more of our attention lately; and the Yearly Meeting of London, in 1861, issued an address to its members recommending missions to the heathen to their particular attention, and reminding them how frequently " George Fox, in his epistles, " exhorts to spread the truth abroad, to instruct and " teach the Indians and negroes, and all others, how that " Christ, by the grace of God, tasted death for every man, " and gave himself a ransom for all, to be testified in due " time."

CHARLES. The genius of Quakerism is against your ever succeeding in missionary work among the heathen. Whilst your missionaries were waiting for the direct movement of the Spirit, the opportunity of acting would, in nine cases out of ten, be lost. In a Quaker missionary college we should witness a constant commentary on the school-boy text,

> " Rusticus expectat dum defluat amnis, at ille
> " Labitur et labetur in omne volubilis ævum."

JOSIAH. I cannot admit this charge. There is nothing in Quakerism, properly understood, which is inconsistent with missionary efforts ; although I do admit that our exertions in this work have not heretofore been properly conducted.

CHARLES. In order to see how very unfit you are to have the charge of a mission to the heathen, one needs only to read the evidence which Elisha Bates, at that time " a minister in good esteem" amongst you, gave before a committee of the House of Commons a few years back, respecting some tribes of North American Indians. These Indians have been under the care of your Society, more or less, since the days of William Penn. They have constantly looked up to you with reverence, as to the children of the great Onas, their dear father, whose words to

them were sweeter than honey, and who never defrauded
them of their lands, or broke faith with them in treaties.
All their traditions would teach them to put faith in your
words. Nor had they any complicated system of idolatry
to be overthrown : like yourselves they acknowledge a
Great Spirit, the Father and Inspirer of all mankind.
They did not indulge, like so many other savage tribes, in
abominable rites. They were intelligent in mind, grave
in deportment, and moral in the relations of social life.
Your friends lived near them, almost within sight of the
smoke of their wigwams. What more promising field
could there be ? Yet, up to the time of Elisha Bates' evidence, nothing had been effected towards introducing
Christianity. Friends were still " waiting till the river
should flow by :" the old story again, " *rusticus expectat.*"
An occasional visit was paid to them ; an occasional meeting was held ; some words of exhortation were spoken ;
presents were exchanged ; the pipe of peace was smoked ;
and there the matter ended. Surely no one but yourselves could look for " growth in the truth" from such
desultory labours as these.

JOSIAH. The error has been in the attempt to civilize
before trying to convert to Christianity—an experiment
which the Moravians also tried, at first, and found to fail.
Therefore the care which our American brethren have,
for many years, extended towards the Indians has had
but little success. This care is still continued ; but the
report, which I have seen, of last year's proceedings
admits that their success has been much less than they
had hoped for, and attributes their failure to causes of
the character to which I have referred.

CHARLES. Contrast for a moment your inefficiency

among these red men, with what other societies have done and are doing, not only among the aborigines of North America, but among the far wilder and more savage races of other lands. Look at the labours of that small and far from wealthy body, the Moravians, in Greenland and in South Africa; or at the great English missionary societies, whether those of the Church, or of the dissenting bodies. Have not these, under God, been the instruments of greatly advancing the civilization of savage man, as well as of extending the bounds of Christianity?

JOSIAH. I am well acquainted with the labours of the missionary societies, and rejoice in their success, although I may think that some of the published reports are somewhat too highly coloured. When we read of the extraordinary results that follow a little preaching, the almost miraculous interpositions of Providence at other times, the deep piety of language attributed to recent converts, and such like circumstances, I sometimes question whether there be not enthusiasm mixed with the zeal, and whether the published accounts may not be too highly coloured.

CHARLES. Allowance must be made for missionaries, as for men shut out from the world and absorbed in one pursuit, which to them is the great concern of life. Perhaps they have laboured long and fruitlessly. In the morning of life they have entered on their toilsome work ; the heat of noon has found them busy ; evening is fast closing in, " when desire fails, and the grasshopper becomes a burden ;" yet the heathen, for whose sake they have been contented to lay down their lives, are still ungathered. If, then, at such a moment, it should please the Lord of the vintage to pour a blessing on the work of his sorely tried, yet faithful and enduring servant, who can wonder at the latter, if he make use of expressions that seem enthusiastic, when read in cold blood, by some supercilious critic, who has never known what it is to be a stranger in a land of strangers?

JOSIAH. Much allowance ought indeed to be made in such cases; nor can we withhold our sympathy from the humblest soldier who stands in the breach, or leads a forlorn hope against the strong places of the enemy.

CHARLES. I speak from some personal observation, having recently (1855) visited the Wesleyan mission stations at the Friendly and Fiji Islands. I know, therefore, something of the work that is actually going forward in the Pacific. And as I am in no way connected with this mission, and, from my predilections as a churchman, not over disposed to sympathise with a body of dissenters, you may, I think, regard me as an unprejudiced witness if I speak favourably of what I have seen.

JOSIAH. And this thou art prepared to do?

CHARLES. I think it is impossible for any Christian man, who has read the accounts that early and later voyagers have given of the heathen state of the Pacific Islanders, to witness what has been effected at the Friendly group, and what is actively and successfully going forward at Fiji, without blessing God that he has put it into the hearts of his Wesleyan children to sound the everlasting Gospel in those unwilling and deaf ears. You must not be deceived in your estimate of the real character of the Friendly Islanders, by the name " Friendly " given them by Cook. They are, for savages, a polished people, full of professions of good will to strangers, hospitable in sharing their food, and winning in their manners; and to Cook, as a great and rich chieftain, from whom much wealth was to be expected, they showed only the sunny side of their character. But with all this, in their heathen state they were avaricious and cruel, indulging in human sacrifices, child murder, and widow strangling; they were liars and thieves, and insatiable and unblushing beggars; and they were constantly at war among themselves. The first band of missionaries, sent among them by the London Society in 1797, were murdered or driven away, after their property, which was considerable, had been begged or stolen. No missionaries revisited them till the Wesleyans settled amongst them in 1823, since which time the mission has been uninterruptedly kept up.

JOSIAH. And what is the present state of this mission field?

CHARLES. There is not a heathen man, woman, or child left in the whole group; there is not a heathen temple nor an idol; but everywhere throughout the islands, "from the rising of the sun to the going down of the same," the name of God is hallowed; and to Him, at morning and evening, in almost every homestead, the voice of prayer and the hymn of praise ascend. The change is as complete as it is wonderful. Nor is it only a change in the outward forms of worship. You see the fruit of the Christian tree gradually ripening everywhere; in the moral habits of the people, in the spread of European comforts and industry among them, in the administration of the laws, in the form of government which has been established. The present king (George*)

---

* There is an excellent engraved portrait of his Majesty, from a daguerreotype, in the Methodist Magazine for January, 1855.

is a man of much ability and of the true Christian stamp. He is indeed the Alfred of his little kingdom ; and has succeeded, by cultivating peace in the spirit of Christian forbearance, in establishing a far more extensive and stable power than any of his predecessors, with all their wars, attained to.

JOSIAH. What a very gratifying picture! I had no idea that the mission had so completely filled the land. But dost thou think that the conversion of the mass of the people is a reality ? May not much of this conformity be owing to policy, in order to win the favour of the king and the good-will of the missionaries ?

CHARLES. I cannot judge people's inmost thoughts or motives. I can only say that, as far as I have seen, " the words which they have heard with their outward ears" appear to have produced among this people " the fruit of good living, to the honour and praise" of their Christian profession. No doubt, there are hypocrites and formalists at Tongataboo as well as elsewhere. But there are all shades of Christian sincerity and enlightenment besides. Proofs of faith, zeal, and love to God and man are seen in the many natives who offer themselves for teachers and assistant missionaries, to be sent to the out-lying islands of the group, as well as to Rotumah, Samoa, and Fiji; not to speak of the still greater numbers who are employed, without fee or reward, in like positions in the home circuits. The mission is managed at present by but five Europeans, who have the general oversight of the work, and who preach in turn at the different chapels. But what I may call the parochial work is chiefly conducted by native deacons, as we should call them, under the supervision of the missionaries. Many of these native teachers have proved themselves faithful through a long ministry, and many more, there is good reason to believe, have " entered into the joy of their Lord."

JOSIAH. I particularly like the system of training teachers from among the natives, and sending them forth to teach other heathen tribes. This is the true working of the leaven of the kingdom. By so doing, the mission will eventually be able to stand alone, and then we may hope to see the people permanently raised to a place among civilized and Christian nations.

CHARLES. Heyday, Josiah! you are forgetting your Quaker principles. These " trained-teachers," remember, are " man-made ministers," sent to preach and to pray, as well as to teach. You would not tolerate them at home; why then allow them abroad?

JOSIAH. And·thou also hast forgotten the necessity of a college education, and of instructing them in Greek and Latin. But as respects these " trained teachers," we do " tolerate them at home." I may instance our Sunday schools, where many of our members, as before stated, act in this capacity.

CHARLES. I never said that a college education was *necessary*, but only that it is highly desirable when it can be had.

JOSIAH. We have already discussed the difference between the gift of " prophecy "—as the apostle Paul terms the highest form of Gospel ministry—and the gift of teaching; and I have shown that in teaching, or in the work of an " evangelist" or missionary, the aid of the Holy Spirit is to be expected by enlightening and· directing the human understanding, in its prayerful efforts after the knowledge of divine things, rather than by the more special guidance which is conferred in the gift of prophecy. Where the object is to explain the principles and duties of Christianity the gift of teaching is peculiarly suitable, and the missionary need not wait for any higher qualification before entering on his work. The address of the Yearly Meeting of London, before alluded to, states in reference to the subject of missions, that " the Scriptural views in regard to the nature of " worship, to the qualification for the Gospel ministry, " and to the authority of Christ in His Church, which " we have ever maintained, so far from offering an im- " pediment to such a service, are peculiarily adapted to " promote it." " How unspeakable the blessing of being " permitted, whether by preaching, by teaching, by the " circulation of the Holy Scriptures, or by any other " means which the Lord may be pleased to appoint, to " bring those ' who are sitting in darkness, and in the " shadow of death,' to the light of the Gospel of Christ."

CHARLES. Well, if *your* scruples are satisfied, I have nothing to object. I have only a few words to say respecting the Fiji archipelago, the heathen natives of which islands are, as you are probably aware, cannibals above any other known race of men, besides being sunk in soul-debasing barbarity of almost every kind. The group has a population of about 200,000, scattered over upwards of eighty islands, some of which are of large size, and all of exuberant fertility and great picturesque beauty—enjoying, for the tropics, a delicious and not unhealthy climate. Here the Wesleyans established a mission about twenty years ago, previously to which time the islands

had only been visited by passing vessels, or by a few
ships trading in *beche-de-mer*,* or by whalers. The
natives, as I have said, were savages of the worst description, cruel and treacherous without parallel. All
conceivable horrors abounded. At their temple-feasts it
was common to have from one hundred to two hundred
human bodies cooked and eaten at once ; and these were
not always the bodies of enemies slain in battle, but often
consisted chiefly of women and defenceless men, who were
kidnapped by hunting parties sent out specially to bring
in meat for the feast. Human flesh was esteemed delicious. Some of the chiefs, were notorious for a lust for
the flesh of young children, who were dressed whole for
their banquets. Endless are the sickening, but alas !
authentic relations of those days. The wildest nursery
tales are not a caricature of the state of Fijian society,
not only when the mission was first established, but for
eighteen long years afterwards. During all this time
Englishmen, with their English wives and families, vexed
their souls day by day with the unrighteous deeds of these
savages, exhorting, imploring, warning them to desist
from their vileness ; and unavailingly ! With a perseve-
rance and moral courage which nothing but the sense of
sacred duty could impart, these pioneers of the Gospel
laboured night and day. Often the wife and children
were left alone for days and weeks, whilst the husband
was absent, in a frail canoe, on some mission of peace to

---

* *Beche-de-mer*—One of the echinoderms called a " sea cucum-
ber" (*Holothuria edulis*, Less.), found on coral reefs in the Pacific.
It is a favourite food of the Chinese, and is brought to China·
chiefly by American trading vessels.

a distant island. And sometimes, on these occasions, a cannibal feast would be held close to the spot where the lonely Englishwoman was left. And, on such occasions, what has not woman achieved? Two faithful women,* mothers, leaving their children in God's care (their husbands being absent on duty), went alone into the midst of the savage multitude, assembled to celebrate heathen orgies at Bau, the chief seat of heathen wickedness in Fiji; and there, in front of the temple reeking with the blood of recently slaughtered victims, stood, and pleaded for the lives of wretched kidnapped women, who were lying in trembling expectation, bound hand and foot, ready to be cooked when the ovens should be sufficiently heated; whilst the heathen danced, and sung, and shouted, brandishing their spears and clubs.

JOSIAH. Such an act of Christian heroism commands our deepest sympathy. But, doubtless, it is had in remembrance by Him who once said, "Verily I say unto " you, wheresoever this Gospel shall be preached in the " whole world, there shall also this that this woman hath " done be told for a memorial of her."

CHARLES. For particulars of the early work in Fiji I must refer you to Mr. Young's "Southern World,"† and

---

* Mrs. Calvert (wife of the Rev. James Calvert) and Mrs. Lyth (wife of the Rev. Richard B. Lyth). They had to cross an inlet of the sea in a small canoe, propelled by a naked savage. Upon their arrival at Bau the work of death was going on. Seven women out of fourteen had already been butchered. Rushing into the presence of Tanoa, the chief, the author of this villany, they succeeded by their bold intercession in saving the lives of five; the two remaining victims were rescued by the interference of the wives of the chiefs Thakombau and Ngavindi.

† *The Southern World.* By Rev. R. Young. London: Mason.

to the annual reports published by the Missionary Society.
Suffice it to say, that, within the last few years, it has
pleased God remarkably to bless the labours of his servants who had so long watered the ground not only with
their tears but with their blood. Some await, in Fijian
graves, a glorious resurrection ; but others, who have for
a long time "gone forth with weeping, bearing precious
seed," "are now returning joyful, bringing their sheaves
with them." Heathenism is everywhere on the decline.
Neither heathen temple nor heathen priest any longer
remains at Bau ! In that late abode of butchery and lust,
the Christian congregation, meeting every Sabbath day,
numbers over a thousand. Some 70,000, throughout the
various islands, are at least nominally Christian ; and
thousands more are willing to come under mission teaching, if only missionaries and native teachers can be sent
to them. The question now is, how can the demand be
sufficiently supplied ? The events of recent years have
crowded so rapidly on each other, that they astonish us by
their magnitude, when we contrast them with the apparent deadness of the past; but the change had long been
preparing under ground. It has been like the burst of
spring after an arctic winter. The people had long been
weary of the darkness of their seers, and the oppressions
and wars of their chiefs. Political changes came, and
some powerful chiefs were laid low ; others joined the
Christian party ; and a visit paid by King George of
Tongataboo to one of the newly converted chiefs has had
a marked influence in furthering the spread of Christianity. There has been a war provoked by the heathen,
but it has ended in their total rout : and if nothing
interfere to blight the present prospects, please God a

few more years will witness the demoniacs of Fiji no longer "naked and cutting themselves with stones," but redeemed to Christ, "sitting, clothed, and in their right mind." *

JOSIAH. What thou has just been saying has brought vividly before my mind the breadth, and height, and depth of the wisdom, mercy, and grace that framed what we may call the central petition of the Lord's prayer: "THY kingdom come. THY will be done." May His kingdom reign over all, both in Europe and in Fiji !

---

* The following statistical table shows the state (1860) of the Wesleyan missions in Tonga, Fiji, and the Navigators' Islands (Samoa) :—

Chapels	462
Other preaching places	167
Ministers and preachers on trial	36
Catechists	232
Day-school masters (not including Fiji) . .	183
Sunday and day-school teachers	2,129
Local preachers	1,161
Class leaders (no return from Fiji) . . .	920
Full and accredited Church members . . .	18,554
On trial for membership	5,837
Sabbath schools.	791
Sabbath scholars of both sexes	34,431
Day-schools	671
Day-scholars	35,019
Attendants on public worship	81,410
Printing establishments	2

The sums contributed by the native converts in aid of the mission funds during the year 1860 are as follows :—

From the Friendly Islands	.	.	£2,500
„ Fiji „	.	.	1,500

The Friendly Island mission is now self-supporting.

CHARLES. Amen. And if you will, let us for once, Churchman and Quaker, unite in a short prayer "for the peace of Jerusalem." Saying, in the words of one of our occasional services :—" O God, the Father of our Lord " Jesus Christ, our only Saviour, the Prince of Peace, " give us grace seriously to lay to heart the great dangers " we [who call ourselves Christians] are in by our un- " happy divisions. Take away all hatred and prejudice, " and whatsoever else may hinder us from godly union " and concord ; that as there is but one Body, and one " Spirit, and one hope of our calling, one Lord, one faith, " one baptism, one God and Father of us all, so we may " henceforth be all of one heart, and of one soul, united in " one holy bond of truth and peace, of faith and charity, " and may with one mind and one mouth glorify Thee ; " through Jesus Christ, our Lord. Amen."

JOSIAH. Our Lord's prayer for his disciples was, "That " they all may be one; as thou, Father, art in me, and I in " thee, that they also may be one in us; that the world " may believe that thou hast sent me :" and even amidst the differences of opinion belonging to a state in which all " see through a glass, darkly," that prayer may yet be an- swered more fully than it has ever been. But still more blessed is the anticipation of that day, when His people shall see as they are seen, and know as they are known. Farewell.

LaVergne, TN USA
05 October 2009
159929LV00003B/125/A